Get a FREE eBook

To register this book, scan the code or go to
www.manning.com/freebook/chiarlone

By registering you get

- **FREE eBook copy**
  download in PDF and ePub
- **FREE online access**
  to Manning's liveBook platform
- **FREE audio**
  read and listen online in liveBook
- **FREE AI Assistant**
  it knows the book and what you are reading when it answers
- **FREE in-book testing**
  fun tests to lock in your knowledge

In Manning's liveBook platform you can share discussions and comments with other readers, add your own bookmarks and highlights, insert personal notes anywhere on the page, see color versions of all the book's graphics, download source code and other resources, and more!
To register, scan the code or go to www.manning.com/freebook/chiarlone

---

MANNING

Server-Side WebAssembly

Server-Side WebAssembly

Building portable and secure multi-language apps

Danilo Chiarlone

Foreword by Brendan Burns
Afterword by Luke Wagner

MANNING
Shelter Island

For online information and ordering of this and other Manning books, please visit www.manning.com. The publisher offers discounts on this book when ordered in quantity.

For more information, please contact

Special Sales Department
Manning Publications Co.
20 Baldwin Road
PO Box 761
Shelter Island, NY 11964
Email: orders@manning.com

Manning Publications Co.
20 Baldwin Road
PO Box 761
Shelter Island, NY 11964

Development editor: Connor O'Brien
Technical editor: Adam S. Chalmers
Review editor: Angelina Lazukić
Production editor: Keri Hales
Copy editor: Kari Lucke
Proofreader: Katie Tennant
Technical proofreader: C. Gerard Gallant
Typesetter: Tamara Švelić Sabljić
Cover designer: Marija Tudor

ISBN 9781633436206
Printed in the United States of America

To my parents, Beatriz, my dear Nonna (1946–2021), Grumpy,
and all my friends who supported this journey

brief contents

contents

foreword

Welcome! I'm excited to have the opportunity to introduce you to *Server-Side WebAssembly*. It goes without saying that the development of web and browser technologies has had a foundational role in shaping the modern internet. Even today, as advancements like mobile and AI have reshaped how we think about interacting with internet services, the core technologies of the web, like HTTP and REST, are at the heart of these advancements. In this book, you will learn how WebAssembly, which started as a component on the client side for the browser, has turned into server-side technology for service development.

I'm old enough to remember a time before browsers came with programming languages built in. Early in the development of the web, it became clear that adding dynamic elements to web pages was a critical part of the browser's evolution from a static content renderer to an application platform. The development of JavaScript and HTML5 changed the browser from a static content renderer to a dynamic application platform. Over time, however, the limitations of JavaScript as a programming language became apparent. A variety of concerns, ranging from the need for other programming languages to the desire to share code between client and server, led to the development of WebAssembly (Wasm) as a foundation for multilanguage code execution in the browser. Much like the Java virtual machine bytecode or the common language runtime, Wasm is a virtual assembly language that can be used as a target for compilers. With Wasm added to browsers, developers could build dynamic web applications in languages from C to Python.

At the same time as the seeds of Wasm were being sown in the browser, a separate development was occurring on the server. The V8 JavaScript runtime that powered the Chromium open source browser was taken and transformed into the Node.js platform for server development in JavaScript. The motivations behind the development of Node.js mirror the things that drove the development of Wasm—particularly, the desire for portability of code between client and server. Instead of developing a new assembly language for the browser, Node.js took the core JavaScript engine out of the browser and made it available on the server. JavaScript (and, more recently, TypeScript) developers could use the same languages and libraries in both places.

With this history in mind, the development of Wasm on the server is a similar migration from client-side browsers to server-side execution. But if you examine the multilanguage value of Wasm to the browser, you might be confused about why there was interest in Wasm on the server. After all, even without Wasm, you still can program servers in a language like C++ and then execute that same code on the browser via Wasm. The motivations for WebAssembly on the server actually come from two additional requirements for browser-based Wasm, particularly security sandboxes and lightweight components.

It should be obvious that code running in the browser must be considered untrusted and therefore must also be isolated (or sandboxed) to protect your computer against code on the internet. Core principles in the design of Wasm, namely, linear memory and a capability-based security model, significantly improve the security profile of code running in the browser. The same value is present on the server in the context of hosting multitenant code. Consider an application like a game that enables user-generated content to add items or other characters. This third-party code for extending the game is inherently untrusted, and thus we need to isolate it from the rest of the code in the game server. Just like in the browser, the Wasm security model is a fantastic way to implement plugins for untrusted code on the server.

The other value of Wasm is small, lightweight components. Because web pages and Wasm are downloaded across the network, the smaller the size of the component, the more responsive the web page and the better the user experience. This same value of small modules applies on the server side as well, especially in the context of things like function-as-a-service, where code is dynamically spun up and down in response to user requests. Wasm can provide an order of magnitude (or more) of a speed-up in terms of starting dynamic code in response to user requests when compared with traditional process execution. This also has significant benefits for server developers.

I hope that this brief history of how web technologies have shaped the internet gives you context and motivation to learn how you can harness the power of Wasm in your server-side applications to power the next generation of the internet!

—Brendan Burns
Co-creator of Kubernetes and Corporate Vice President
of Azure Cloud Native Open Source at Microsoft

preface

My experience with WebAssembly (Wasm) started with server-side applications rather than browser-based ones. While Wasm was initially created for web performance, I focused on its applications in cloud computing. I worked on SpiderLightning—a collection of WebAssembly Interface Types definitions that simplified application development by abstracting away environmental complexities. This work evolved into wasi-cloud-core, a set of cloud interaction interfaces that's now part of the WASI standards, where I contribute as a champion.

The idea for this book emerged from one of my talks at WasmCon, where Manning editor Jonathan Gennick approached me about writing a comprehensive guide to server-side Wasm. The timing felt right—Wasm was gaining significant traction beyond the browser, but documentation and learning resources remained scarce. While AI topics dominate technical conferences, Wasm actually rated higher than AI in engagement at KubeCon EU 2024 in Paris, highlighting the community's hunger for knowledge in this space.

Currently, I work on Hyperlight, which, through its sister project Hyperlight-Wasm, enables Wasm adoption in public clouds like Azure by providing hardware-based isolation for multi-tenant workloads. This work has exposed me to different perspectives on where Wasm might fit in the server-side landscape, particularly in isolation-critical environments.

What excites me most about Wasm is its promise of true portability and security without sacrificing performance. The ability to compile code from multiple languages into a secure, sandboxed format that runs consistently across different environments represents a fundamental shift in how we think about server-side development. Wasm enables us to break free from vendor lock-in, reduce cold start times in serverless environments, and deploy the same code from cloud to edge with confidence.

This book reflects my belief that Wasm's server-side capabilities deserve to be more accessible to developers. Throughout these pages, you'll not only learn the technical details of working with Wasm modules and components but also gain practical experience building real applications. By switching between languages like Rust, JavaScript, and Python in our examples, I hope to demonstrate Wasm's true language-agnostic nature and help you see how it can fit into your existing development workflow.

I hope this book helps make Wasm technology more approachable and encourages more developers to experiment with its capabilities. The future of server-side computing is being written now, and Wasm is playing a crucial role in that story.

acknowledgments

Writing this book has been an incredible journey that wouldn't have been possible without the support, guidance, and patience of many people.

First and foremost, I want to thank my girlfriend, Beatriz. You've been my rock throughout this intensive writing process, taking over household responsibilities without complaint, showing endless understanding when I had to work through weekends and vacations, and always believing in me even when deadlines felt impossible. Your support means everything to me.

I owe immense gratitude to my editorial team at Manning. Connor O'Brien, development editor: thank you for your exceptional guidance throughout this project, your patience with my questions, and for fighting battles with publishing on delivery schedules. Your advocacy made this book possible. Adam Chalmers, technical editor: your insights and thorough reviews elevated the technical accuracy and clarity of every chapter. Your attention to detail is remarkable. Gerard Gallant: your meticulous work as technical proofreader polished every detail and ensured the code examples work flawlessly. Angelina Lazukić, review editor: you orchestrated the extensive review process that brought diverse perspectives to strengthen this book.

To Courtney Kimball and Manning's marketing team—especially Aira Dučić, Ana Romac, Robin Campbell, Divya Mudaliar, and Sam Wood—thank you for your invaluable support in helping me share this book with the community through conferences and other promotional opportunities.

This book benefitted enormously from the numerous reviewers who provided feedback throughout its development: Advait Patel, Beatriz Gascón Lourenco, Sergio Britos, David Justice, David Paccoud, Denis Saripov, Fahrudin Paljus, Heng Zhang, German Gonzalez-Morris, Ikko Ashimine, James Haring, Jeremy Lange, Joe Zhou, Joel

Dice, John Guthrie, Jonathan Womack, Jorge Prendes, Juan Camilo Cifuentes, Clyde Kallahan, Liam Randall, Lîm Tsú-thuàn, Luke Wagner, Mario-Leander Reimer, Mark Fisher, Max Sadrieh, Michael Bright, Miley Fu, Mohammad Shahnawaz Akhter, Olivier Ducatteeuw, Peter Hampton, Piotr Jastrzebski, Piotr Sarna, Pradeep Saraswati, William Ko, Ronald Borman, Sander Zegveld, Shantanu Kumar, Simeon Leyzerzon, Thomas Lockney, Thorsten Hans, Tom Oeste, Vojta Tuma, Wayne Mather, William E. Wheeler, Zachary Manning, and Zbigniew Curylo. Each of you helped shape this book, catching errors, suggesting improvements, and ensuring the content serves its intended audience. Your collective wisdom made this a much better resource for the WebAssembly community.

I'd also like to thank the broader WebAssembly community, particularly the Bytecode Alliance team and the WebAssembly Community Group. Your work on Wasmtime, WASI specifications, and tooling provides the foundation that makes server-side WebAssembly possible. Special thanks go to those who answered my questions on forums and GitHub issues as I worked through challenging technical details.

To Jonathan Gennick, who first approached me after my WasmCon talk—thank you for seeing the potential for this book and for believing that the developer community needed a comprehensive guide to server-side WebAssembly.

Finally, thank you to the entire production team at Manning who worked behind the scenes to transform my manuscript into the polished book you're reading today. Aleksandar Dragosavljevic facilitated my connection with this exceptional team. Keri Hales, production editor, expertly guided the book through the production process. Kari Lucke, copy editor, refined my prose and ensured consistency throughout. Katie Tennant, proof manager, coordinated the final quality checks that caught countless details. Tamara Švelić Sabljić, typesetter, brought the technical content to life with clean, readable layouts. Your professionalism and dedication to quality are evident on every page.

about this book

Server-Side WebAssembly: Building portable and secure multi-language apps teaches you how to make use of WebAssembly (Wasm) beyond the browser to build efficient, secure, and portable server-side applications. Rather than presenting abstract concepts in isolation, this book takes a hands-on approach: you'll build a complete smart content management system (SmartCMS) from the ground up, with each chapter introducing new Wasm concepts through practical implementation. This approach ensures you not only understand the theory but also gain real-world experience applying Wasm's unique capabilities for cloud computing, edge deployment, and cross-language interoperability.

Who should read this book

This book is for backend developers, systems architects, and DevOps engineers who want to use Wasm for server-side development. While the book primarily uses Rust for examples, readers comfortable with any modern programming language can follow along—the concepts translate across languages that compile to Wasm. You should have basic familiarity with server-side development concepts, containerization basics, and command-line tools. No prior Wasm experience is required.

How this book is organized: A road map

The book contains nine chapters divided into two parts. Part 1: WebAssembly for Architects (chapters 1–5) introduces Wasm from a systems perspective, covering the fundamental concepts and architecture:

- Chapter 1 introduces Wasm's evolution from browser technology to server-side platform, exploring its performance characteristics, security model, and ideal use cases for serverless and edge computing.

- Chapter 2 demonstrates building server-side applications with Wasm modules, diving deep into Wasm's memory model and the guest-host architecture that enables system interaction.
- Chapter 3 introduces Wasm components, showing how they enhance portability and security through higher-level abstractions and cross-language interoperability.
- Chapter 4 explores interfacing Wasm with underlying systems through WASI, demonstrating capabilities management and component composition.
- Chapter 5 showcases advanced applications, including machine learning inference with wasi-nn and database integration, highlighting Wasm's versatility.

Part 2: WebAssembly for Developers (chapters 6–9) focuses on practical development and deployment:

- Chapter 6 covers creating production-grade applications using standardized interfaces and prebuilt hosts, emphasizing best practices for real-world deployments.
- Chapter 7 introduces Wasm containers, demonstrating how to package and deploy Wasm workloads using familiar containerization tools.
- Chapter 8 explores Kubernetes integration for Wasm applications, covering orchestration, scaling, and management in cloud environments.
- Chapter 9 examines the future of Wasm, including emerging proposals, ecosystem developments, and the potential effects on cloud computing.

While the book is designed to be read sequentially, with each chapter building on previous concepts, experienced developers can jump to specific topics. The SmartCMS project that runs throughout the book provides hands-on experience with each concept as it's introduced.

About the code

This book contains many examples of source code both in numbered listings and in line with normal text. In both cases, source code is formatted in a `fixed-width font like this` to separate it from ordinary text.

In many cases, the original source code has been reformatted; we've added line breaks and reworked indentation to accommodate the available page space in the book. In some cases, even this was not enough, and listings include line-continuation markers (➥). Additionally, comments in the source code have often been removed from the listings when the code is described in the text. Code annotations accompany many of the listings, highlighting important concepts.

You can get executable snippets of code from the liveBook (online) version of this book at https://livebook.manning.com/book/server-side-webassembly. Source code for the examples in this book is available for download from the Manning website at https://www.manning.com/books/server-side-webassembly and from the GitHub repository at https://github.com/danbugs/serverside-wasm-book-code. The repository includes all code examples, the complete SmartCMS project, and additional resources.

The book primarily uses Rust for Wasm examples, with JavaScript and Python for demonstrating cross-language capabilities. You'll need the following software to run the examples:

- Rust (versions 1.84.0 and 1.85.0 or later)
- Node.js (version 22 or later) with npm
- Python (version 3.12 or later)
- Docker (version 28.0.0 or later)
- Various Wasm tools (installation instructions provided in each chapter)

Detailed setup instructions are provided in appendix A, and each chapter includes specific toolchain requirements as needed.

liveBook discussion forum

Purchase of *Server-Side WebAssembly* includes free access to liveBook, Manning's online reading platform. Using liveBook's exclusive discussion features, you can attach comments to the book globally or to specific sections or paragraphs. It's a snap to make notes for yourself, ask and answer technical questions, and receive help from the author and other users. To access the forum, go to https://livebook.manning.com/book/server-side-webassembly/discussion. You can also learn more about Manning's forums and the rules of conduct at https://livebook.manning.com/discussion.

Manning's commitment to our readers is to provide a venue where a meaningful dialogue between individual readers and between readers and the author can take place. It is not a commitment to any specific amount of participation on the part of the author, whose contribution to the forum remains voluntary (and unpaid). We suggest you try asking the author some challenging questions lest his interest stray! The forum and the archives of previous discussions will be accessible from the publisher's website as long as the book is in print.

Other online resources

For additional learning and support:

- WebAssembly Community Group: https://www.w3.org/community/webassembly/
- WASI proposals and status: https://github.com/WebAssembly/WASI/blob/main/Proposals.md
- Bytecode Alliance (maintaining Wasmtime and other tools): https://bytecodealliance.org/
- Wasm language support: https://developer.fermyon.com/wasm-languages/webassembly-language-support

about the author

Danilo (Dan) Chiarlone is a champion of multiple WebAssembly System Interface (WASI) proposals and works at Microsoft on cloud and virtualization technologies. He is a passionate educator who offers free lessons on Rust and WebAssembly through his YouTube channel and is a frequent conference speaker at events such as WasmCon and RustConf.

about the cover illustration

The figure on the cover of *Server-Side WebAssembly*, “Marchand d’Outres à Pulque,” or “Merchant carrying pulque-filled wineskins,” is taken from a book by Claudio Linati published in 1828. Linati’s book includes hand-colored lithographs depicting a variety of civil, military, and religious costumes of Mexican society at the time.

In those days, it was easy to identify where people lived and what their trade or station in life was just by their dress. Manning celebrates the inventiveness and initiative of the computer business with book covers based on the rich diversity of regional culture centuries ago, brought back to life by pictures from collections such as this one.

Part 1

WebAssembly for architects

WebAssembly began its life in the browser, promising near-native performance for web applications. But today, its most transformative potential lies beyond the browser—in the cloud, at the edge, and everywhere that server-side applications run. As WebAssembly matures from a browser technology to a universal runtime, it's reshaping how we think about portable, secure, and efficient computing.

This first part of the book introduces you to WebAssembly from an architect's perspective, building your understanding from the ground up. You'll discover why WebAssembly's unique combination of performance, security, and language agnosticism makes it ideal for modern server-side development, particularly in serverless and edge-computing environments, where cold starts and resource efficiency matter most.

Chapter 1 explores WebAssembly's evolution and its advantages for server-side development, from its sandboxed security model to its remarkable startup times. Chapter 2 takes you inside WebAssembly modules, revealing the low-level building blocks of linear memory and basic types that form the foundation of all WebAssembly applications. Chapter 3 introduces WebAssembly components, showing how they elevate the developer experience through higher-level abstractions and enable seamless cross-language interoperability. Chapter 4 demonstrates how WebAssembly interfaces with underlying systems through WASI, teaching you to manage capabilities and compose components. Finally, chapter 5 showcases real-world applications, from machine learning inference to database integration, illustrating WebAssembly's versatility across diverse workloads.

By the end of this part, you'll understand not just what WebAssembly is but why it represents a fundamental shift in how we build and deploy server-side applications. You'll have the architectural knowledge needed to design systems that use WebAssembly's unique strengths.

1 Introducing Wasm on the server

This chapter covers

- The evolution of Wasm from a browser-based tool to a versatile technology for server-side development
- The key attributes of Wasm: Performance, security, and flexibility
- Practical scenarios where Wasm excels
- The limitations and challenges of adopting Wasm in server-side development

WebAssembly, commonly abbreviated as Wasm, is a construct that is akin to an instruction set architecture (ISA) like x86_64, aarch64 (also known as arm64), and others. In the same way you can compile your code to such architectures, you can compile your code to Wasm. But, unlike x86_64 or aarch64, you can't go to the store and buy a computer that contains a Wasm chip. Wasm is not a real or physical platform. As illustrated in figure 1.1, it can be thought of as an entirely agnostic hardware abstraction layer over the hardware itself. Wasm can then be transformed into native code for the specific hardware it is running on. In fact, one of Wasm's goals is to serve as a common denominator across different ISAs.

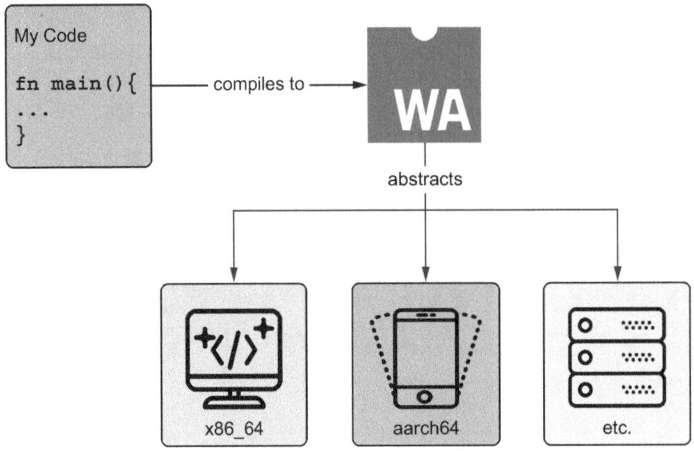

Figure 1.1 Wasm as an abstraction layer virtualizing over various kinds of hardware

Wasm was released as a minimum viable product in 2017, and it was created to meet the performance demand for increasingly hard computational tasks that people wanted to run in the browser, like 3D applications, audio and video software, and games, which JavaScript (i.e., the web's only universally supported native programming language) could not handle due to its inconsistent performance and various other pitfalls. Unlike earlier attempts, such as Java applets—which also aimed to bring high-performance code to the browser but struggled with security vulnerabilities, plugin dependencies, and, still, inconsistent performance—Wasm offers a modern solution. As a W3C standard, Wasm is an official language of the web, alongside JS, HTML, and CSS. To address the web's performance challenges (as illustrated in figure 1.2), Wasm was designed to let developers compile code written in high-performance languages like C, C++, Rust, and others to run safely in the browser at near-native speeds.

Figure 1.2 Compiling to Wasm from various languages

With this idea in mind, some of Wasm's design goals were established for it to be

- Fast, with predictable, near-native execution
- Safe, designed for efficient, secure verification and isolation of untrusted code
- Hardware independent
- Language independent

People quickly realized that these characteristics could also benefit the server side. In 2019, the WebAssembly System Interface (WASI) was released. It defined an interface that Wasm runtimes can implement to enable Wasm to communicate with an operating system (OS) and run outside the web. In a browser, Wasm relies on the browser itself as its environment; outside the browser, a Wasm runtime—often referred to as a host—serves the same role, providing the necessary system interactions.

1.1 What is the server side and where does Wasm fit in?

It's easy to get overwhelmed when developing server-side applications today. Unlike before, where you most probably just crafted a monolithic (i.e., nonmodularized) application that ran on a single server, today, you have to think about microservices, serverless, containers, and edge computing. And, with all these options, it's hard to know which one best fits the needs of your project.

Aside from managing your own hardware, there are three primary levels of abstraction for server-side development:

- *Infrastructure as a service (IaaS)* is when you rent, say, a virtual machine (VM), and you are responsible for managing everything on it, from the OS to your application, while the cloud provider manages the physical hardware.
- *Platform as a service (PaaS)* is when the cloud provider is responsible for managing the OS and the hardware, and you are only responsible for your application, which is often deployed in a container.
- *Serverless or function as a service (FaaS)* is when you don't have to worry about the OS, the hardware, or particular details of your application—like scaling. Instead, you write a function, and the cloud provider manages its execution in response to events. With that, FaaS has the unique advantage of being able to scale to zero, meaning if no one is using your application, you don't have to pay for it, which is achieved by the cloud provider deprovisioning the containers running your code after a specific period of inactivity and relaunching them when a request comes in.

Containers are essentially lightweight, portable packages that bundle your application code with all its dependencies—libraries, runtime, system tools, and configuration files—into a single unit that can run consistently across different environments. Think of them like shipping containers for software: just as a shipping container can be moved from truck to ship to train without unpacking its contents, a software container can move from your laptop to a staging server to production without worrying about compatibility problems. This consistency and portability make containers the backbone of modern PaaS and FaaS platforms.

Solomon Hykes, the founder of Docker, once famously said: "If WASM+WASI existed in 2008, we wouldn't have needed to create Docker. That's how important it is. WebAssembly on the server is the future of computing." As implied by this quote and its context in relation to containers, you might deduce that Wasm is particularly impactful for both abstraction levels that have containers at their core—PaaS and FaaS. And if you did, you would be right!

In 2022, Docker announced its Docker+Wasm Technical Preview (https://mng.bz/vZQa), which allows you to run Wasm workloads within their platform using the same containerization technologies. While these "Wasm containers" still adhere to the Open Container Initiative (OCI) image format and runtime specifications, they use Wasm's unique capabilities for running lightweight, secure, and portable applications.

> **NOTE** The OCI image format is a standardized way to package and distribute containerized applications, ensuring compatibility across different runtimes and platforms. Originally designed for traditional containers, this format defines how filesystem layers, metadata, and configurations are structured within an image. By adhering to this format, Wasm workloads can integrate with existing container tools while still benefiting from Wasm's advantages.

In the upcoming section, we will explore the advantages of using Wasm and try to answer why you might want to use a Wasm container over a traditional Docker container.

1.2 The advantages of Wasm for server-side development

"Write once, run anywhere" (WORA), while being a very fitting slogan for Wasm, was first said in 1995 while describing the cross-platform benefits of the Java programming language. This shows that Wasm's benefits (for this example, its portability) are not new ideas. So, what is Wasm's differentiator, and why should you care about it?

1.2.1 Language agnosticism

Java allows you to WORA by the fact that, when you compile your Java application, it gets translated to Java bytecode, which, just like Wasm, is entirely platform independent. Then, the Java bytecode can be run by the Java Virtual Machine (JVM), which serves the same role as a Wasm runtime in converting agnostic instructions to platform-specific ones. The parallels between Java and Wasm are shown in figure 1.3.

The main difference between the two, as you can see in figure 1.3, is that Java bytecode, while it does aid portability, is primarily designed for Java and a few other languages with similar execution models (e.g., Kotlin). Wasm, on the other hand, is built as a truly language-agnostic binary format. While over 40 languages can be compiled to Wasm (see https://mng.bz/YZNj for more details on whether your language is supported), the key advantage is not just the breadth of language support but the

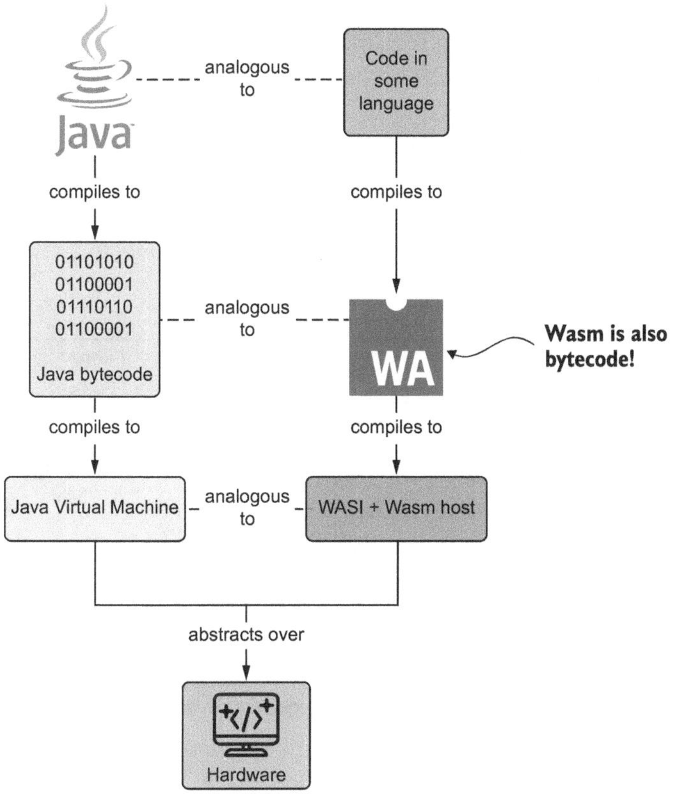

Figure 1.3 Java and Wasm's similarities

lightweight nature of the runtime. Unlike the JVM, which requires a heavyweight VM, Wasm's design avoids the need for a complex execution environment, making it well suited for languages like C, C++, Rust, and Zig.

This architectural difference also means Wasm can more easily support languages like Python, which rely on C-based components, whereas running Python on the JVM requires reimplementation from scratch. Additionally, Wasm's simple instruction set and stack-based execution model were intentionally designed for broad compatibility across languages, unlike JVM, which was originally optimized for Java.

Another important distinction is that Wasm is an open standard developed through the W3C with multivendor collaboration; it is not controlled by any single company. This contrasts with Java, where Oracle maintains considerable influence over the language's direction. Interestingly, Oracle also owns the JavaScript trademark, but this is purely nominal.

Wasm's broad language support, in theory, sounds fantastic, but in practice, it can sometimes mean that the support for a particular language is not as mature as it is for others. One reason for a possible difference in support is that, for a long time, Wasm did not have garbage collection, which is a feature of many languages that allows a program to have automatic memory management by the fact that any allocated memory that is no longer referenced is recognized and reclaimed. This meant that languages that rely on garbage collection, like Kotlin, PHP, and Java, needed to first compile their entire runtime to Wasm so that the runtime can be shipped together with a Wasm application written in that same language. Let's take PHP as an example. As illustrated in figure 1.4, using PHP Wasm without garbage collection meant that a large chunk of your Wasm-compiled app is really just the PHP runtime, which, say, in the context of the browser, will run side by side with JavaScript's runtime garbage collector.

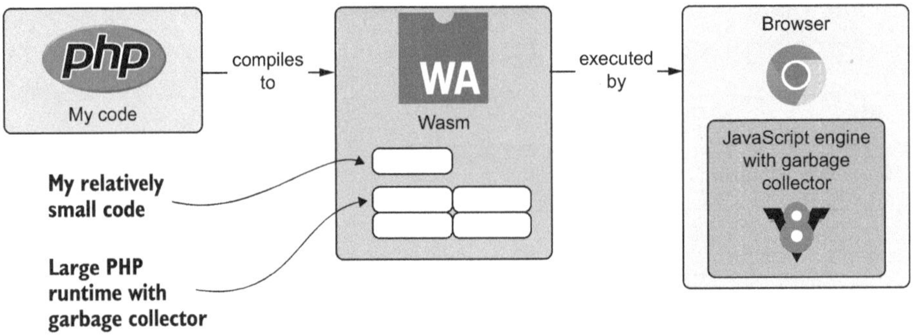

Figure 1.4 Running a PHP Wasm without garbage collection application in the browser

Running PHP's own garbage collector alongside JavaScript's is inefficient and redundant. A better approach is to enable Wasm to work with the host environment's garbage collection infrastructure. This is exactly what WasmGC—a proposal by the WebAssembly Community Group—aims to address.[1] It introduces garbage-collected reference types that can be managed by the host, reducing the need to bundle a complete garbage collection system within each language's runtime.

However, this doesn't mean the entire PHP runtime can be removed when compiling to Wasm. Components like the interpreter, support for dynamic evaluation, and other necessary features still need to be included in the Wasm binary to ensure proper execution. Language support for Wasm is a constantly evolving landscape. Throughout this book, while we primarily use Rust in the examples, we will also explore writing applications in higher-level languages like JavaScript and Python.

1.2.2 Performance

When it was released for the web, Wasm promised near-native performance. This means if you compile a C application to a native binary and run it on your desktop environment and then compare that benchmark to running the same application

[1] Steiner, Thomas (2023). WebAssembly Garbage Collection (WasmGC) now enabled by default in Chrome. Chrome for Developers. https://developer.chrome.com/blog/wasmgc.

compiled to Wasm but running on the browser, you should see that it performs just about the same. Does that still hold true for the server side? To answer that question, there are a couple of scenarios we can compare.

Wasm app vs. x86_64 app

In this scenario, we are comparing single-threaded benchmark applications compiled to both the x86_64 architecture and Wasm. The x86_64 binary runs directly atop the native OS, while the Wasm app runs in a Wasm runtime that implements WASI atop the native OS. Spies and Mock[2] showed that the Wasm app, on average, performed only 14% slower than the x86_64 app, which, all in all, is close to near-native performance.

But in practice, apps are often containerized. Next, let's compare a Wasm app's performance to the same app running in a container.

Wasm app vs. short-running workload in a container

In this scenario, we are looking at a Wasm application running on a Wasm runtime versus a containerized application running with Docker. Long et al.[3] showed that Wasm runtimes running a simple application that reads a file and exits perform at least 10× faster than Docker running the same application from cold start (i.e., meaning the time it takes for the container to start for the first time or from a fully deprovisioned state). And when running other benchmarking applications, Wasm was found to usually perform 10% to 50% faster than the same app containerized even on warm start (i.e., the time it takes for the container to start after it has been previously initialized but is currently inactive).

This, while impressive, does not necessarily paint an accurate picture of how Wasm will perform in the real world with more complex applications like, say, running an HTTP server. So let's explore further in the next scenario.

Wasm container vs. Docker container

In this scenario, we will compare two container types: a traditional Docker container and the newly introduced Wasm container. This time, both applications were written to run a simple HTTP server that will listen for requests and provide a response after querying a SQL database. Sondell[4] showed that, when stressing such a system with 50 concurrent clients making requests, the Wasm application showed a worst-case latency of about 15.2 seconds, while the Docker container showed a worst-case latency of 0.881 seconds. This means that the Docker container was about 17× faster than the Wasm one. So what's going on? Is the containerization of Wasm creating that much overhead? The answer is no. In fact, when running the same application outside the container and just atop the respective Wasm runtime (i.e., simply eliminating containerization), the Docker container was

---

[2] Spies, Benedikt, and Mock, Markus (2021). An evaluation of WebAssembly in non-web environments. 2021 XLVII Latin American Computing Conference (CLEI), Cartago, Costa Rica, pp. 1–10. https://doi.org/10.1109/CLEI53233.2021.9640153.

[3] Long, Ju, et al. (2020, October 13). A lightweight design for serverless function-as-a-service. https://arxiv.org/abs/2010.07115.

[4] Sondell, Per (2024). An evaluation of performance and usability of WebAssembly containers in cloud computing. Umeå University. https://mng.bz/Kwgg.

still almost 13× faster. The answer here lies in Wasm's lack of support for multithreading. That is, the Docker container, when stressed, increased its CPU utilization to 11 cores, while Wasm, due to its current single-threaded nature, only utilized one core.

Wasm's threading proposal is still in the works. But, while still being a significant limitation, this is not the end of the road for Wasm. In fact, with a modern setup, it's very common for multithreading to be handled by the Wasm runtime through having each request handled by starting a new Wasm instance entirely. Regardless, Sondell (2024) showed that, while latency was left to be desired with this setup, the cold start time of a Wasm container was about 160% faster than that of a Docker container. This is particularly true because Wasm containers are much smaller (upwards of 80% smaller!) than Docker containers, as they are never packaged together with an OS (e.g., Linux), which consequently reduces the data volume required to be pulled and accelerates download speeds. This is illustrated in figure 1.5, which depicts two Dockerfiles: one for a Docker container and one for a Wasm container.

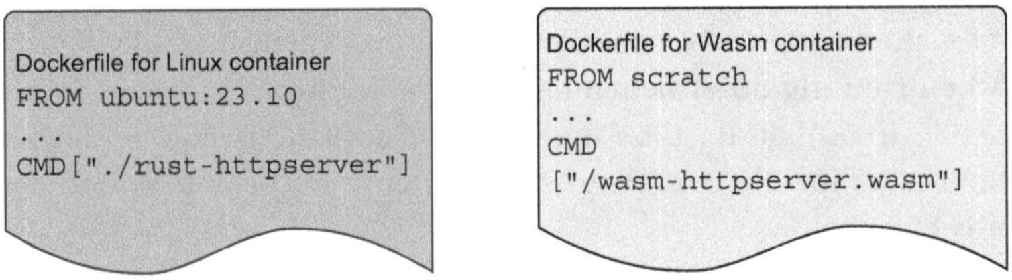

Figure 1.5 Dockerfiles for a Docker container and a Wasm container

As you can see, the Wasm container starts from scratch (i.e., a special empty image), while the Linux container begins with a base Ubuntu v23.10 image. This means the Wasm container includes only the application itself, whereas a typical Docker container includes both the application and the OS. While traditional containers can sometimes reach several gigabytes in size, Wasm containers are typically just a few megabytes. We will explore Wasm containers in more detail in chapter 7.

Is FROM scratch possible outside Wasm?

Yes. Docker containers don't necessarily have to be packaged together with an OS. You can avoid specific OS bits by using a static native binary along with `FROM scratch`, which is not entirely uncommon for some Rust- or Go-based containers. This section just illustrates with `FROM ubuntu:23.10` to display a commonly used setup.

The improved cold start times are a big deal, particularly for serverless applications that must constantly deprovision and reprovision containers to accommodate scaling to zero. This process often results in frequent cold starts.

As described by Hall and Ramachandran,[5] serverless applications suffer from the *cold start problem*, where startup times typically begin at around 300 milliseconds and can be significantly longer depending on factors like networking configurations (e.g., service meshes) and initialization processes. In the same paper, they compared the performance of non-Wasm versus Wasm serverless applications under varying access patterns and found that, for applications experiencing periods of inactivity, Wasm's improved cold start times led to 70% faster response times for moderate tasks and 90% faster response times for basic tasks.

Plus, Shillaker and Pietzuch,[6] when combining serverless and Wasm, managed to speed up training a machine learning model by 2× and utilized 10× less memory. So, as it stands, it's clear that Wasm's sweet spot in server-side development really is powering this new wave of applications.

Later in this book, we will explore for ourselves how to write Wasm applications that use HTTP servers and machine learning.

WASM DENSITY IN KUBERNETES

Until now, we have mostly focused on the runtime and cold start aspects of performance. However, another equally important facet is *density*—specifically, how many workloads (in our case, Wasm instances) can be packed onto a given set of hardware. Greater density is crucial because it directly translates to cost savings. For example, the company ZEISS was able to reduce its Node.js Express app deployment size from 423 MB to 2.4 MB by leveraging Wasm, resulting in over 50× greater workload density per Kubernetes node. This higher density allows for more efficient use of resources, reducing the need for additional hardware and lowering overall infrastructure costs.

1.2.3 Hardware agnosticism

Another great benefit of Wasm is the fact that it is completely independent of platform or hardware. The bytecode makes no assumptions about the underlying system, and it is entirely up to WASI to fill in the gaps. This has various benefits. For one, it means you can compile your application on an x86_64 machine and run it on an arm64 one without any changes. This has the potential to save countless DevOps hours that would be spent creating pipelines with runners to build your application for the various platforms you want to support. Instead, with Wasm, you build once and run anywhere.

But, what's more, Wasm's hardware agnosticism combined with its low memory footprint makes it particularly well suited for *edge computing*—a field that aims to bring computing closer to the sources of data (like mobile devices, vehicles, sensors, and so on) in an attempt to reduce latency and bandwidth usage. Edge environments are very

---

5 Hall, Adam, and Umakishore Ramachandran (2019). An execution model for serverless functions at the edge. IoTDI '19: Proceedings of the International Conference on Internet of Things Design and Implementation, pp. 225–226. https://doi.org/10.1145/3302505.3310084.

6 Shillaker, Simon, and Peter Pietzuch (2020). FAASM: Lightweight isolation for efficient stateful serverless computing. 2020 USENIX Annual Technical Conference (USENIX ATC 20). https://mng.bz/GwXA.

different from the cloud, where we essentially assume unlimited resources. Instead, for the edge, we need to support a large number of different devices with limited resources. Wasm perfectly fits this requirement and has the potential to power things like self-driving cars and smart cities through edge computing.

1.2.4 Security

Wasm is designed to run within a memory-safe sandboxed execution environment. By itself, it cannot interact with or access the native OS except through specific, tightly controlled capabilities provided by the Wasm runtime. For example, if the Wasm runtime grants the Wasm binary access to standard output to print "Hello, World," that controlled interaction is the only way the Wasm binary can communicate with the native OS, all while remaining within its sandbox. As illustrated in figure 1.6, this is in stark contrast to native applications that have full access to the native OS system calls (i.e., the fundamental interfaces that allow applications to request services from the OS, such as file manipulation, process control, and network communication) and the native OS memory.

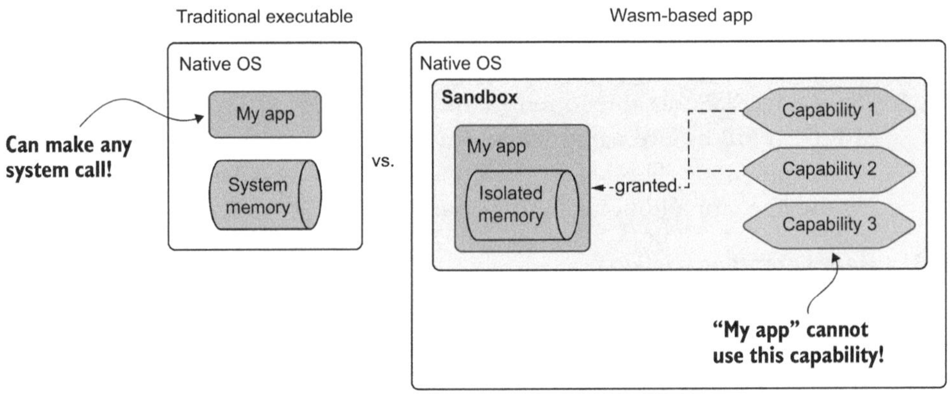

Figure 1.6 A native (traditional) application security model versus Wasm's capability-based security model

This isolation is especially crucial in the context of cloud computing, where supply-chain attacks are becoming increasingly common. Supply-chain attacks occur when a vulnerability in one component can potentially compromise the entire system, as all parts of the application often share the same environment and resources. However, with Wasm's sandboxed execution, each component operates independently, significantly reducing the risk that a compromised module could affect the rest of the application.

1.2.5 Standards-based and vendor neutrality

One of the compelling advantages of Wasm and WASI for server-side development is their foundation on open standards. Unlike many current serverless offerings that are tied to proprietary platforms, Wasm and WASI provide a vendor-neutral environment, allowing organizations to build serverless applications without being locked into a specific vendor's ecosystem.

This standards-based approach gives enterprises the flexibility to move their applications across different environments, whether on premises, in the cloud, or at the edge, without needing to rearchitect or redeploy their entire application stack. For organizations looking to adopt serverless technologies while avoiding vendor lock-in, Wasm offers a path to lower operational burden and increased portability, ensuring that their applications remain future-proof and adaptable to changing infrastructure needs.

1.3 When and where to use Wasm (and when not to)

As discussed, Wasm can be pivotal for serverless and edge computing. Particularly, it has great advantages for serverless as it is, on average, 80% faster than traditional serverless technologies. In addition, the same low memory footprint that gives Wasm the edge with serverless when paired with its hardware agnosticism makes it a great fit for edge computing, which relies on executing code at the edge of the network on a variety of devices with limited resources.

In addition to these areas, Wasm has also found its footing in

- *Mobile and desktop applications*—Wasm's cross-platform nature allows developers to share the same code across different platforms, such as an app's mobile and desktop versions, similar to how JavaScript frameworks like Electron enable cross-platform development.
- *Microcontrollers*—Microcontrollers are tiny, single-chip computers embedded in everything from household appliances to industrial machinery and vehicles. The microcontroller field is heavily dominated by low-level languages like C, which can make debugging and porting code across different microcontrollers challenging. Wasm has gained popularity in this space for its ability to serve as a middle ground between high-level languages—often too slow for microcontrollers—and low-level languages, enabling developers to write performant, debuggable, and portable code. Beyond immediate development benefits, Wasm also has the potential to improve the long-term maintainability of embedded software. Modern cars, for instance, contain dozens of microcontrollers managing everything from engine control to entertainment systems. The average lifespan of a European car, including its second life in Eastern Europe, is around 30 years. This means vehicles on the road today may still rely on software built during the Windows 95 era. With Wasm, manufacturers could more efficiently and securely update and maintain such software over decades, reducing technical debt and improving long-term sustainability.
- *Application plugins*—Wasm's natural sandboxing capabilities make it an ideal choice for developing secure and portable application plugins. Its ability to safely execute code in isolation from the host application reduces the risk of security vulnerabilities.

Honorable mentions also go to Wasm's effects in areas like smart contracts (i.e., blockchain) and polyglot programming, where it serves as a bridge to interoperate between various languages.

On the other hand, due to the lack of multithreading support, Wasm's performance can struggle in traditional PaaS-type applications. But these effects can be reduced if you use a containerized application that is orchestrated with Kubernetes and scale your application horizontally. In chapter 8, we will discuss how to deploy Wasm applications in Kubernetes.

Wasm's true struggle, however, lies in its ecosystem maturity. Even with Rust, which has always treated Wasm as a first-class citizen, the experience of trying to utilize an external package (i.e., a crate in Rust-speak) and finding out that it is not compilable to Wasm is a common one. This puts the developer in a position where they potentially have to choose between using the package they are comfortable with and dropping Wasm altogether, or instead, when it exists, using another equivalent package that does compile to Wasm. In the worst-case scenario, the developer may choose to set themselves on a quest to compile the original package to Wasm, which is often nontrivial and most likely heavily deviates from the original project's goal. Another significant challenge stemming from the ecosystem's maturity is the lack of integrated debugging tools in most languages, which further complicates the development process and can increase the time needed to identify and resolve problems.

Wasm is constantly evolving. While this means that support for a package you want to use may be coming soon, it also means that many tools and libraries are still maturing and may not yet be fully stable. However, ongoing work on Wasm itself is actively addressing many of these limitations. As new proposals are implemented, constraints that currently prevent some packages from being compiled to Wasm will gradually be removed, making the ecosystem more capable and versatile over time.

While these limitations are real, it's important to understand that Wasm offers capabilities that simply cannot be achieved with existing technologies. Table 1.1 compares Wasm across key dimensions.

Table 1.1 Comparing Wasm to traditional technologies across key dimensions

Capability	Wasm	Traditional technologies
Sandboxed execution	Built-in, lightweight isolation	Containers (not as secure), VMs (heavy/slow), or language-specific (Java, .NET)
Cold start	Microseconds	Containers: seconds; VMs: minutes
Artifact size	KBs to low MBs	Containers: 100s of MBs; traditional: varies widely
Portability	Compile once, run anywhere	Docker (platform-specific builds); interpreted languages (performance penalty)
Memory footprint	Minimal overhead	Containers/VMs: significant overhead
Multithreading	Limited (proposals in progress)	Well supported

Table 1.1 Comparing Wasm to traditional technologies across key dimensions (*continued*)

Capability	Wasm	Traditional technologies
Ecosystem maturity	Growing (many packages incompatible)	Mature
Debugging tools	Improving but limited	Well established
Runtime performance	Near-native	Varies (native to interpreted)

To stay up to date with upcoming features and improvements, you can check the status of Wasm and WASI proposals at https://github.com/WebAssembly/proposals (Wasm proposals) and https://mng.bz/z2V6 (WASI proposals).

1.4 How to navigate this book

This book is structured as a gradual progression, starting with low-level details and steadily moving toward a more accessible and streamlined developer experience. The early chapters focus on the fundamentals of Wasm, giving you a deep understanding of how it works under the hood. As you move forward, each chapter builds on the last, introducing higher-level tooling and abstractions that make working with Wasm easier. By the end, you'll be using Wasm in practical, real-world scenarios with a much smoother development experience.

The book is divided into two parts:

- Part 1: WebAssembly for architects (chapters 1–5) explores how Wasm works behind the scenes—ideal for understanding the inner workings for debugging, system design, or building a solid foundation.
- Part 2: WebAssembly for developers (chapters 6–9) shifts to practical development, covering everything from HTTP servers to machine learning workloads, Wasm containers, and Kubernetes deployment.

NOTE For a detailed breakdown of each chapter, see the "about this book" section of the introduction.

Throughout this book, we'll also develop a SmartCMS project, applying our newly learned skills as we go. The code from all chapters can be found on GitHub: https://github.com/danbugs/serverside-wasm-book-code. If you run into any problems, please open an issue on the repository—feedback is always appreciated!

Summary

- Wasm is akin to an ISA like x86_64 in the sense that your code can target it for compilation. But it is not a real platform and instead just virtualizes actual hardware.
- Wasm apps can run outside of a browser primarily through the WASI, which allows communication with the OS.

- Docker supports running two types of containers: the traditional Docker container and the newly introduced Wasm container.
- Wasm's language agnosticism makes it so that more than 40 languages can be compiled to it, but that is a double-edged sword, as support for a particular language might not be as mature as it is for others.
- While benchmarks show that standalone Wasm apps can be 10% to 50% faster than containerized apps, real-world applications can struggle due to Wasm's lack of support for multithreading.
- Wasm, when paired with serverless and its scale-to-zero requirement, leads to 80% faster execution times on average when compared to traditional serverless technologies.
- A Wasm binary is completely independent of the platform or hardware where it is built and can theoretically run on any system due to its hardware-agnosticism property.
- Wasm employs a capability-based security model that restricts the binary to access the native OS only through specific capabilities made available by the Wasm runtime.
- Aside from serverless and edge computing, Wasm has found its footing in mobile and desktop applications, microcontrollers, smart contracts, and polyglot programming.
- When targeting Wasm, it is commonplace to make sacrifices of particular packages that do not support Wasm.

2 Building server-side applications with Wasm modules

This chapter covers

- Building a Wasm "Hello, World" with Rust
- Understanding Wasm memory and data types
- Understanding the guest-host architecture of server-side Wasm applications
- Writing and compiling Rust code to Wasm
- Executing a Wasm module with a custom Wasm runtime

In this chapter, we're going to build a simple "Hello, World" application. As illustrated in figure 2.1, our app will take a string as input and output that string with `"Hello, "` in front of it. While this example might seem straightforward, implementing it in Wasm is far from trivial—Wasm doesn't have a built-in `String` type, so handling text requires a low-level approach.

Before exploring more advanced features, we'll work through this challenge using Wasm's raw capabilities. This will give us a deep understanding of how data is managed at this level and lay the groundwork for appreciating the more efficient techniques introduced later.

Figure 2.1 High-level view of our "Hello, World" application

2.1 Understanding Wasm's building blocks

We begin by rolling up our sleeves and working with the fundamental elements that Wasm offers out of the box: linear memory and four primitive data types (i.e., integers and floats, both in 32- and 64-bit sizes).

Linear memory is a contiguous and growable array of bytes that forms the memory space used by a Wasm program. This model is direct, meaning that the program interacts with memory in a straightforward manner, using explicit byte offsets to read and write data. It is low-level because it operates without higher-level abstractions, giving developers precise control over how memory is managed and accessed.

Unlike most languages that contain high-level types, raw Wasm requires us to engage with primitives directly. Wasm's integers and floats are the bedrock upon which we can construct more elaborate data structures. While this might feel low-level now, we'll later see how Wasm provides mechanisms to work with richer types more easily.

Consider our seemingly straightforward task of prefixing a user input with `"Hello, "`. In most high-level languages, this would be a trivial string concatenation. However, as mentioned, in Wasm, we don't have a string data type. So how do we represent a string using only integers and raw memory? One solution, as depicted in figure 2.2, is to

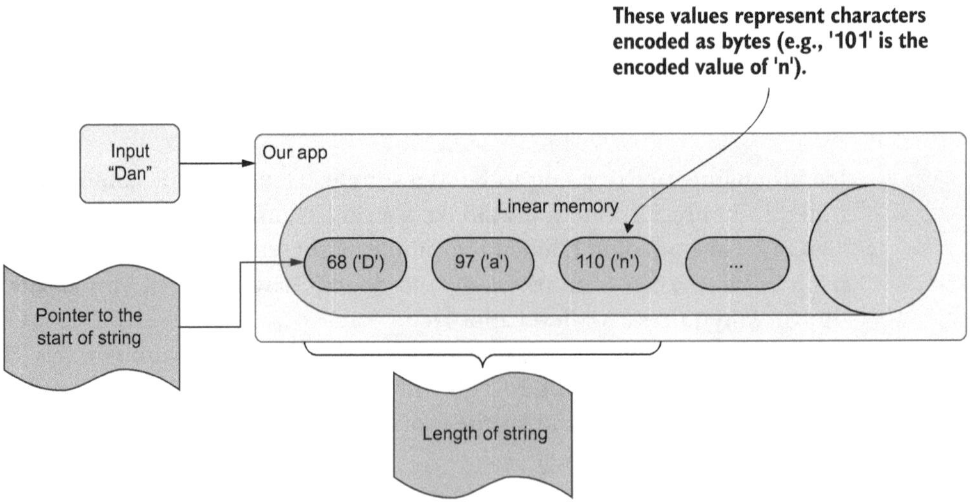

Figure 2.2 Representing a string with Wasm's linear memory and basic types

employ two integers. The first integer acts as a pointer to the start of the string, which is stored as an array of encoded (ASCII/UTF-8) bytes in linear memory, and the second represents its length.

By storing the string as an array of bytes, we can manipulate it as needed. When we wish to prepend `"Hello, "` to any user input, we encode the prefix (i.e., `"Hello, "`) and the user input as bytes, store them sequentially in linear memory, and use our two integers to keep track of their location and combined length. This approach may seem rudimentary when compared to the abstractions offered by higher-level languages, but it is precisely this simplicity that gives Wasm its speed and flexibility. By controlling exactly how memory is allocated, accessed, and combined, we can optimize performance in ways that higher-level abstractions might not allow. Moreover, this method of string handling is not just a workaround; it offers a window into understanding how higher-level languages (and, as we will see later, Wasm itself) abstract away such details.

2.2 Understanding the guest-host architecture of server-side Wasm

In the browser, Wasm runs within the web's native ecosystem, using the browser's features and resources. Similarly, on the server, Wasm needs a host to provide access to system resources. This role is typically filled by a Wasm runtime, which acts as the execution environment for Wasm applications.

To illustrate, let's consider the structure of our "Hello, World" app. This app is designed as a guest application, meaning it is built to run within said host, which provides the necessary runtime capabilities.

For demonstration, I've developed a custom host. Let's call it HelloWorldHost. This HelloWorldHost acts as a lightweight intermediary between the guest application and the Wasmtime runtime—a prominent open source Wasm runtime known for its performance, versatility, and security.

The architecture of our setup, as visualized in figure 2.3, operates in a four-step process:

1. HelloWorldHost injects the input string into the linear memory of the Wasm binary (i.e., our guest application).
2. HelloWorldHost then invokes the execution of our guest application—specifically, a function we will name `greet`.
3. The `greet` function first determines the amount of memory needed for the new string. Then it writes the updated content directly into memory, constructing the final greeting in place.
4. Once the `greet` function has done its work, HelloWorldHost re-engages, reading the newly formed greeting directly from the linear memory.

Next up, we'll dive into constructing our guest in Rust. You'll be guided through writing the code, compiling it into a Wasm module, and finally, executing it within HelloWorldHost.

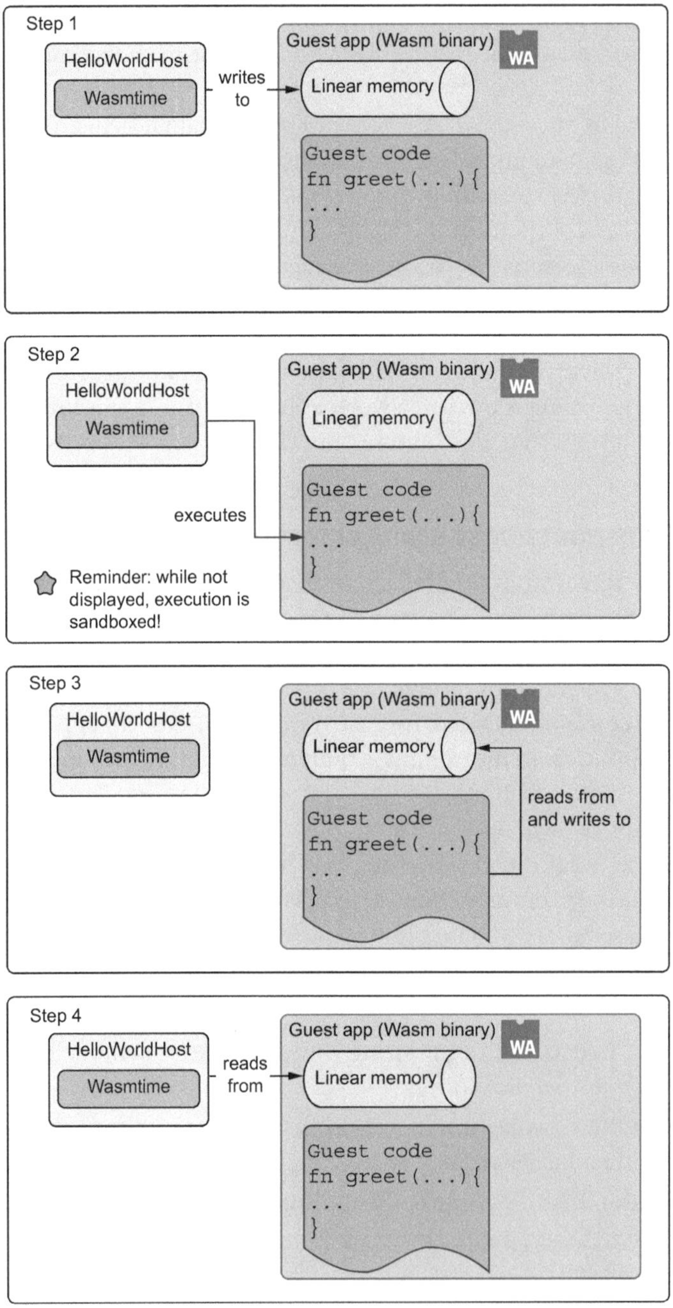

Figure 2.3 Illustration of interactions between our "Hello, World" guest and its custom host

2.3 Creating a Wasm app using Rust

Before getting into the meat and potatoes of our application, let's address a fundamental question: why Rust? The choice is practical—Rust's support for Wasm is the most mature among modern languages, and its safety guarantees align well with Wasm, simplifying our development process significantly. Don't worry if Rust isn't your first language; we'll break down each code snippet and process step by step.

For setup assistance, follow the instructions at https://www.rust-lang.org/learn/get-started to install Rust. This guide also includes information on setting up Rust with different editors like VS Code.

> **NOTE** The recommended Rust version for working through this book is `rustc 1.84.0 (9fc6b4312 2025-01-07)`. This version is important because it ensures we're using Rust edition 2021, which keeps our code stable and compatible with the tooling used throughout the book. You can check your current version with `rustc --version`. To install 1.84.0 specifically, after having some other version installed, you can run `rustup install 1.84.0` and set your default Rust version to it with `rustup default 1.84.0`.

2.3.1 Creating a Rust library project

In Rust, when you start a project, you're faced with a choice: build a library or a binary. As highlighted in the title of this section, we've opted for a library. This choice means our code is compiled into a reusable package, which is exactly what we need since our application doesn't require an executable `main` function like what you'd find in binary projects. Instead, our project centers around a `greet` function, designed to be called by HelloWorldHost.

Before we create the library, let's set up a consistent structure for all the book's code:

1. Create a top-level folder for the book: `serverside-wasm-book-code/`.
2. Inside this folder, create chapter-specific subfolders: `chapter02/` through `chapter08/`.
3. Within each chapter's folder, we'll create project-specific directories. For now, inside `chapter02/`, create `hello_world/`.

> **TIP** If you'd like to just follow along with the examples without coding them yourself or doing all this setup, you can instead clone the book's code repository with `git clone` https://github.com/danbugs/serverside-wasm-book-code. Some files in the repository are stored using Git Large File Storage (LFS), which is designed to handle large or binary files more efficiently. To make sure those files are available, first install Git LFS (see https://git-lfs.com/ for instructions), then run `git lfs install` followed by `git lfs pull` from the root of the cloned repo. This repository also uses Git submodules. To initialize them, run `git submodule update --init --recursive`.

Finally, navigate into the project folder and initialize the Rust library using the following command:

```
cargo new --lib hello_world_guest
```

This command uses Cargo, the Rust package manager and build system, to create a new Rust library project called `hello_world_guest`. The project's files will be placed in a new directory with the same name.

To keep all of the book's Rust projects organized, we'll also set up a Cargo workspace. This helps autocomplete and related features work more effectively when opening the entire book's folder at once, making navigation and development smoother. Inside `serverside-wasm-book-code/`, create a `Cargo.toml` file and populate it with the contents of the following listing.

Listing 2.1 Workspace `Cargo.toml` file

```
[workspace]
resolver = "2"
members = [
    "chapter02/hello_world/hello_world_guest",
]
```

With this set and after creating the project, you'll need to navigate into your new project directory:

```
cd hello_world_guest
```

> **NOTE** If you are planning on using a Cargo workspace as well, unless specified otherwise, after creating any of the upcoming Rust projects in the book, make sure to add their path to this file.

2.3.2 Specifying compilation to a Wasm module

In the `hello_world_guest` directory, there's a `src` folder, and inside it, a `lib.rs` file. This file is where we'll write the code for our Wasm application. You'll also find a `Cargo.toml` file in the `hello_world_guest` directory, which is the manifest file for your Rust project. It holds metadata about your project and defines how your project should be compiled.

To make sure our code compiles into a *Wasm module*, we need to edit the `Cargo.toml` file in the `hello_world_guest` directory.

> **NOTE** The term "Wasm module" specifically refers to core, or what we've been calling raw, Wasm. This distinction will become more relevant as we explore higher-level expansions onto core Wasm, like Wasm components, in chapter 3.

Open the `Cargo.toml` file in your preferred text editor and add the following snippet:

```
[lib]
crate-type = ["cdylib"]
```

The addition of `crate-type = ["cdylib"]` under the `[lib]` section guides the Rust compiler to generate a dynamic library. With the correct target settings, which we will discuss shortly, this ensures the output is a `.wasm` file compatible with our Wasm runtime.

Your `Cargo.toml` file, after including the necessary modifications to compile as a Wasm module, should appear as in the following listing.

Listing 2.2 `hello_world_guest Cargo.toml` file

```
[package]
name = "hello_world_guest"
version = "0.1.0"
edition = "2021"

[lib]
crate-type = ["cdylib"]

[dependencies]
```

> **NOTE** Parts of this book were developed using Rust's 2021 edition. If you're Rust version 1.85 or later, you might see `edition = "2024"` (or, in the future, later) in your `Cargo.toml` files.

2.3.3 *Writing the code for our application*

Let's edit the `lib.rs` file next. Clear out the default contents to start with a clean slate. Our first task is to define the `greet` function. This function will accept two arguments: a pointer to the beginning of a string in linear memory and the string's length (as shown previously in figure 2.2). The signature of the `greet` function should look like this:

```
#[no_mangle]
pub fn greet(ptr: i32, len: i32) {
  ...
}
```

The `#[no_mangle]` attribute is critical. It's a directive to the Rust compiler, ensuring the function name remains unchanged after compilation. This step is necessary for HelloWorldHost to find and invoke the `greet` function correctly.

Now let's move on to constructing our greeting. We'll start by creating the prefix string `"Hello, "`, and then we'll convert our two integer parameters (`i32s`) into the types that Rust uses for memory operations: a pointer and a length. Type this code into the `greet` function body we wrote previously:

```
let hello = "Hello, ";

let input_ptr = ptr as *mut u8;
let input_len = len as usize;
```

It's worth mentioning that even though Wasm itself doesn't support a string type directly, we're able to utilize it here (i.e., with `"Hello, "`). This is possible because Rust's compiler translates high-level types like `String` into low-level Wasm types, effectively bridging the gap between Rust strings and the byte representations required by Wasm.

This same principle applies to our use of `*mut u8` for pointers and `usize` for sizes. Even though Wasm doesn't directly recognize these Rust-specific types, Rust's compilation process handles these conversions smoothly. This highlights again why we chose Rust for this project. As mentioned earlier, its strong support for Wasm makes these low-level interactions easier to manage. Still, we keep the function signature utilizing `i32` types directly because that's part of the implicit contract with our HelloWorldHost—it invokes our function with two `i32` parameters.

Next, we can calculate the new length of our string, which will include the length of the `"Hello, "` prefix:

```
let new_len = input_len + hello.len();
```

Given this new length, we access the linear memory using an `unsafe` block, which is necessary for any operations in Rust that could potentially lead to safety problems, such as memory corruption or data races.

NOTE A data race happens when two or more threads access the same memory at the same time, at least one of them writes to it, and there's no synchronization to keep things in order. It's like multiple people editing the same document simultaneously without talking to each other—chaos, and potentially corrupted data.

This is especially pertinent when dealing with the low-level aspects of Wasm's linear memory:

```
let output = unsafe {
  core::slice::from_raw_parts_mut(0 as *mut u8, new_len)
};
```

By invoking `core::slice::from_raw_parts_mut`, we're effectively grabbing a mutable slice of memory from a raw pointer and a specified length. This allows us to write to a specific segment of memory (i.e., from `0` to `new_len`), facilitating the addition of our greeting to the existing string.

With the memory accessible, we can now construct our greeting by copying the `"Hello, "` prefix and the original string into the linear memory:

```
    output[..hello.len()].copy_from_slice(hello.as_bytes());
    output[hello.len()..]
        .copy_from_slice(unsafe {
          core::slice::from_raw_parts(input_ptr, input_len)
        });
```

In these lines, we first we set the beginning of the slice to `"Hello, "`. Then, we place our input string right after it. This operation, though straightforward in high-level languages, showcases the meticulous control over memory that working with Wasm and Rust allows, all while maintaining efficiency and safety within our application's context.

Overall, the `greet` function, with all its components, should look like the following listing.

Listing 2.3 The `greet` function (`lib.rs` file)

```
#[no_mangle]
pub fn greet(ptr: i32, len: i32) {
    let hello = "Hello, ";

    let input_ptr = ptr as *mut u8;
    let input_len = len as usize;

    let new_len = input_len + hello.len();

    let output = unsafe {
      core::slice::from_raw_parts_mut(
        0 as *mut u8, new_len)
    };

    output[..hello.len()].copy_from_slice(hello.as_bytes());
    output[hello.len()..]
        .copy_from_slice(unsafe {
          core::slice::from_raw_parts(
            input_ptr, input_len) });
}
```

- `#[no_mangle]`: Adds a compiler directive to keep the function name intact post-compilation
- `let input_ptr` / `let input_len`: Explicitly casts the i32 values to pointer and size types for Rust memory operations
- `let new_len`: Calculates the new length to accommodate the "Hello, " prefix
- `let output`: Grabs a slice of memory from 0 to new_len
- `output[..]`: Constructs the greeting by copying "Hello, " and the provided string into linear memory

2.3.4 Compiling the Rust code into a Wasm module

Before we compile our Rust library into a Wasm module, we need to ensure our toolchain is set up for targeting Wasm. Run the following command in your terminal:

```
rustup target add wasm32-unknown-unknown
```

This tells Rust to install the necessary components for compiling to the `wasm32-unknown-unknown` target. In Rust, target triples (e.g., `wasm32-unknown-unknown`) typically specify the architecture, vendor, and operating system for compiled code. In this case, `wasm32` indicates that we're targeting Wasm, and `unknown-unknown` signifies that there are no designated operating system or underlying platform dependencies.

This highlights one of Wasm's key strengths—its OS- and architecture-agnostic nature, which is what allows code to run consistently across different environments.

With that set and now that our `greet` function is in place, it's time to compile our Rust library into a Wasm module, making it ready for execution by HelloWorldHost. Navigate to the `hello_world_guest/` folder if you're not already there, and execute the following command:

```
cargo build --release --target wasm32-unknown-unknown
```

By specifying `--release`, we're asking Cargo to compile our project in release mode, which applies optimizations to make the resulting Wasm module more efficient. The `--target wasm32-unknown-unknown` part of the command explicitly tells Cargo to compile the project for a generic Wasm target, which, again, is what ensures our Rust code is transformed into a Wasm module compatible with any Wasm runtime, including our HelloWorldHost.

2.3.5 Executing the Wasm module with the custom host

At this stage, our Wasm module resides in the `target/wasm32-unknown-unknown/release/` folder of our root workspace. For easier access, we'll copy it to the root of the `hello_world_guest/` directory:

```
cp ../../../target/wasm32-unknown-unknown/release/hello_world_guest.wasm
➥hello_world_guest.wasm
```

This step positions the `.wasm` file conveniently for the next operation: execution.

To facilitate running our module without much hassle, I've packaged our HelloWorldHost into a Docker image. This setup requires only Docker to be installed on your machine.

You can install Docker in one of two ways:

- *Docker Engine* (lightweight, CLI-focused) https://docs.docker.com/engine/install/
- *Docker Desktop* (includes Docker Engine with a GUI) https://docs.docker.com/desktop/

NOTE The recommended Docker version for working through this book is `Docker version 28.0.0, build f9ced58`. You can check your current version with `docker --version`.

So, finally, always from `chapter02/hello_world/hello_world_guest/`, we can execute our guest application using the following command:

```
docker run --rm -v ".:/data"
➥ghcr.io/danbugs/serverside-wasm-book-code/hello-world-host:latest
➥/data/hello_world_guest.wasm 'Dan'
```

TIP These images are pushed to the GitHub Container Registry (GHCR) and are tied to the book's code repository. If you'd like to inspect the image, you can view it here: https://mng.bz/Ww8l.

Let's break down this command:

- `--rm` ensures that the Docker container, serving as our temporary host application environment, is removed after use, keeping your system clean.
- `-v` mounts a local directory to the container. This step requires specifying the path to the directory where `hello_world_guest.wasm` is located (i.e., obtained with '`.`'), enabling the Docker container to access the Wasm module.
- The final part executes our `hello_world_host:latest` Docker image. It requires two arguments: the path to the `.wasm` file within the mounted directory (`/data/hello_world_guest.wasm`) and a string parameter (`'Dan'`).

Upon successful execution, you'll observe the following output:

```
Initial Memory:
[0, 0, 0, 0, 0, 0, 0, 0, 0, 0, 0, 0, 0, 0, 0, 0]
Memory After Host Writes 'Dan':
[0, 0, 0, 0, 0, 0, 0, 0, 0, 0, 0, 0, 0, 68, 97, 110]
Memory After Host Calls `greet`:
[72, 101, 108, 108, 111, 44, 32, 68, 97, 110, 0, 0, 0, 68, 97, 110]
Hello, Dan
```

Aside from displaying the final `"Hello, Dan"` string we were expecting, HelloWorld-Host provides us with a view of the linear memory at several critical junctures:

- *Initial memory*—To start off, the memory is empty, signified by a series of zeros. This represents the untouched state of our linear memory before any operations are performed.
- *Memory after host writes* `'Dan'`—After the HelloWorldHost writes the string `'Dan'` into the memory, those characters are represented as ASCII/UTF-8 values in the memory space. Each character's ASCII/UTF8 value replaces the corresponding zeros in the initial memory layout. More specifically, HelloWorldHost, arbitrarily, wrote the bytes at index `input_len+10` to give us enough space to subsequently write `"Hello, Dan"` before it.
- *Memory after host calls* `greet`—Once the `greet` function is invoked, it prepends `"Hello, "` to the existing string `"Dan"`. In practice, as per the code we've written, that is actually copying two memory segments (`"Hello, "` and `"Dan"`) starting from `0` (i.e., due to `core::slice::from_raw_parts_mut(0 as *mut u8, new_len)`). The memory now reflects this change, showcasing the updated ASCII/UTF-8 values corresponding to `"Hello, Dan"`. Note that `"Dan"` still exists at `new_len+10`.

Congratulations! You've successfully built and executed your first Rust Wasm application executing in a non-web environment. Now let's take a moment to reflect on the challenges and limitations encountered during this process.

2.3.6 Reflecting on the "Hello, World" application

The completion of our "Hello, World" application serves not just as an introductory exercise but also as a practical demonstration of the complexities involved in Wasm's manual memory management. While we've managed to perform basic string manipulation, the process has illuminated notable limitations related to the following:

- *Handling complex data types*—The exercise of manipulating a simple string begs the question: how would one manage more complex data structures, such as classes/structs? The manual handling of memory for strings already introduces potential for error and complexity; extending this to more complex types would exponentially increase the difficulty and risk.
- *Memory assumptions risks*—The strategy assumes a certain memory layout and availability, which can lead to overwriting important data if those assumptions don't hold. For example, our code assumes that we can write to the memory slice from `0` to `new_len`, and our HelloWorldHost assumes the output will be written there—if you modify our code to write to a different memory slice (say, from 7 to `new_len`), you'll note the output displayed by the HelloWorldHost will be incorrect! Additionally, this approach assumes that the length of the `"Hello, "` string remains the same. If you modify it to a longer prefix, the output will no longer be valid, as the shifted memory will not account for the extra space. This risk is further exacerbated when considering the interaction of multiple modules, possibly written in different languages, each with unique memory management assumptions. Such interactions can lead to unpredictable behaviors and compromise application integrity.

These challenges underscore the need for a more robust and higher-level approach to data management within Wasm modules, and we're going to explore that throughout the book—starting with the first part of the story right now!

NOTE If you'd like to play with the HelloWorldHost yourself a bit, the code is available on GitHub at https://mng.bz/8XK5.

2.4 Building on Wasm's simple types with WebAssembly Interface Types

Core Wasm keeps its type system intentionally simple, relying on fundamental numeric types and linear memory. This minimalism is a strength—it ensures efficiency, portability, and broad compatibility across different execution environments. However, as Wasm adoption grows, so does the need for higher-level abstractions that make working with structured data more intuitive.

Enter WebAssembly Interface Types (WIT). Rather than working around Wasm's constraints, WIT builds on this solid foundation to enable more expressive module interactions. It serves as an interface definition language, allowing developers to define software component interfaces in a way that is agnostic to programming languages. This facilitates smoother communication between different parts of a Wasm application—or even between Wasm and the host runtime (e.g., HelloWorldHost)—by abstracting complex data types and simplifying module interactions.

WIT enhances the developer experience and broadens Wasm's applicability by introducing a wide array of new interface-level types in its interface definition language, beyond just the four number types mentioned earlier. These include Booleans (`bool`), signed and unsigned integers of various sizes (`s8`, `s16`, `s32`, `s64`, `u8`, `u16`, `u32`, `u64`), floating-point numbers (`f32`, `f64`), characters (`char`), and strings. Rather than adding new core Wasm primitives, WIT standardizes how to describe and marshal (i.e., convert between representations for communication across boundaries) richer data representations via the *Canonical ABI,* effectively lifting and lowering between Wasm and the interface layer.

> **NOTE** *ABI* stands for *application binary interface.* In this context, the Canonical ABI defines a standard way to translate values between Wasm and the other environments—whether that's the host or another Wasm guest. Think of it as the agreed-upon rules for how data gets packaged and unpackaged when crossing the Wasm boundary.

Beyond these primitives, WIT extends its type system to support lists (e.g., `list<u8>`), optional values (e.g., `option<string>`), error handling through results (e.g., `result<string, string>`), and tuples for grouping values (e.g., `tuple<string, u32>`).

Moreover, WIT introduces constructs for defining complex, user-defined types that closely mirror data structures found in high-level programming languages. These include records for structured data (e.g., `record person { name: string, age: u32 }`), enums for enumerating possible values (e.g., `enum color { red, green, blue }`), variants that are like enums but their properties can hold onto data (e.g., `variant error { server-error(u64), not-authorized, unknown(string) }`), and flags for bitwise combinations of options (e.g., `flags permissions { read, write, execute }`). Additionally, WIT supports type aliases to create new names for existing types and functions to define callable operations.

All these newly introduced types describe values that are copied in and out of memory. In addition to these, WIT also introduces resources, which are things that aren't copyable and, instead, are passed by handle (i.e., similar to how file descriptors or database connections are managed in operating systems).

Finally, WIT introduces higher-level constructs to organize and group functionalities. The concept of "worlds" is akin to namespaces or modules, organizing the exports and imports of interfaces or specific functions in a cohesive manner. Interfaces, which group related functions, will be further explored in future examples.

Revisiting our "Hello, World" application with the addition of WIT allows us to imagine a version where the complexities of manual memory management are abstracted away. With WIT, the `greet` function can be more intuitively defined, utilizing high-level types directly, as shown in the following listing.

Listing 2.4 The "Hello, World" application's WIT

```
package component:hello-world-guest-wit;

world example {
    export greet: func(name: string) -> string;
}
```

NOTE We've adjusted the `greet` function to return a string, eliminating the need for direct memory manipulation. This adjustment highlights WIT's capacity to simplify the interface for developers by abstracting lower-level details.

So, instead of having to create a function that takes in two integers representing a pointer and a length for a string and directly manipulating memory, transforming Wasm's basic types to higher-level ones, you can write this interface and create your program off it, utilizing abstractions provided by Wasm directly.

But there's no need to rush into creating a file for this interface just yet; we'll dive deeper into that in the next chapter. That said, this does lead us to a crucial consideration: how exactly do we bring this interface to life? The implementation specifics can differ across programming languages, yet the essence of working with WIT remains consistent. Once your interface is defined, it enables the generation of boilerplate code that navigates the intricacies of memory management for you. This method shifts the developer's focus from wrestling with low-level details to purely concentrating on the business logic, which, in our example, is fleshing out the `greet` function. This significant shift streamlines the development workflow, making it more efficient and focused on the core functionality.

2.5 Building the foundation of a smart content management system

Throughout the course of this book, we're going to apply what we learn by constructing a practical project: a smart content management system (CMS) for children's stories. A CMS is essentially a software application that allows users to create, edit, and manage digital content. In our case, it will enable the crafting and curation of engaging stories for children, making it easy to add new stories and present them.

The SmartCMS will be structured with a straightforward frontend where users can input and view stories. However, the core functionality will reside in the backend, which is where Wasm's capabilities will be harnessed to full effect. Our backend will consist of the following components:

- *Key-value store component*—This will be the repository for storing all the stories, which can be persisted to disk, Redis, or others.
- *HTTP component*—This will act as the API gateway, allowing the frontend to communicate with the backend.

- *Machine learning component*—This will serve as the story generator, using machine learning to create new stories. More specifically, we will be using a WIT interface for neural networks.

Our ultimate goal is to deploy this system on Kubernetes—an open source platform for automating deployment, scaling, and management of containerized applications—with dedicated Wasm containers. The architecture diagram in figure 2.4 visualizes the interaction between the user, the frontend, and the various backend components, all orchestrated within a Kubernetes environment.

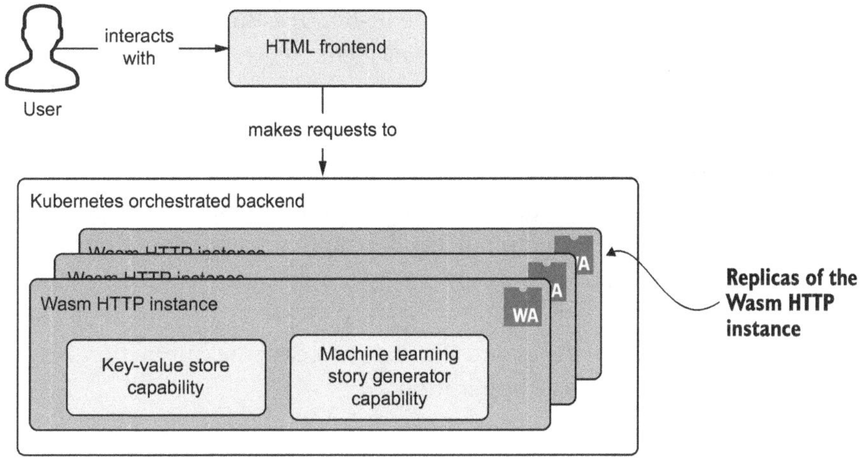

Figure 2.4 The basic architecture for our SmartCMS application

Let's begin by laying the groundwork for our key-value store component with WIT. Our initial interface, as seen in the following listing, will focus on the foundational operations of any key-value store: retrieving (`get`) and storing (`set`) data.

Listing 2.5 The SmartCMS's key-value store WIT

```
package component:smartcms-kvstore;

world kvstore {
    export get: func(key: string) -> string;
    export set: func(key: string, value: string);
}
```

The `get` function will take a `string` representing the key and return a `string` containing the value associated with that key. This will be used to retrieve stories from our store. The `set` function will accept two `string` parameters: one for the key and another for its corresponding value. This function won't return any value, reflecting the action of adding a new story to the store.

By defining these operations in WIT, we create an interface that can be universally understood and utilized by any language or tool that supports WIT, ensuring interoperability and flexibility.

With this in place, we close this chapter. In the following one, we'll dive into the implementation of the interface, bringing our key-value store component to life and running our first component.

Summary

- Wasm's core is formed by linear memory and four primary data types: integers and floats, each available in 32- and 64-bit sizes. Building complex data structures requires utilizing these foundational elements.
- Rust provides good support for working with Wasm as it can compile directly to it.
- Server-side Wasm applications need a specific execution runtime like Wasmtime, which is designed to enable interaction with system resources.
- Manual management of Wasm's limited foundational datatypes is intricate and susceptible to errors, emphasizing the importance of more sophisticated abstractions, such as WIT.
- WIT offers a versatile, language-agnostic type system, enabling the crafting of complex data structures and interfaces to ease the interaction between various components of a Wasm application.

3 Enhancing portability and security with Wasm components

This chapter covers

- How Wasm components provide enhanced portability and security
- Building a Wasm component with JavaScript
- Building a custom runtime for a Wasm component with Python
- Implementing host-side functionality from a WIT file in Rust

In chapter 2, we built our first Wasm app and compiled it into a Wasm module—the thing most people think of when they hear "Wasm." But, as we saw, a module on its own is stuck with only simple types like integers and floats. You can build more complex types from those, but that means both the guest and the Wasm runtime need to agree on the exact memory layout. For any real application, that's a headache.

This is where WebAssembly Interface Types (WIT) comes in. It gives us a way to define higher-level types without all the manual layout work. But WIT isn't the whole story. It's part of something bigger: the Wasm Component Model. The model uses

WIT as its interface definition language and serves as a wrapper around Wasm modules. The goal is to let different Wasm applications talk to each other without all the manual memory wrangling or those fragile, implicit agreements about where structures live in linear memory.

3.1 Benefits of Wasm components

The capability of components to lift from low- to high-level types (like going from two integers to a string) and lower from high- to low-level types brings several key benefits that aren't always obvious at first glance. These include cross-language portability, shared-nothing security, and only-what-you-need security with faster vulnerability mitigation. Let's break down each of these and see how they come into play.

3.1.1 Cross-language portability

Imagine you're developing a JavaScript application but want to use a machine learning library written in Python. How would you do that today? Most likely, you would create a Python microservice and possibly introduce a network stack into your application to communicate with it. This approach has two major drawbacks:

- You are forced to write code in Python, which you may not be familiar with, increasing the cognitive load.
- You are adding the complexity and overhead of a network stack to your application, which includes not only network communication but also the serialization and deserialization of data for communication between the two languages, such as using formats like JSON.

As shown in figure 3.1, Wasm components allow you to write applications in different languages and then compose or link them together to form a single `.wasm` file.

This means that with components, Wasm is not only language agnostic—meaning it doesn't rely on specific language features for compilation—but it is also now portable across languages. Languages with completely different paradigms or memory layouts can interact with one another as if they were one and the same. Imagine the number of person hours saved by not having to replicate the same feature across different languages!

Also, it's important to emphasize that Wasm components are really nothing more than a wrapper around Wasm modules. This is useful because it means we don't have to change our existing pipelines to utilize components. The only difference is the added linking/composing step.

3.1.2 Shared-nothing security

Wasm components also address another pain point of Wasm modules: the lack of a standard way to interact between modules/components or with a Wasm runtime. As we saw in our previous application, the way to communicate with our Wasm module was to directly interact with its exported memory. This approach is error prone because

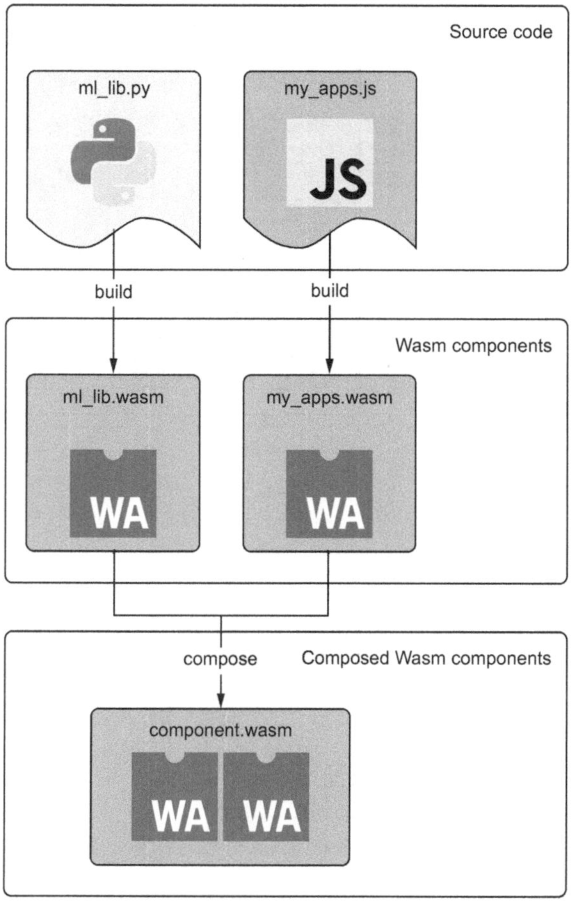

Figure 3.1 An example of cross-language portability with Wasm components

it requires the Wasm runtime (or another module) and our module to agree on the memory layout. Wasm components, on the other hand, follow the principle of shared nothing, meaning a Wasm runtime/module and our module do not share memory. Instead, they communicate exclusively through imports and exports of the Wasm component.

Let's walk through the example shown in figure 3.2 to see how we can achieve shared-nothing interactivity. In this example, we have two components: `my_app.wasm`, which imports a `secret-store` and retrieves a secret from it, and `my_secret_store.wasm`, which exports the `secret-store` interface containing a `get` method. And remember, both components are completely isolated and contain their own memory space.

To start, `my_app` calls the `get` method with a `my-key` value. That key is copied from `my_app`'s linear memory into `my_secret_store`'s linear memory. From there, `my_secret_store` can access its own linear memory to handle the `get` function call. But `get` returns a `Secret` resource, which is an opaque type—it doesn't directly expose its data like

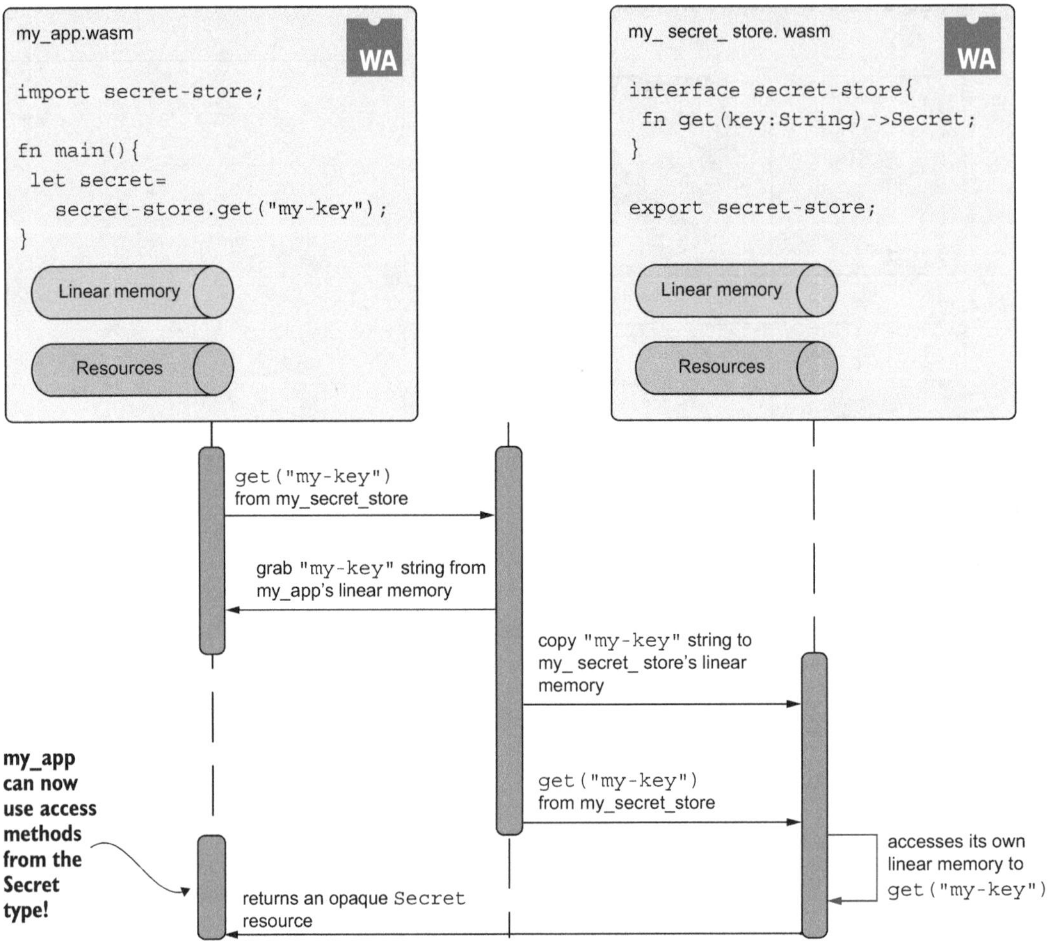

Figure 3.2 The interaction between two isolated Wasm components starting from a function call to communicating with an adapter component, doing required memory copies, and returning a resource that can be accessed via a resource table

strings or integers, and you interact with it through specific functions. That said, it can't be copied by value, so `my_secret_store` returns a *resource handle* instead. This handle is just an integer that points to the resource in a resource table—a separate memory space alongside linear memory.

Now, with that handle, `my_app` can call functions on the `Secret` type, like, say, some method to actually get the `Secret`'s data. If the idea of resource tables still feels a bit unclear, don't worry—we'll dig deeper into this with a hands-on example in chapter 4.

This process closely resembles interprocess communication, which might seem complicated but overall helps us understand the inner workings of Wasm components.

This complexity is hidden from the programmer consuming the interface—from the perspective of the programmer writing `my_app.wasm`, `secret-store.get` is just a simple function call.

This is a big shift in how we understand Wasm. That is, initially, we learn of it as being simply a compilation target—often compared to x86_64, arm64, RISC-V, etc. But Wasm components, while retaining that function, add a lot of structure around component-to-component or component-to-Wasm runtime communication, which much more closely resembles the idea of microservices. So now we can think of components as something that can be developed and deployed independently and interact with one another as part of a larger application.

3.1.3 Only-what-you-need security and improved vulnerability mitigation response

Another security benefit highlighted by Wasm components is that each component only ever has access to its specified imports. There are no unexpected or unauthorized dependencies that the component could access.

The best way to illustrate why this is important is by looking at Sysdig's 2023 Cloud-Native Security & Usage Report (https://mng.bz/4nVQ). That states that 87% of container images running in production have a critical or high severity vulnerability, but only 15% of high or critical severity vulnerabilities with an available fix are in use at run time. This means that most app code and, more importantly, most vulnerable code is not actually our app logic but rather some hidden dependency.

Now, of course, just because our components only have access to specific imports, it doesn't mean we are now vulnerability free. The few capabilities we have access to could still have bugs in them, but even in that scenario, Wasm components offer a benefit in terms of mitigation response, as shown in figure 3.3.

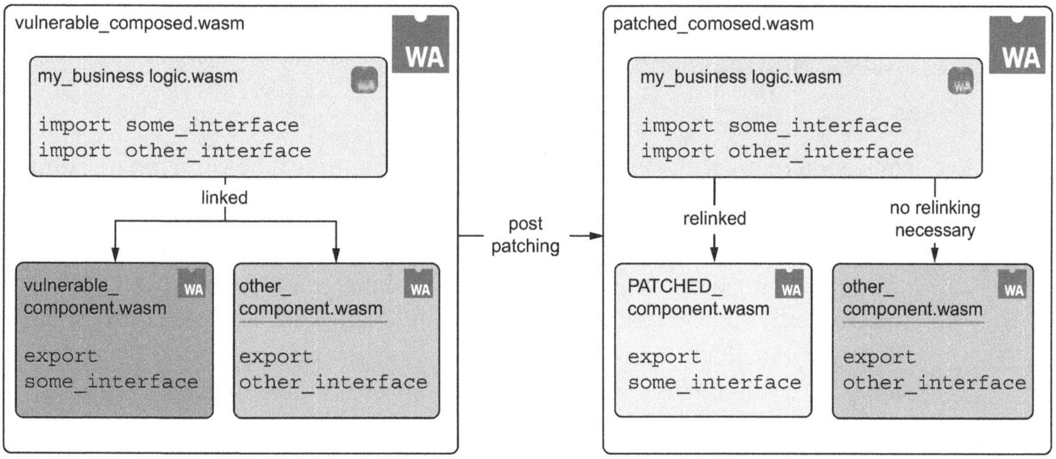

Figure 3.3 An example of improved mitigation response with Wasm components

Why only relink the vulnerable component? Because Wasm components are isolated and communicate through explicit interfaces, you can swap out just the vulnerable component with a patched version—no rebuild of your business logic needed. The vulnerable component and the other component are completely separate components that connect via imports/exports. Your business logic (`my_business_logic.wasm`) never changes, so there's nothing to recompile. You simply replace the vulnerable component and reestablish the connection.

This is different from traditional approaches where dependencies are often baked into your compiled binary. Even with dynamic libraries (like `.dll` or `.so` files), while you can replace them without rebuilding, they have full access to your application's memory and global variables. Wasm components use a shared-nothing isolation model—each component only accesses its specified imports and cannot share memory with other components. This means the effect or "blast radius" of a vulnerable component is contained. Figure 3.4 illustrates this difference in mitigation approaches.

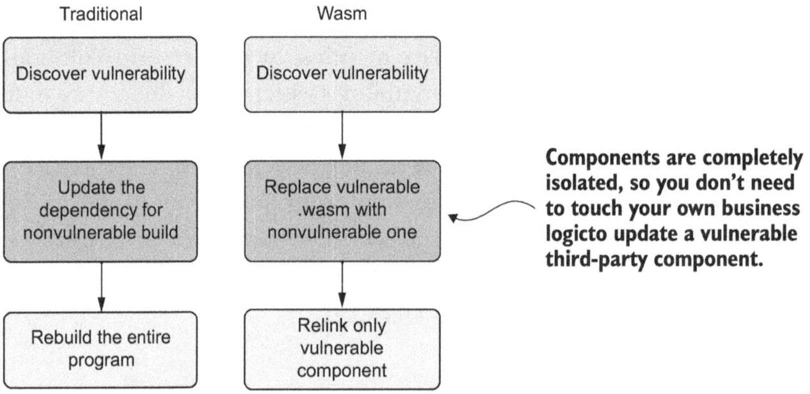

Figure 3.4 Illustrated difference between traditional architectures and one using Wasm components in terms of vulnerability mitigation

Let's consider a real-world scenario: imagine you're running an e-commerce platform and discover a critical vulnerability in your PDF-generation library:

- *Traditional approach*—You update the library version, rebuild your entire application (which includes your checkout logic, inventory management, user authentication, etc.), run your full test suite, and deploy a new release. Even with dynamic libraries, that PDF library has access to your entire application's memory—meaning a vulnerability could potentially expose customer data or credentials.
- *Wasm components approach*—You swap out just the PDF component with a patched version and relink it. Your checkout logic, inventory system, and authentication never get touched or recompiled. And because the PDF component was already

isolated to only its specified imports (like file-writing capabilities), even before patching, it couldn't accidentally leak customer data or access your database.

The isolation and composability of Wasm components turns vulnerability mitigation from an application-wide event into a surgical replacement.

3.2 Building a componentized "Hello, World" guest application with JavaScript

Now that we understand the benefits of Wasm components, let's pick up where we left off in chapter 2 and build a componentized "Hello, World" application. And because we already used Rust in the previous chapter, let's use JavaScript to create our Wasm component.

3.2.1 Setting up the project and installing the toolchain

We left off having crafted the WIT for our "Hello, World" application as displayed in the following listing.

Listing 3.1 The WIT file for our "Hello, World" application (`greet.wit`)

```
package component:hello-world-guest-wit;

world example {
    export greet: func(name: string) -> string;
}
```

To use this WIT file to create a component with JavaScript, we will need to set up the JavaScript Wasm toolchain. First, make sure you have Node and NPM installed. The Node.js documentation recommends using Node Version Manager (nvm) to handle this.

If you're on Linux, macOS, or Windows Subsystem for Linux, you can install nvm by running

```
curl -o- https://raw.githubusercontent.com
➥/nvm-sh/nvm/v0.40.2/install.sh | bash
```

Once that's done, restart your terminal and install Node version 22 (along with npm) by running

```
nvm install 22
```

If you're on Windows, you can grab the nvm installer from https://github.com/coreybutler/nvm-windows and follow the same steps.

After Node and npm are set up, install the JavaScript component toolchain (jco) globally:

```
npm install -g @bytecodealliance/jco@1.10.2
```

You'll also need the componentization tooling that jco uses:

```
npm install -g @bytecodealliance/componentize-js@0.17.0
```

With that done, from inside our `chapter03/` folder, let's create a folder for our project and call it `hello_world_component/`. In it, place the WIT file (`greet.wit`) from listing 3.1 and an empty JavaScript file called `greet.js`.

3.2.2 Implementing the component logic

As explicitly stated in the WIT file, our component will have a single function called `greet` that takes a `name` (`string`) and returns another `string` (i.e., the name prepended with `"Hello, "`). Let's implement this function in our JavaScript file as per the following listing.

Listing 3.2 The JavaScript file for our "Hello, World" component (`greet.js`)

```
export function greet(name) {
    return `Hello, ${name}!`;
}
```

Note that, unlike before, we are no longer walking on eggshells with memory by managing pointers and offsets. Instead, we are working directly with high-level types like strings. This is because the Wasm component wrapping handles the memory layout for us. We only need to focus on the logic of our component.

3.2.3 Compiling the Wasm component

Finally, let's componentize. To do this, we will use the JavaScript Wasm toolchain we set up earlier. Run the following command in the terminal inside your `hello_world_component` folder:

```
jco componentize greet.js --wit greet.wit --world-name
➥ example --out greet.wasm --disable stdio random clocks http
```

> **NOTE** Remember the security benefits we talked about in chapter 1 where Wasm only has access to the native OS via specific tightly controlled capabilities? You can see a bit of that with this command where we explicitly disable access to `stdio`, `random`, `clocks`, and `http`.

This command will bundle our JavaScript file into a Wasm component, utilizing the WIT file as a reference for imports and exports, creating a file called `greet.wasm`. Note, we need to provide the WIT file together with the JavaScript code, because our guest code does not provide a full picture of what needs to be linked for this component—for example, say we specified in our WIT that we want to import a capability to print to `stdout`; `jco` would only know that from our WIT. Next, let's move on to creating a custom Wasm runtime where we will execute our component.

3.3 Building a Python host for a JavaScript-bundled Wasm component

To run our component, we will need a host. And we will not use the HelloWorldHost from chapter 2 because that host meddled with memory directly, which goes against the whole point of Wasm components. So let's create a new host ourselves using Python, which will also serve to demonstrate how straightforward it is to call our JavaScript function cross-language from Python.

3.3.1 Setting up the project and installing the toolchain

Before we start building our Python app, we need to set up the Python environment. If you don't have Python installed, you can find installation instructions at https://wiki.python.org/moin/BeginnersGuide/Download. At the time of writing, I installed and am using Python version 3.12.3.

> **NOTE** Python projects typically use a virtual environment to manage dependencies and avoid interfering with your global Python setup. Before starting any Python project in this book, it's recommended to create a dedicated virtual environment for that project. You can do this by running `python -m venv venv` in the root directory of the specific Python project you're working on. Once that's done, you can activate the environment from the same directory. On Windows, use `.\venv\Scripts\activate` and on Linux or macOS, use `source venv/bin/activate`. When you're finished and want to return to the global Python environment, simply run `deactivate`.

To start, inside our `chapter03/` folder, create a new folder called `hello_world_python_host` at the same level as our `hello_world_component` folder and place an empty Python file called `main.py` in it.

Next, create a `requirements.txt` file in the `hello_world_python_host` folder and add the following line to it:

```
wasmtime==30.0.0
```

This will allow us to use the Wasmtime runtime in our Python host. We can then install the required package by running the following command in the terminal:

```
python -m pip install -r requirements.txt
```

> **NOTE** Depending on your Python installation, you may need to use `python3` or `py` instead of `python` to run commands. On Linux, you might also need to install pip using `apt-get install python3-pip`.

3.3.2 Implementing the host logic

Now let's implement the logic for our Python host. This step, as illustrated in figure 3.5, involves embedding the Wasmtime runtime to load our Wasm component and directly call the `greet` function.

To start, let's import some necessary modules. The first is the runtime itself, and the second is a loader module, which will help us load our Wasm component. In `main.py`, write

```
import wasmtime, wasmtime.loader
```

Next, copy the `greet.wasm` file from our `hello_world_component` folder to our `hello_world_python_host` folder.

With that done, we can directly load our `greet.wasm` file directly from disk, like so:

```
import greet
```

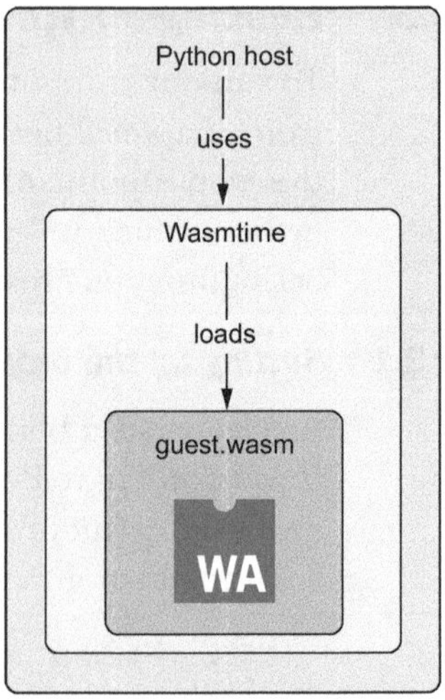

Figure 3.5 The host is a thin wrapper around Wasmtime, which we will use to load our guest component and execute the functions it implements.

Next, we set up a store—a Wasmtime construct for storing data related to a component or module—and attach or "root" it to the greeter component we bundled earlier from JavaScript:

```
store = wasmtime.Store()
component = greet.Root(store)
```

Now we have everything we need to call the `greet` function from the component we wrote earlier. Let's do that:

```
print(component.greet(store, "World"))
```

Finally, the following listing shows the full Python file for our "Hello, World" host.

Listing 3.3 The Python file for our "Hello, World" host (`main.py`)

```
import wasmtime, wasmtime.loader
import greet

store = wasmtime.Store()
component = greet.Root(store)
print(component.greet(store, "World"))
```

3.3.3 *Running the Python host*

The Python host can then be run like any other Python file:

```
python main.py
```

If everything went well, you should see the output `"Hello, World!"`. Let's take a moment to reflect on what happened here with figure 3.6.

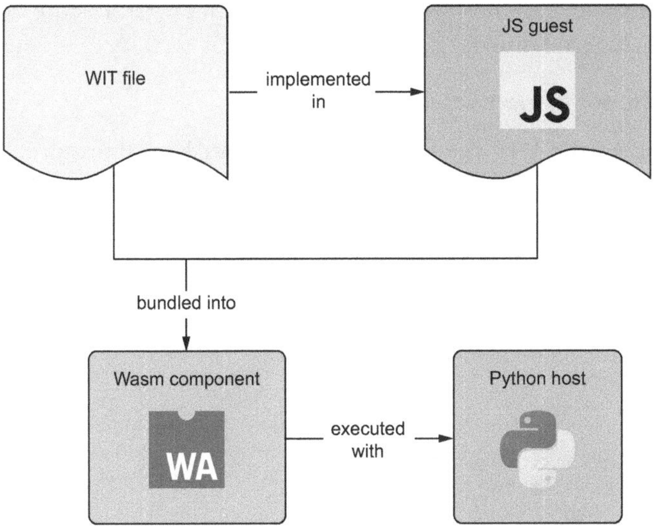

Figure 3.6 The flow of our "Hello, World" application with a Wasm component

Take a moment to pat yourself on the back. You have come a long way! Starting only with a WIT file that defined a `greet` function, we implemented the functionality in JavaScript, bundled it into a Wasm component, and loaded that in a self-made Python host that embedded Wasmtime to call a function cross-language. It was a lot of work, and, in fact, maybe too much work. Constantly creating WIT files and custom hosts can be cumbersome and is much more effort than a conventional project. As app developers, we should only be concerned with our JavaScript Wasm component and not with crafting WITs or dealing with Wasmtime. So, in subsequent chapters, we will see how to do just that when we discuss some standardized WIT interfaces and even prebuilt generic Wasm runtimes that simplify the process of making an app. But, for now, let's dig even deeper into Wasm components and establish some solid foundational knowledge.

3.4 Expanding the example project with Wasm components

In chapter 2, we introduced the smart content management system (CMS) for children's stories that we'll build throughout this book. We started by crafting a simple, initial WIT file for interacting with the key-value store that will hold those stories. Now, before expanding on that, let's talk about where we're putting that key-value store logic. In this case, we're going to implement the functionality in the host so that the guest can import and use it.

This might feel different from our "Hello, World" example, where the host mostly acted as an entry point and the component contained all the logic. But here, we're treating the host as the provider of the environment and supporting functions the guest needs during execution. By placing this logic in the host, guests can stay focused on using that functionality rather than defining it, which also makes it easier to swap in generic hosts later on. So let's see how we can implement our key-value store in the host and have the guest service call into it.

3.4.1 Improving the WIT file for the key-value store

In chapter 2, we created the WIT file in listing 3.4 for our key-value store. To begin using the interface, copy the contents of listing 3.4 into a new file named `smart_cms.wit`. Save this file inside a folder called `smart_cms/`, which should be located within the `chapter03/` directory.

Listing 3.4 The preliminary WIT file for our key-value store (`smart_cms.wit`)

```
package component:smartcms-kvstore;

world kvstore {
    export get: func(key: string) -> string;
    export set: func(key: string, value: string);
}
```

Now that we have a better mental model for how the application will work, let's move the `get` and `set` methods to a unique `kvstore` interface to be called like so:

```
// ...
interface kvstore {
    get: func(key: string) -> string;
    set: func(key: string, value: string);
}
// ...
```

We are doing this because we will modify our existing `world`. We'll rename it to `app` and have it import the `kvstore` interface we just created. This is particularly important because it indicates that a host is responsible for implementing the key-value store functionality, which is different from before, where we `exported` functions that were to be implemented by the guest:

```
// ...
world app {
    import kvstore;
}
// ...
```

We will also add a new `export` for a `run` function that is meant to be implemented by a guest. This function will be the entry point for the guest's execution, and it will return a `string` so that we can see some output from calling into the guest:

```
// ...
world app {
    import kvstore;
```

```
    export run: func() -> string;
}
// ...
```

Lastly, let's update the package name of our WIT file to be `component:smartcms`:

```
package component:smartcms;
// ...
```

Overall, our updated WIT file should look like the following listing.

Listing 3.5 The updated WIT file for our key-value store (`smart_cms.wit`)

```
package component:smartcms;

interface kvstore {
    get: func(key: string) -> string;
    set: func(key: string, value: string);
}

world app {
    import kvstore;
    export run: func() -> string;
}
```

- **kvstore was moved to its own interface.**
- **world app imports kvstore, meaning a host must implement it.**
- **world app exports run, meaning a guest (i.e., a Wasm component) must implement it.**

3.4.2 *Creating the SmartCMS host*

Now let's try our hand at using Rust to create the host for our SmartCMS. To reiterate, we are doing this for two main reasons:

- We don't currently have an environment for our guest to run in, so we have to handcraft one.
- We need to implement the host functionality for the key-value store that our guest is expecting to be capable of importing.

By the end of this, we will have a full-fledged host to load our component in and execute the guest's `run` function from.

Inside our `smart_cms/` folder, we can set up our new project by running the following command in the terminal:

```
cargo new smartcms_test_host
```

Next, let's move our newly created `smart_cms.wit` file to the `smartcms_test_host` folder.

Then open the project with your IDE of choice, and let's edit the `Cargo.toml` file to add the dependency we need to utilize Wasmtime. This is all very similar to how we built our Python host just prior:

```
# ...

[dependencies]
wasmtime = "30"
```

Next, let's look at the autogenerated `main.rs` file and delete all its contents. Then we can start implementing our host by making a call to `wasmtime::component::bindgen!` at the top of our file, which will generate a bunch of glue code for us to be able to implement the key-value store functionality:

```
wasmtime::component::bindgen!({
    path: "./smart_cms.wit",
    world: "app",
});
```

This call will give us access to a `Host` trait that we can implement for our own type. If you're not familiar with traits, think of them as interfaces in Go and Java or protocols in Python and Swift. Our own type will be a `struct` called `KeyValue` that will serve as the implementor for our `kvstore` interface. To keep things simple, we will use a `HashMap` as the backing to store our key-value pairs, like so:

```
// ...
struct KeyValue {
    mem: std::collections::HashMap<String, String>,
}
```

Next, let's implement the host interface. We can do so like this:

```
impl component::smartcms::kvstore::Host for KeyValue {
    // ...
}
```

Inside the `impl` block, we need to implement the `get` and `set` functions. Let's start with `get`:

```
impl component::smartcms::kvstore::Host for KeyValue {
    fn get(&mut self, key: String) -> String {
        self.mem.get(&key).cloned().unwrap()
    }
}
```

In here, we will access the `mem` field of our `KeyValue` instance, which, of course, is a `HashMap`, so we can call its very own `get` method. Next, we clone that value and `unwrap` it. This is because `get` from `HashMap` returns an `Option<String>`, which is Rust's way of handling `null` values (i.e., for when the key isn't present). In our usage, `unwrapping` means we are assuming that the key will always be present. If it isn't, our code will `panic`/crash, which isn't particularly graceful error handling. Let's get rid of this assumption by slightly modifying our WIT file to have our `get` function match the `HashMap`'s `get` function:

```
// ...
interface kvstore {
    get: func(key: string) -> option<string>;
    set: func(key: string, value: string);
}
// ...
```

Then we can modify our get implementation and remove that `unwrap` call:

```
// ...
    fn get(&mut self, key: String) -> Option<String> {
        self.mem.get(&key).cloned()
    }
// ...
```

Next, let's implement the `set` function. It is very similar to the `get` function except for the `&mut self` parameter (i.e., Rust's way to indicate that the function will be able to modify the `KeyValue` instance it is called on) and the fact that, instead of returning a value, it will set a value, like so:

```
// ...
    fn set(&mut self, key: String, value: String) {
        self.mem.insert(key, value);
    }
// ...
```

Now that we are done implementing the `Host` interface, let's implement the `main` function. The `main` function will be the entry point of our host. So, there, we will be configuring Wasmtime to execute our components. We can start on that by first creating the configuration object for Wasmtime:

```
fn main() {
    let mut config = wasmtime::Config::default();
    config.wasm_component_model(true);
}
```

Note that we are utilizing default configuration for the runtime, but we are also setting the `wasm_component_model` feature to `true`. This is because we are using Wasm components, and we need to enable this to use them.

Next, we will create the `Engine` object to that configuration, which is essentially Wasmtime itself, where our component will be executed:

```
fn main() {
    // ...
    let engine = wasmtime::Engine::new(&config).unwrap();
}
```

One of the last items we need to create is the `Store` object, which, like in our Python host, is where we will store the data related to our component or module. Before, we didn't really have any data to store, but now we have all the data inside our key-value component. So the store configuration is a little different. For starters, let's create a new `struct` to collect our runtime state and call it `State`. Right now, this `struct` is a bit redundant because the only possible state we can have is related to our key-value store, so we could make do with just `KeyValue`. But, by creating `State`, we are being future-proof, so we can build upon our host in the future. `State` will look like this:

```
struct State {
    key_value: KeyValue,
}
```

Now, back in `main`, we can initialize our store with such state:

```
// ...
fn main() {
    // ...
    let mut store = wasmtime::Store::new(&engine, State {
        key_value: KeyValue {
            mem: std::collections::HashMap::new(),
        }
    });
}
```

And, finally, we can load the component that this host will run:

```
// ...
fn main() {
    // ...
    let component = wasmtime::component::Component::from_file
    ➥ (&engine, "guest.wasm").unwrap();
}
```

`guest.wasm` will be the file name of the Wasm guest component we will be building in the next section, which will implement our `run` function.

Finally, the last thing that we need to do is start our `Linker` object. The linker is in charge of connecting our host and guest: it is what will allow our guest to access the functions we implemented in our host:

```
// ...
fn main() {
    // ...
    let mut linker = wasmtime::component::Linker::new(&engine);
    component::smartcms::kvstore::add_to_linker
    ➥ (&mut linker, |state: &mut State| &mut state.key_value).unwrap();
}
```

The second parameter to the `add_to_linker` function is a closure/lambda/anonymous function that will return a mutable reference to our `KeyValue` instance, which is how we are able to give our guest access to the host's key-value store implementation. Next, we can simply instantiate the guest and call the `run` function, which we will be wrapping in a `println` so we can see the output `string` the guest will return:

```
// ...
fn main() {
    // ...
    let app = App::instantiate(&mut store, &component, &linker).unwrap();
    println!("{:?}", app.call_run(&mut store).unwrap());
}
```

And that's it! We have our host ready to go. In the following listing, you can see the full `main.rs` file.

Listing 3.6 The full `main.rs` file for our SmartCMS host

```
wasmtime::component::bindgen!({
    path: "./smart_cms.wit",
    world: "app",
});

struct KeyValue {
    mem: std::collections::HashMap<String, String>,
}

impl component::smartcms::kvstore::Host for KeyValue {
    fn get(&mut self, key: String) ->
    ➥ Option<String> {
        self.mem.get(&key).cloned()
    }

    fn set(&mut self, key: String, value: String) {
        self.mem.insert(key, value);
    }
}

struct State {
    key_value: KeyValue,
}

fn main() {
    let mut config = wasmtime::Config::default();
    config.wasm_component_model(true);

    let engine = wasmtime::Engine::new(&config).unwrap();

    let mut store = wasmtime::Store::new
    ➥ (&engine, State { key_value: KeyValue { mem:
    ➥  std::collections::HashMap::new() } });

    let component = wasmtime::component::
    ➥ Component::from_file(&engine, "guest.wasm").unwrap();
```

Annotations:
- We use macros to create glue code to facilitate our host implementation.
- The implementation of our kvstore world, using a HashMap to store key-value pairs
- The get function now returns an Option<String> for better error handling.
- The runtime state containing our KeyValue struct
- Enables the component model feature to indicate that we are using components instead of modules
- Sets our runtime state in the Store object

```
    let mut linker = wasmtime::component::Linker::new(&engine);
    component::smartcms::kvstore::
    ➥add_to_linker(&mut linker, |state: &mut State| &mut
    ➥ state.key_value).unwrap();

    let app = App::instantiate(&mut store,
    ➥&component, &linker).unwrap();

    println!("{:?}", app.call_run(&mut store)
    ➥.unwrap());
}
```

Links our kvstore host implementation together with its respective state

The App symbol isn't defined by us, but rather it is implemented by wasmtime::component::bindgen!

Calls the run function that will be implemented in the guest

Now let's move onto creating the guest component.

3.4.3 Implementing and running a guest Wasm component inside our SmartCMS host

To store our guest code, let's create a new folder called `smartcms_kvstore_guest`. It should be a sibling to `smartcms_test_host`. Inside of it, we will make a new file called `guest.js` where we will be creating another JavaScript guest component. This guest code won't be incredibly meaningful and, for now, will just demonstrate we can do a full roundtrip from the host to the guest and back—all while using the key-value store we implemented in the host, which, in particular, uses types that are not present in JavaScript (like Rust's `Option` type).

First, let's bring in the imports from the host. We can do so like this:

```
import { get, set } from "component:smartcms/kvstore";
```

Next, let's implement the `run` function. It will simply set a key-value pair, then get it, and return that value:

```
export function run() {
    set("guest-hello", "Hello from the Guest!");
    return get("guest-hello");
}
```

The full file can be seen in the following listing.

Listing 3.7 The full `guest.js` file for our SmartCMS guest

```
import { get, set } from "component:
➥smartcms/kvstore";

export function run() {
    set("guest-hello", "Hello from the Guest!");
    return get("guest-hello");
}
```

The guest only has access to what is provided to it (i.e., the functions from kvstore).

The guest communicates through its imports; it does not meddle with memory directly.

We can't print here because we never granted the guest access to standard output.

But remember: our `run` function returns a `string`, so how can this work with our `get` function returning an `option<string>`? Let's try componentizing it. To componentize, run the following command from inside the `smartcms_kvstore_guest` folder:

```
jco componentize guest.js --wit ../smartcms_test_host/smart_cms.wit --
➥world-name app -o ../smartcms_test_host/guest.wasm --
➥disable stdio random clocks http
```

And—it all works! To figure out what is going on here, let's run `jco transpile`. This will allow us to provide our `.wasm` component back to `jco` so it can spit out the generated JavaScript glue code. This way, we can see how the types are being handled:

```
jco transpile ../smartcms_test_host/guest.wasm --out-dir transpile
```

Now, inside `transpile/interfaces`, we can see our WIT interface defined as a TypeScript declaration file at `transpile/interfaces/component-smartcms-kvstore.d.ts`. There, we will see what is displayed in the following listing.

Listing 3.8 The TypeScript declaration file for our key-value store interface

```
/** @module Interface component:smartcms/kvstore **/
export function get(key: string): string | undefined;
export function set(key: string, value: string): void;
```

Aha! This is what allows our JavaScript guest to still work. The `Option` type has been translated to `string | undefined`, with `undefined` aligning to `Option`'s `None` variant. So, essentially, the signature of `run` is still fulfilled and the code works.

> **NOTE** The `run` function signature is technically fulfilled—but only at run time, not statically. Since our key-value store has a value for `guest-hello`, everything works fine. But if it didn't, and `undefined` were returned, the app would crash.

To finish off, let's run this component. Back in our host folder, execute the following in the terminal:

```
cargo run --release
```

If everything went well, you should see the output: `"Hello from the Guest!"`.

Again, that was quite a bit of work, but it highlighted several important pieces of the puzzle coming together. Primarily, we saw how we can now utilize high-level types, in high-level languages, across different languages. But we also saw some notable security principles in practice. For example, we saw only-what-you-need security being displayed with our guest utilizing nothing but the `kvstore` interface—that is, our guest, did not even have access to standard output, which is why I deferred displaying the result of `get` to our host. And we also saw the shared-nothing principle in action, where our guest and host did not share memory but instead communicated through the `kvstore` interface that manipulated the runtime state.

Throughout this chapter, we put on a lot of different hats. While designing interfaces, we acted as architects. While implementing the host, we acted as system engineers. And, while implementing the guest, we acted as application developers. This, of course, is not how developing a server-side Wasm application is supposed to be. Most of the time, we will be using standardized interfaces and prebuilt generic hosts, so we can dedicate ourselves to simply caring about the business logic. But, hopefully, by going through this process, we now have a much better understanding of the system as a whole, which will be invaluable when things don't go exactly as planned.

Summary

- Wasm components are a wrapper around Wasm modules that allow us to use higher-level types.
- Wasm components add a new level of portability to Wasm by allowing easy cross-language communication.
- Wasm components enforce a shared-nothing principle between components or within the host. They communicate exclusively through imports and exports and do not share memory.
- Wasm components improve security by only allowing access to specific imports and exports, and they contain no hidden dependencies.
- Wasm components improve mitigation response by allowing us to update components simply by relinking the patched component without rebuilding the entire project.
- There are language-specific toolchains for creating Wasm components that take care of generating the glue code needed to interact across languages.
- Developers generally use standardized interfaces and prebuilt generic hosts to run Wasm components.

4 Interfacing Wasm with the underlying system

This chapter covers

- Implementing APIs with WASI
- The new capabilities of WASI 0.2
- Converting a Wasm module to a Wasm component
- Using WASI-Virt to restrict or allow component capabilities
- Composing Wasm components together

At this point in our exploration of Wasm for server-side development, we have a somewhat clear picture of what Wasm modules and Wasm components are, together with the differences between the two, as illustrated in figure 4.1.

Wasm modules are core Wasm. They are what we got from the base implementation of the Wasm spec (https://webassembly.github.io/spec/core/): a binary format with four basic types and a linear memory block that sets the stage for very quick (near-native) and safe (sandboxed) execution of code—be it in a JavaScript engine (on the browser) or in a Wasm runtime (on the server).

Wasm components, on the other hand, build on top of Wasm modules to expand their versatility and make certain interactions much smoother. While Wasm modules are intentionally low-level—giving developers the freedom to build exactly what they need—components take that foundation and add a clear, standardized way for different Wasm programs (or a Wasm program and its host) to talk to each other.

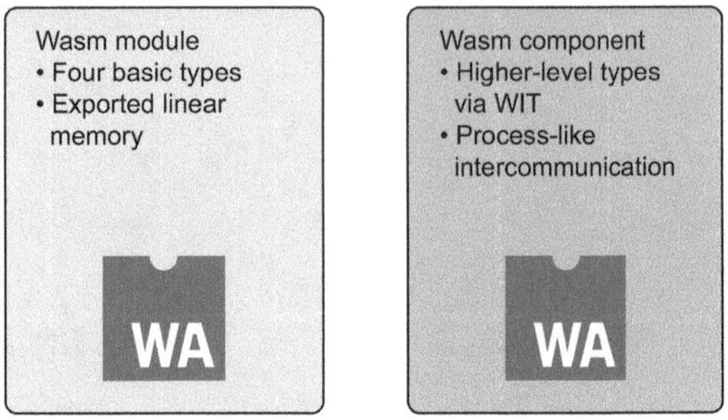

Figure 4.1 Comparing Wasm modules and Wasm components

Without components, these interactions required a custom contract, defining how to use a module's linear memory block to represent anything beyond the four basic Wasm types. For instance, in chapter 2, we showed how to handle strings this way. Components simplify all that by introducing the Canonical ABI: a ready-made agreement for passing data around in Wasm binary form. The Canonical ABI defines how to lift those four basic Wasm types into richer, more complex data structures and lower them back down again. This shift—from the manual handling we used in chapter 2 to the streamlined process enabled by the Canonical ABI—is shown in figure 4.2.

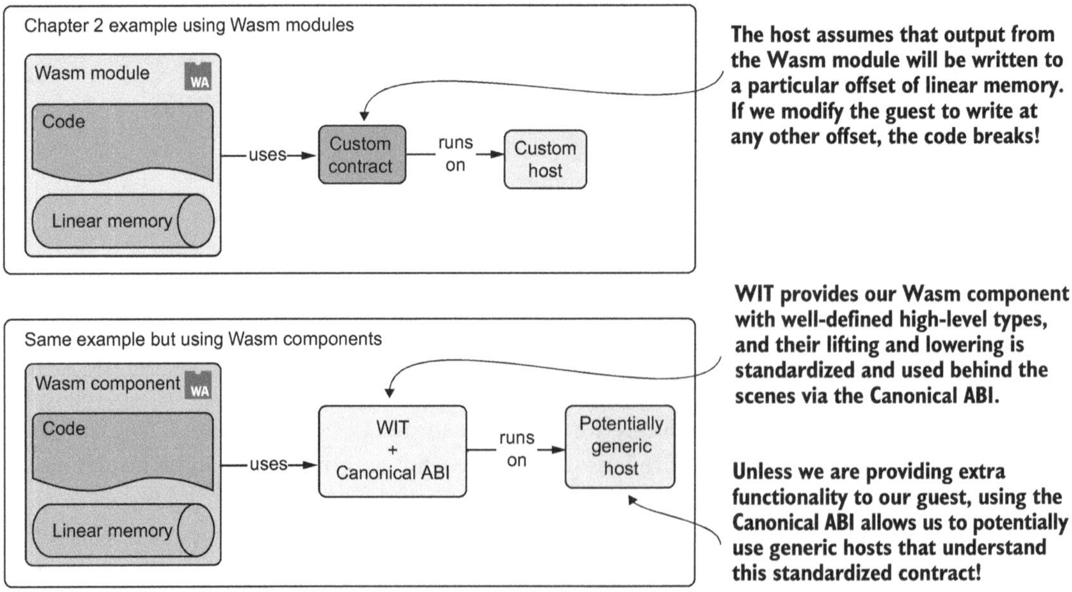

Figure 4.2 Comparing how data flows in chapter 2's Wasm module example versus using Wasm components. The top diagram shows the manual setup, with a custom contract between the module and a custom host. The bottom diagram shows how components rely on WebAssembly Interface Types (WIT) and the Canonical ABI, making it possible to interact with a potentially generic host without custom wiring.

But components go beyond just data handling. Once you factor in how they let you interface with the underlying system itself, the differences between Wasm modules and components really start to stand out. Let's dig into that next.

4.1 The WebAssembly System Interface

Wasm, as we've established, is platform agnostic, meaning it makes no assumptions on what platform it will be running, and that's one of its main superpowers. This is what makes it possible for it to run anywhere, from the browser to an on premises server, cloud, or edge devices. But if Wasm is platform agnostic, what happens when you actually want to interact with the platform your Wasm is running on? How can a Wasm program ever open a file or print to `stdout`?

If you've ever used Wasm in a browser, you might remember that browsers provide a Wasm JavaScript API. With this API, you can write functions in JavaScript and make them available for your Wasm module to use, under whatever names you choose. In other words, when your Wasm code calls these functions, it's really calling JavaScript functions behind the scenes! You set this up by instantiating the Wasm module with an object that maps Wasm function names to JavaScript functions, as shown in figure 4.3.

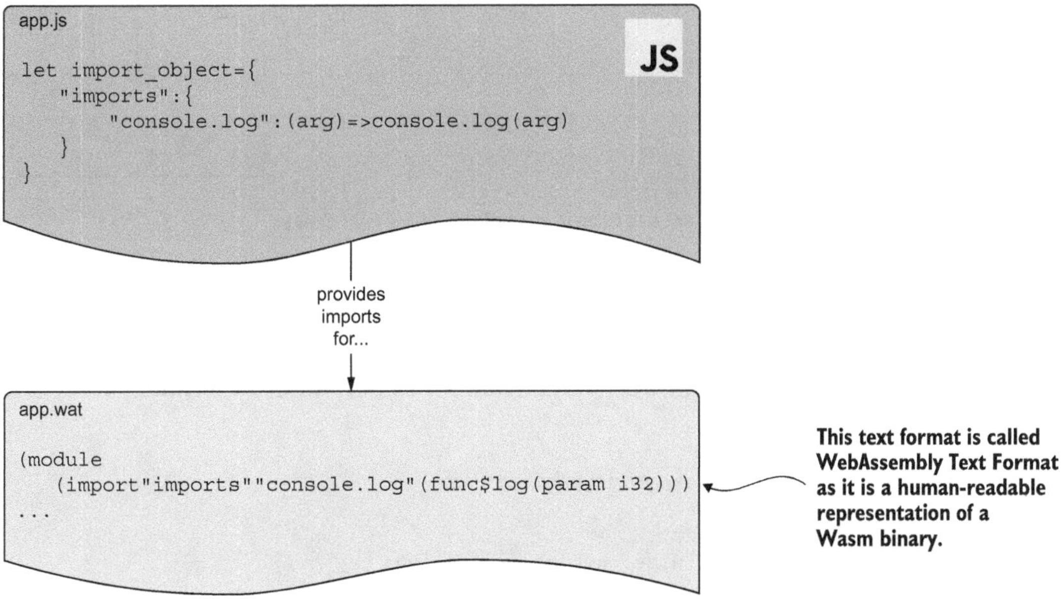

Figure 4.3 JavaScript API providing access to host capabilities to a Wasm guest

With this mechanism, it is very easy to expose something like the `console.log` function and have it work in Wasm. This is great in the browser, because Wasm's purpose there is to be embedded within a larger application for complex processing that is too slow to do in JavaScript—for example, calculations for rendering a large 3D game.

On the server side, to some extent, Wasmtime (and any other Wasm runtime) serves the purpose of the browser. It is where we embed our Wasm, and it is the engine where it runs. So, equally, it should be in charge of providing the necessary APIs for Wasm to interact with its environment. This is where the WebAssembly System Interface (WASI) comes in. WASI establishes the set of APIs that Wasm runtimes implement to provide Wasm programs with the necessary system calls to interact with the setting in which they are placed, as illustrated in figure 4.4.

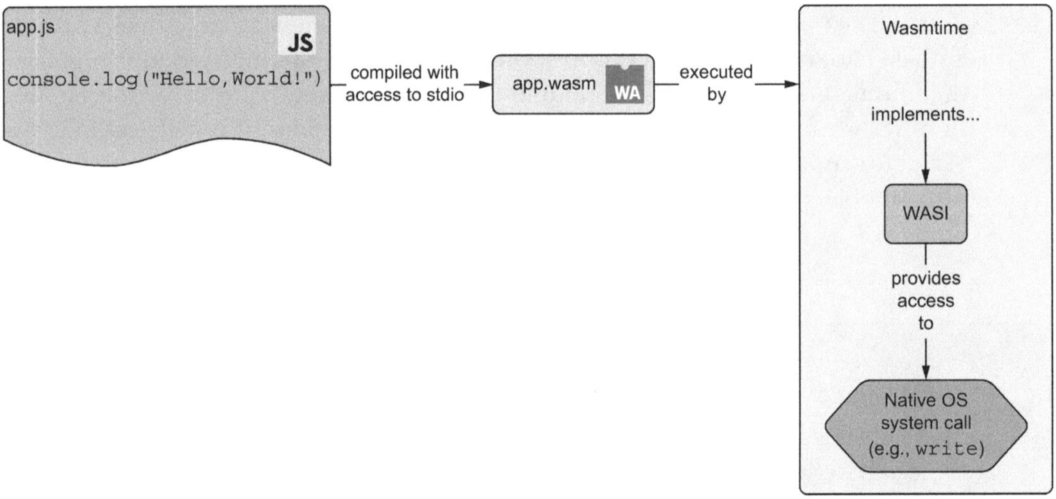

Figure 4.4 Wasmtime/WASI providing access to host capabilities to a Wasm guest

Let's take a look at how we can make use of WASI to interact with our system's standard output.

Previously, when crafting our componentized "Hello, World" application, we created the following WIT file:

```
package component:hello-world-guest-wit;

world example {
    export greet: func(name: string) -> string;
}
```

Then, our implementation got the name parameter and prepended `"Hello, "` to it:

```
export function greet(name) {
    return `Hello, ${name}!`;
}
```

Finally, we created a Python host to instantiate and call our `greet` component and function.

With WASI, our WIT definition no longer has to return a string. Instead, in `greet`, we can directly print to the standard output. This is possible because WASI provides access to system capabilities—things like printing to standard output, reading environment variables, or working with files—that a plain Wasm component wouldn't have on its own.

To get started, copy the `greet.js` and `greet.wit` files we created in the previous chapter to a new directory (say, `chapter04/hello_world_wasi/hello_world_wasi_guest`). Then modify the `greet.wit` file to look like the following listing. And, for organization's sake, let's put our `greet.wit` file inside a directory at `hello_world_wasi_guest/wit/`.

Listing 4.1 Modified WIT file for guest component (`greet.wit`)

```
package component:hello-world-guest-wit;

world example {
    export greet: func(name: string);    // greet no longer returns a string.
}
```

Then modify the `greet.js` file to look like the following listing.

Listing 4.2 Modified implementation of guest component (`greet.js`)

```
export function greet(name) {
    console.log(`Hello, ${name}!`);    // We can utilize console.log to print to the standard output.
}
```

Now let's try compiling our component using `jco` like we did in section 3.2.3. From the `hello_world_wasi_guest/` folder:

```
jco componentize greet.js --wit wit/greet.wit
➥ --world-name example --out greet.wasm --disable http
```

But note this time we are only disabling the `http` capability. Disabling `http` makes sense here because our simple greeting application doesn't need network access. We are not disabling `stdio`, though—with WASI, we can now interact with the system's standard output, and we want to make use of that.

Next, because `wasmtime-py` (i.e., the Python bindings for Wasmtime) does not currently fully support WIT, we will not be able to use the Python host we worked on prior to call the `greet` function and, instead, we'll have to create a Rust host.

Let's start by creating a new Rust project at the same directory level from the `hello_world_wasi/` folder:

```
cargo new hello_world_wasi_host
```

Then let's add the `wasmtime` and `wasmtime-wasi` dependencies to our `Cargo.toml` file:

```
[dependencies]
wasmtime = "30"
wasmtime-wasi = "30"
```

We can then delete all the contents of the `src/main.rs` file and start our host implementation by using `wasmtime`'s `bindgen` macros, like so:

```
wasmtime::component::bindgen!({
    path: "../hello_world_wasi_guest/wit",
    world: "example",
});
```

Next, we can create our `State` struct. Just like in our SmartCMS test host, we'll use this struct to keep the state associated with our application, but, unlike the SmartCMS test host state, which only held our key-value's store state, this host's state will hold our WASI context and the resource table associated with WASI and component usage. Remember the resource tables we talked about when going over figure 3.2 in the last chapter? This is where they come into play:

```
// ...
struct State {
    wasi: wasmtime_wasi::WasiCtx,
    table: wasmtime_wasi::ResourceTable,
}
```

Next, we need to update our `State` struct to implement two traits: `WasiView` and `IoView`. `WasiView` will give access to the WASI context, and `IoView` will provide access to the resource table:

```
// ...
impl wasmtime_wasi::WasiView for State {
    fn ctx(&mut self) -> &mut wasmtime_wasi::WasiCtx {
        &mut self.wasi
    }
}

impl wasmtime_wasi::IoView for State {
    fn table(&mut self) -> &mut wasmtime_wasi::ResourceTable {
        &mut self.table
    }

}
```

Then we can finally implement the entry point of our host: the `main` function. This function will be responsible for loading our component, creating an instance of it, and calling the `greet` function.

To start off, just like we did with the SmartCMS test host, we'll create a `Config` and an `Engine` object. The `Config` object will hold the configuration for our Wasmtime engine (e.g., a flag specifying we are dealing with components), and the `Engine` object will be the engine itself, where we will load and run our component:

```
// ...
fn main() {
    let mut config = wasmtime::Config::default();
    config.wasm_component_model(true);

    let engine = wasmtime::Engine::new(&config).unwrap();
}
```

Next, always inside the `main` function, we can create a `Linker` object associating our `State` with the engine and linking `wasmtime_wasi` to our setup:

```
fn main() {
    // ...
    let mut linker = wasmtime::component::Linker::<State>::new(&engine);
    wasmtime_wasi::add_to_linker_sync(&mut linker).unwrap();
}
```

Then, we can create our `WasiCtx` and, in it, specify we want to tie the context's standard output stream (i.e., whatever we get from components running within our engine) to the host's standard output:

```
fn main() {
    // ...
    let wasi = wasmtime_wasi::WasiCtxBuilder::new()
        .inherit_stdout()
        .build();
}
```

With that done, we are finally ready to create our `Store` object and load our component from a file:

```
fn main( ) {
    // ...
    let mut store = wasmtime::Store::new
    ➥(&engine, State { wasi, table:
    ➥wasmtime_wasi::ResourceTable::new() });
    let component = wasmtime::component
    ➥::Component::from_file(&engine,
    ➥"../hello_world_wasi_guest/greet.wasm").unwrap();
}
```

Now all that's left is to instantiate our component and call the `greet` function:

```
fn main() {
    // ...
```

```
    let app = Example::instantiate
    ➥ (&mut store, &component, &linker).unwrap();

    app.call_greet(&mut store, "World").unwrap();
}
```

And that's it! As seen in the following listing, we now have a Wasm component that interacts with the system's standard output.

Listing 4.3 Rust host for guest component (`main.rs`)

```
wasmtime::component::bindgen!({
path: "../hello_world_wasi_guest/wit",
world: "example",
});

struct State {
    wasi: wasmtime_wasi::WasiCtx,
    table: wasmtime_wasi::ResourceTable,
}

impl wasmtime_wasi::WasiView for State {
    fn ctx(&mut self) -> &mut wasmtime_wasi::WasiCtx {
        &mut self.wasi
    }
}

impl wasmtime_wasi::IoView for State {
    fn table(&mut self) -> &mut wasmtime_wasi::ResourceTable {
        &mut self.table
    }
}

fn main() {
    let mut config = wasmtime::Config::default();
    config.wasm_component_model(true);
    let engine = wasmtime::Engine::new(&config).unwrap();
    let mut linker = wasmtime::component::Linker::<State>::new(&engine);
    wasmtime_wasi::add_to_linker_sync
    ➥ (&mut linker).unwrap();

    let wasi = wasmtime_wasi::WasiCtxBuilder::new()
        .inherit_stdout()
        .build();

    let mut store = wasmtime::Store::new(&engine,
    ➥ State { wasi, table:
    ➥  wasmtime_wasi::ResourceTable::new() });
    let component = wasmtime::
    ➥ component::Component::from_file(&engine,
    ➥ "../hello_world_wasi_guest/greet.wasm").unwrap();

    let app = Example::instantiate
```

Annotations:
- Our State struct now contains a WASI context and a resource table.
- We link WASI to our setup.
- We inherit standard output from the host environment.

```
    ➥(&mut store, &component, &linker).unwrap();

    app.call_greet(&mut store, "World").unwrap();
}
```

Then, from the `hello_world_wasi_host/`, we can run this with

```
cargo run --release
```

We should see the output `Hello, World!` printed to the standard output, showing that we successfully provided our Wasm component with the ability to interact with its environment.

4.2 What can you build with WASI?

Upon its release in 2019, WASI or, more specifically, WASI 0.1/WASI Preview 1 (i.e., what is used by Wasm modules), was essentially a super portable subset of the Portable Operating System Interface (POSIX), which is a standard maintained to ensure compatibility and interoperability between UNIX-like operating systems (e.g., Linux, macOS, etc.). POSIX defines a set of APIs that a conforming operating system must provide to be POSIX compliant. Users can run various commands and programs on any POSIX-compliant system without worrying about compatibility problems or receiving different results.

This means that, with WASI 0.1, you could develop applications you are used to because WASI would essentially provide you access to the same APIs or system calls you'd normally expect to have. But, as WASI grew, its focus shifted from mirroring expectations to trying to go beyond them and create something fundamentally lighter, faster to start, and more secure.

Enter WASI 0.2, also known as WASI Preview 2. This new version introduced Wasm components, making it possible for Wasm to use a much broader set of interfaces—or, more specifically, worlds defined via WIT—than the limited POSIX-style subset offered by WASI 0.1. WASI 0.1's interfaces were just a foundational base layer. In contrast, WASI 0.2's interfaces are aimed at the kinds of applications developers actually want to build. These differences are highlighted in figure 4.5.

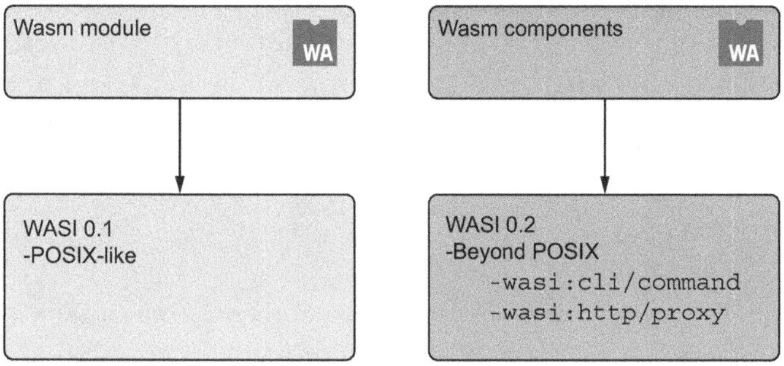

Figure 4.5 Comparison of WASI 0.1 (a more POSIX-like interface) to WASI 0.2 that defines higher-level interfaces

As Oscar Spencer (coauthor of the Grain programming language) put it, WASI has evolved from being just a WebAssembly System Interface to more of a *WebAssembly Standard Interfaces* collection. Now it bundles together standardized ways of doing things like running on the cloud with SQL database access or even performing machine learning inference.

That said, WASI 0.2, by itself, defined two worlds:

- *Command world* (i.e., `wasi:cli/command`), which resembles a traditional POSIX command-line application with access to the filesystem, sockets, and the terminal
- *HTTP proxy world* (i.e., `wasi:http/proxy`), which can send and receive HTTP requests and responses

But these two worlds are just the beginning. There are already several proposals in progress for WASI 0.3 and beyond, some of which we'll discuss in chapter 5.

To start, let's see how much easier it is to create a "Hello, World!" application when we utilize WASI 0.2.

4.2.1 Creating a CLI application

Let's create a new component using Rust's toolchain. We'll use the `cargo component` tool, which is Rust's official tooling for building and working with Wasm components. If you don't have it installed yet, you can install it with this:

```
cargo install cargo-component@0.20.0 -locked
```

NOTE `cargo component` is being deprecated in favor of the native Rust toolchain, but it's not yet archived and still offers convenient functionality that isn't available out of the box with the native approach. For now, this book uses `cargo component` for its ease of use. To see how the native toolchain works, check out the example at https://mng.bz/26do. Future editions of this book may switch to the native toolchain once its usage is more established.

Then, from our `chapter04/` folder, create a new directory called `wasi02/` and, inside it, run

```
cargo component new --bin hello_world_wasi02
```

In this project, by inspecting its `Cargo.toml`, you will see that, while we have a dependency for `wit-bindgen-rt` in our `Cargo.toml` for code generation of WIT files, we don't have any visible WIT. This is because `cargo component` abstracts away a lot of the setup work that we'd have to do to provide a more streamlined developer experience. Next, from inside `hello_world_wasi02/`, let's run

```
cargo component build --release
```

Now you should see `hello_world_wasi02.wasm` at `target/wasm32-wasip1/release`. But wait a minute! `wasm32-wasip1` (i.e., Wasm 32–WASI Preview 1)? Doesn't that mean we are using WASI 0.1? At first glance, you're right—it does! This is because, as of writing this book, the `wasm32-wasip2` target (i.e., the target for WASI 0.2) is still experimental. However, this doesn't necessarily mean we are using WASI 0.1. In fact, the way `cargo component` works right now is that, while it does compile to `wasm32-wasip1`, it also utilizes an adapter module to convert to WASI 0.2 during the compilation process. So, in reality, we are using WASI 0.2. To confirm this, we can use `wasm-tools`—a command-line interface that provides a set of tools useful for working with Wasm. You can install it with the following:

```
cargo install wasm-tools@1.227.1 --locked
```

Then run

```
wasm-tools component wit <path-to>/hello_world_wasi02.wasm
```

> **NOTE** If you're using a Cargo workspace and have added the path to `hello_world_wasi02/` to your workspace's `Cargo.toml`, the `<path-to>` from inside `hello_world_wasi02/` should be `../../../target/wasm32-wasip1/release/hello_world_wasi02.wasm`.

At the start of the output, you should see the contents of the following listing.

Listing 4.4 Output of `wasm-tools component wit`

```
package root:component {
  world root {
    import wasi:cli/environment@0.2.0;
    import wasi:cli/exit@0.2.0;
    import wasi:io/error@0.2.0;
    import wasi:io/streams@0.2.0;
    import wasi:cli/stdin@0.2.0;
    import wasi:cli/stdout@0.2.0;
    import wasi:cli/stderr@0.2.0;
    import wasi:clocks/wall-clock@0.2.0;
    import wasi:filesystem/types@0.2.0;
    import wasi:filesystem/preopens@0.2.0;

    export wasi:cli/run@0.2.0;
  }
}
```

This is the meat and potatoes of the WIT output: the `root world`. It specifies all our application has access to (i.e., the `imports`) and what we are implementing ourselves (i.e., the `export`). The rest of the WIT is just the definition of the `import/export` interfaces themselves, which you could still use as a reference for the APIs you can use. In addition, you can see all `imports/exports` are versioned at `0.2.0`, which is a pretty strong indication we are using WASI 0.2 APIs.

Next, we can see we are `exporting` the `wasi:cli/run` function. This function is the entry point of our application, and it is tied to the `main` function in `main.rs`. Now, how can we run the code to verify that? Do we have to create our own host yet again? No! In fact, Wasmtime provides a way to directly run applications that `export` the `wasi:cli/run` function. To try it out, first install Wasmtime like this:

```
cargo install wasmtime-cli@30.0.0 --locked
```

And then run

```
wasmtime <path-to>/hello_world_wasi02.wasm
```

That's it! We now have a "Hello, World" application that utilizes WASI 0.2.

4.2.2 Creating libraries

What if you'd like to create an application that has access to all WASI 0.2 capabilities we saw earlier but does not necessarily export the `wasi:cli/run` function? With Rust, you can do so very easily. From the `wasi02` directory, run

```
cargo component new --lib wasi02_lib
```

This will create a new library project. In it, you will be provided with a WIT file, so you can define your own exports to implement. By default, `cargo component` provides you with a `hello_world` function specified in WIT and implemented in `src/lib.rs`. As usual, from inside `wasi02_lib/`, you can build it with

```
cargo component build --release
```

Let's use `wasm-tools` again to extract the WIT and compare the differences between a `bin` and a `lib` project. Run

```
wasm-tools component wit <path-to>/wasi02_lib.wasm
```

At the end of the output, you should see the contents of the following listing.

Listing 4.5 Output of `wasm-tools component wit`

```
package root:component {
  world root {
    import wasi:cli/environment@0.2.0;
    import wasi:cli/exit@0.2.0;
    import wasi:io/error@0.2.0;
    import wasi:io/streams@0.2.0;
    import wasi:cli/stdin@0.2.0;
    import wasi:cli/stdout@0.2.0;
    import wasi:cli/stderr@0.2.0;
    import wasi:clocks/wall-clock@0.2.0;
```

```
    import wasi:filesystem/types@0.2.0;
    import wasi:filesystem/preopens@0.2.0;

    export hello-world: func() -> string;
  }
}
```

The only difference here is that we are exporting the hello-world function instead of the wasi:cli/run function. This is because, in a library project, you are not expected to have an entry point function. Instead, you are expected to provide a set of functions that can be utilized by other applications.

4.2.3 Creating HTTP proxies

Another world that became a standard in WASI 0.2 was the wasi:http/proxy world. With it also came a new command to Wasmtime: wasmtime serve. This command spins up an HTTP server that directs requests directly to our component. Now, while we do have the convenience of wasmtime serve, there is no easy way of creating an HTTP proxy application that doesn't require a lot of manual setup with cargo component. So we will leave creating HTTP Wasm applications for when we introduce other generic hosts that are tailored particularly for improved developer experience.

NOTE For an example application using the wasi:http/proxy world, see https://github.com/sunfishcode/hello-wasi-http.git.

4.3 Converting a Wasm module to a Wasm component

Now we have a better idea of the differences between Wasm modules and Wasm components, not just in theory, but also in practice. Up until this moment, every Wasm we've created, except the very first one, has been a Wasm component. But say you've been working with Wasm modules for a while and now you want to make use of the benefits of Wasm components, like WASI 0.2. How can you convert a Wasm module to a Wasm component? Surely, it should be simple. After all, Wasm components were designed to be wrappers around modules. And, indeed, they are!

For this example, let's take our very first "Hello, World" Wasm module: hello_world_guest.wasm. This is the module we created that dealt with integers to extract a string added to linear memory by the host.

We can use wasm-tools to check what type of Wasm it is, like so:

```
wasm-tools metadata show <path-to>/hello_world_guest.wasm
```

The output of this command should look like figure 4.6.

Under kind, you see module. To convert it to a component, do the following:

```
wasm-tools component new <path-to>
➥/hello_world_guest.wasm -o
➥<wherever>/hello_world_guest_component.wasm
```

KIND	NAME	SIZE	SIZE%	LANGUAGES	PARENT
module	hello_world_guest.wasm	20.8k	100%	Rust	<root>

KIND	VALUE
name	hello_world_guest.wasm
kind	module
range	0x0..0x516f
language	Rust
processed-by	rustc [1.84.0 (9fc6b4312 2025-01-07)]

Figure 4.6 The output from inspecting the metadata of our Wasm binary with `wasm-tools`, showing details like the module name, size, language, and the Rust compiler version used to build it

Now let's run `wasm-tools metadata show` on the newly created `hello_world_guest_component.wasm`:

```
wasm-tools metadata show <path-to>/hello_world_guest_component.wasm
```

The output of this command should look like figure 4.7.

As you can see, it shows we now have a component acting as a wrapper over a "child" module! If you try to run this component with the custom host we used in chapter 2, you will get

```
Error: failed to parse WebAssembly module

Caused by:
    Unsupported feature: component model
```

So that's it! You've successfully converted a Wasm module to a Wasm component, which means we now have access to modern component model features and tooling.

It's important to note that this conversion didn't give us access to Preview 2 APIs; we've simply wrapped the module as a component. Because our module was compiled to the `wasm32-unknown-unknown` target, it didn't originally have access to any WASI APIs. You can verify this by running the following:

```
wasm-tools component wit hello_world_guest_component.wasm
```

KIND	NAME	SIZE	SIZE%	LANGUAGES	PARENT
component	unknown(0)	20.9k	100%	-	<root>
module	hello_world_guest.wasm	20.8k	>99%	Rust	unknown(0)

KIND	VALUE
name	<unknown>
kind	component
range	0x0..0x51c0
processed-by	wit-component [0.227.1]
child	hello_world_guest.wasm [module]

KIND	VALUE
name	hello_world_guest.wasm
kind	module
range	0xc..0x517b
language	Rust
processed-by	rustc [1.84.0 (9fc6b4312 2025-01-07)]

Figure 4.7 The output from inspecting the metadata of our Wasm binary with `wasm-tools`, now showing that the Wasm binary includes a component kind created by `wit-component`

The output should show an empty world:

```
package root:component;

world root {
}
```

If we want to convert and adapt to Preview 2 APIs, we could go back to our chapter 2 example (at `chapter02/hello_world/hello_world_guest/`) and recompile it as a module with WASI access:

```
cargo build --target wasm32-wasip1 --release
```

Then we can create a component using an *adapter component,* which translates the module's Preview 1 WASI imports into Preview 2 component imports. You can download the adapter component directly from Wasmtime releases:

```
curl -L -O https://github.com/bytecodealliance/wasmtime/
➥ releases/download/v30.0.0/
➥ wasi_snapshot_preview1.reactor.wasm
```

NOTE If your module was created as a binary project (i.e., with a main function), you'd want to use this link instead: https://mng.bz/15dQ.

Next, run the same conversion command we used before, but provide both the adapter and your newly compiled Wasm module (let's call it `p1-hello_world_guest`):

```
wasm-tools component new <wherever>/
➥ p1-hello_world_guest.wasm --adapt
➥ wasi_snapshot_preview1=wasi_snapshot_preview1
➥ .reactor.wasm -o p1-hello_world_guest_component.wasm
```

You can verify the adapted component now has Preview 2 API access by running

```
wasm-tools component wit p1-hello_world_guest_component.wasm
```

This time, you should see Preview 2 imports like `wasi:cli/environment`, `wasi:filesystem/types`, and others.

And there we go! We've now converted our previous `wasm32-unknown-unknown` Wasm module to, essentially, a `wasm32-wasip2` Wasm component.

Now, if you think about it, this whole process may seem a bit roundabout. After all, just like we went back and recompiled to a `wasm32-wasip1` target, we could have recompiled directly to `wasm32-wasip2` and avoided the conversion and adaptation steps entirely. This would be the ideal approach when you have access to source code and your language has good Wasm support like Rust does.

However, this conversion process becomes valuable in situations where

- You're working with legacy code or third-party modules without source access.
- Your language doesn't yet support `wasip2` directly.
- You need to gradually migrate a large codebase to components.

In these cases, you can use WASI Preview 1 support, Wasm tooling, and Wasmtime-provided adapters to bridge the gap and get a working component with Preview 2 APIs!

4.4 Managing component capabilities

As we have seen in listing 4.4, the WIT output for our "Hello, World" WASI 0.2 application specified all the capabilities our application has access to. But what if we want to restrict some of these capabilities? For example, what if we want to restrict our application from actually accessing the standard output? To do so, aside from creating our own custom worlds, we can utilize a tool called WASI-Virt. WASI-Virt is a tool that allows you to encapsulate a Wasm component and virtualize its capabilities to either restrict or allow them.

Let's see it in practice. To install WASI Virt, run

```
cargo install wasi-virt --git https:
➥//github.com/bytecodealliance/WASI-Virt
➥--rev b662e419 --locked
```

Then copy the component we created from the "Hello, World" WASI 0.2 application (i.e., the `hello_world_wasi02.wasm` file from `target/wasm32-wasip1/release/`, where the `target/` directory is located at the same level as your chapter folders when using the workspace setup) to a new directory (say, `wasi_virt/` inside `wasi_02/`). Then, from that directory, run

```
wasi-virt ./hello_world_wasi02.wasm -o
➥./hello_world_wasi02_fully_restricted.wasm
```

If you try running this `hello_world_wasi02_fully_restricted.wasm` with `wasmtime`, you will get a panic (the program will crash). This is because, by default, virtualization will deny all capabilities and will cause a panic on an attempt to use any of them—e.g., standard output usage from `println!("Hello, World!")`.

Let's try seeing what the WIT output of this new Wasm component is. Run

```
wasm-tools component wit ./hello_world_wasi02_fully_restricted.wasm
```

At the end of the output, you should see the contents of the following listing.

Listing 4.6 Output of `wasm-tools component wit`

```
package root:component;

world root {
  export wasi:cli/run@0.2.0;
}
package wasi:cli@0.2.0 {
  interface run {
    run: func() -> result;
  }
}
```

It shows that, after virtualization, we restricted all capabilities, and their imports are gone. Now, to only allow the `stdout` capability, run

```
wasi-virt ./hello_world_wasi02.wasm --stdout=allow -o
➥./hello_world_wasi02_stdout_allowed.wasm
```

Then running this new Wasm component with `wasmtime` should work as expected.

Once again, checking the WIT output of this new Wasm component, at the end, you should see the contents of the following listing.

Listing 4.7 Output of `wasm-tools component wit`

```
package root:component {
  world root {
    import wasi:io/error@0.2.0;
    import wasi:io/poll@0.2.0;
    import wasi:io/streams@0.2.0;
    import wasi:cli/stdin@0.2.0;
    import wasi:cli/stdout@0.2.0;
    import wasi:cli/stderr@0.2.0;
    import wasi:cli/terminal-input@0.2.0;
    import wasi:cli/terminal-output@0.2.0;
    import wasi:cli/terminal-stdin@0.2.0;
    import wasi:cli/terminal-stdout@0.2.0;
    import wasi:cli/terminal-stderr@0.2.0;

    export wasi:cli/run@0.2.0;
  }
}
```

This shows we are only bringing the capabilities necessary to use `stdout`. And that's it! You've successfully restricted and allowed capabilities for a Wasm component.

But this only scratches the surface of what you can do with WASI-Virt. Under the hood, WASI-Virt works through composition—the same component model composition we'll explore in the next section. Your original component still imports WASI interfaces internally, but WASI-Virt composes it with an adapter component that provides implementations of those interfaces. When you restrict an interface, the adapter provides a deny-all implementation. When you allow it, the adapter either passes calls through to the host or provides a virtualized implementation—for example, you could mount a read-only filesystem directly into the component. The resulting composed component only imports what the adapter itself requires from the host. This is why our fully restricted component had no imports at all—the adapter satisfied all of the original component's imports internally, so the final composition doesn't need anything from the host. You can also use it to set environment variables, mount virtual filesystem directories, and more. Figure 4.8 illustrates the capabilities of WASI-Virt.

Further uses for WASI-Virt

While we didn't explore much of the `wasi:http/proxy world`, WASI-Virt could actually be very helpful with it. In particular, due to the fact that `wasi:http/proxy` was made to be able to run in many different environments, it doesn't import the filesystem API. But, if you wanted to serve some files, you could utilize WASI-Virt to bundle a filesystem with the component and use it as such.

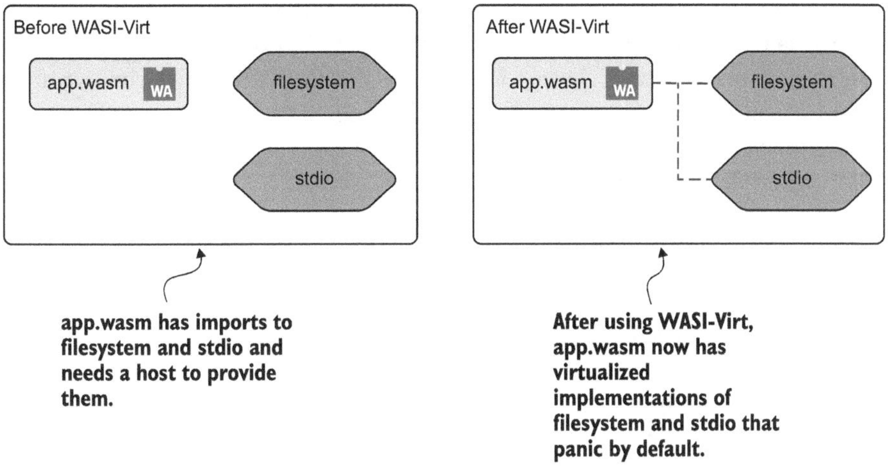

Figure 4.8 Utilizing WASI-Virt to restrict capabilities of a Wasm component

4.5 Composing components together

You have heard me say quite a lot that one of the main benefits of Wasm components is that they allow for easy interaction between two Wasms or a Wasm and a host. But, up until now, we didn't actually get to directly compose any components together. So, in this section, let's do just that.

To display composability, we'll compose a binary component together with a library component. And, for convenience, we will reuse the components we created earlier. Figure 4.9 illustrates the architecture we want to create.

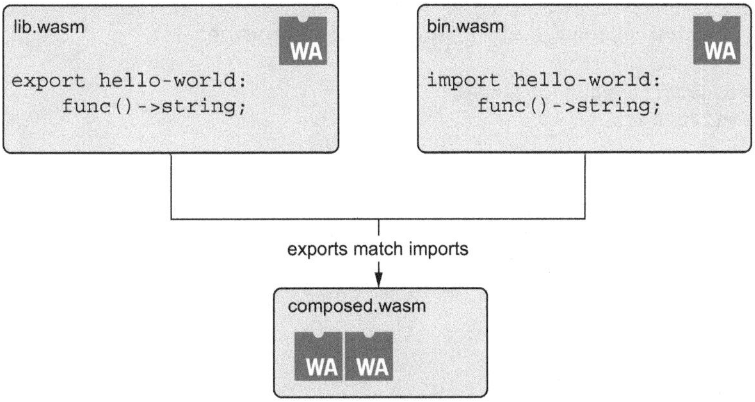

Figure 4.9 Composing a library component with a binary component and displaying matching imports and exports

Inside `chapter04/`, create a new directory called `composability/`. Then copy the `hello_world_wasi02/` directory to inside `composability/` and rename it from `hello_world_wasi02/` to `composability_bin/`. Equally, we'll reflect the name changes in the `Cargo.toml` file by changing the `name` field to `composability_bin`:

```
name = "composability_bin"
```

In addition, we will modify the `package` field under the `[package.metadata.component]` section to

```
package = "composability:bin"
```

Binaries created with `cargo component` by default hide their WIT file from the user. But, in this instance, we need access to the WIT file because we will be modifying it to import some library function. So, at the same level as `composability_bin/`, create a folder called `wit/` and, inside this new folder, create a WIT file called `bin.wit` with the contents of the following listing.

Listing 4.8 WIT file for our binary component (`bin.wit`)

```
package composability:bin;

world bin {
    import hello-world: func() -> string;
}
```

- `package composability:bin;` — The package name we defined earlier in the Cargo.toml file
- `import hello-world: func() -> string;` — Imports some hello-world function, supposedly coming from a library

Note that we don't need to specify all the WASI dependencies (e.g., `stdio`, etc.) because `cargo component` will take care of all of that for us during the build process. So, conveniently, we just need to specify the extra interfaces or functions our component will be using.

Then, inside our `Cargo.toml` file, we need to specify the path to this WIT file we've just created. Open the `Cargo.toml` file and add the following:

```
[package.metadata.component.target]
path = "../wit/bin.wit"
world = "bin"
```

Finally, our `Cargo.toml` file should look like the following listing.

Listing 4.9 `Cargo.toml` file for our binary component

```
[package]
name = "composability_bin"
version = "0.1.0"
edition = "2021"

[dependencies]
```

```
wit-bindgen-rt = { version = "0.41.0", features = ["bitflags"] }

[profile.release]
codegen-units = 1
opt-level = "s"
debug = false
strip = true
lto = true

[package.metadata.component]
package = "composability:bin"

[package.metadata.component.dependencies]

[package.metadata.component.target]
path = "../wit/bin.wit"
world = "bin"
```

Now let's try building the binary component with `cargo component build --release` run from inside `composability_bin/`. With everything running smoothly, we can then make use of our new `import` inside our `main.rs`, as in the following listing.

Listing 4.10 `main.rs` file of our binary component

```
#[allow(warnings)]
mod bindings;

use bindings::hello_world;

fn main() {
    println!("{}", hello_world());
}
```

- `use bindings::hello_world;` — Brings the hello_world function from our generated bindings
- `println!("{}", hello_world());` — Uses it and prints the result to the standard output

Then, with these changes, build again.

NOTE What is `mod bindings`? It's autogenerated Rust code that refers to a sibling file to our `main.rs` called `bindings.rs`. This `bindings.rs` file contains all the glue code needed for our Rust program to interact with the functions and types defined in our WIT files. In other words, it connects the `world` we defined in WIT to the actual Rust code we write.

Now, for convenience, let's reuse the `wasi02_lib` project we created earlier—this will be the provider of that `hello-world` function. Copy that entire directory to inside `composability/`. Then move the `world.wit` file from the `wasi02_lib/wit/` folder to the `composability/wit/` folder. With that done, rename the `world.wit` file to `lib.wit`. Then open the `Cargo.toml` file from `composability/wasi02_lib/` and add the following:

```
[package.metadata.component.target]
path = "../wit/lib.wit"
world = "lib"
```

Note that we modified the `world` name. So let's reflect that in our WIT. Overall, the `lib.wit` file should look like the following listing.

Listing 4.11 WIT file for our library component (`lib.wit`)

```
package composability:lib;            ◄── We changed the package name.

world lib {                           ◄── We changed the world name.
    export hello-world: func() -> string;
}
```

You can then delete the `wit/` directory from `composability/wasi02_lib`.

Now we need to distinguish between the two `wasi02_lib` projects. Let's rename the one in `composability/` to `composability_lib/`. And, just like we did for `composability_bin`, in the `Cargo.toml` file, change the `name` field to `composability_lib`:

```
name = "composability_lib"
```

Change the `package` field under the `[package.metadata.component]` section to

```
package = "composability:lib"
```

Finally, our `Cargo.toml` file should look like the following listing.

Listing 4.12 `Cargo.toml` file for our library component

```
[package]
name = "composability_lib"
version = "0.1.0"
edition = "2021"

[dependencies]
wit-bindgen-rt = { version = "0.41.0", features = ["bitflags"] }

[lib]
crate-type = ["cdylib"]

[profile.release]
codegen-units = 1
opt-level = "s"
debug = false
strip = true
lto = true

[package.metadata.component]
package = "composability:lib"

[package.metadata.component.dependencies]

[package.metadata.component.target]
path = "../wit/lib.wit"
world = "lib"
```

Now let's also modify the `lib.rs` file to look like the following listing.

Listing 4.13 `lib.rs` file of our binary component

```
#[allow(warnings)]
mod bindings;

use bindings::Guest;

struct Component;

impl Guest for Component {
    fn hello_world() -> String {
        "Hello from Lib!".to_string()
    }
}

bindings::export!(Component with_types_in bindings);
```

We modified the hello_world function to return a different string.

This string modification, of course, is an optional change, but it can serve as validation that we are composing the two components together.

From inside `compatibility_lib/`, you can then also build the library component with

```
cargo component build --release
```

Now we are finally ready to compose the two components together. To do so, we can use another Wasm tool called `wac` (pronounced "whack") that stands for Wasm composition. `wac` is a powerful tool that even provides its own composition language for complex linkage scenarios (e.g., matching specific component imports and exports). You can install it with

```
cargo install --locked wac-cli@0.6.1
```

Now, for our simple use case, we can simply plug the two compiled components together. So, at the same level as `composability/`, run

```
wac plug <path-to>/composability_bin.
➥ wasm --plug <path-to>/
➥ composability_lib.wasm -o composability.wasm
```

`wac` metaphorically refers to "plugs" that get plugged into "sockets"—in other words, Wasm exports that can be used as Wasm imports. In this example, the library exports a plug that gets put into the appropriate socket in our binary.

Then, because the two components are bundled together, we don't need to provide any custom host functionality. Instead, we can just run the two components with `wasmtime` from `composability/` like so:

```
wasmtime composability.wasm
```

And you should get

```
Hello from Lib!
```

That's it! You've successfully composed two components together.

When we ran `wac plug`, the tool created a new component that embeds both of our original components inside itself. The binary component's import for `hello-world` gets wired to the library component's export of that same function internally. The resulting `composability.wasm` is a standalone component that no longer imports `hello-world` from the outside world—all the dependencies are resolved within the composed component itself.

This is why we could run it with just `wasmtime composability.wasm` without any custom host setup. The component model's Canonical ABI ensures that data flowing between the two components works seamlessly, even though they were compiled separately. This build-time composition approach creates tightly coupled components that are deployed as a single unit.

4.6 Expanding our example project with WASI and composability

In this section, we will expand upon our SmartCMS project. In particular, our main goal will be to create a fake machine learning component together with its usage and composition with our existing architecture. Figure 4.10 illustrates the architecture we want to create.

This machine learning component will utilize WASI to access the host's filesystem, load a text file containing one-liner stories, and randomly select one story to return to our `smartcms_kvstore_guest`, which will then add that story to the host's key-value store and return the result of `get` for that story's key back to the host. Plus, we will be composing this fake machine learning component and the `smartcms_kvstore_guest` component together, which will be putting into practice all we learned about composability. In the future, we'll replace this fake component with a real machine learning model to generate children's stories.

We will be working on our existing SmartCMS implementation. So feel free to work from the existing project or copy your work from chapter 3 onto a new directory (i.e., `chapter04/`) if you want to keep each chapter's work separate.

NOTE If you're copying over your work from the SmartCMS in chapter 3 and have both the chapter 3 and chapter 4 SmartCMS projects in your workspace, it's a good idea to suffix each host's name (in their respective `Cargo.toml`) with the chapter number. This helps avoid any naming clashes. For example, you could name it `smartcms_test_host_chapter04`.

With that done, let's start by creating a new library component for our machine learning component. At the same directory level as `smartcms_kvstore_guest/` and `smartcms_test_host`, run

```
cargo component new --lib smartcms_ml_guest
```

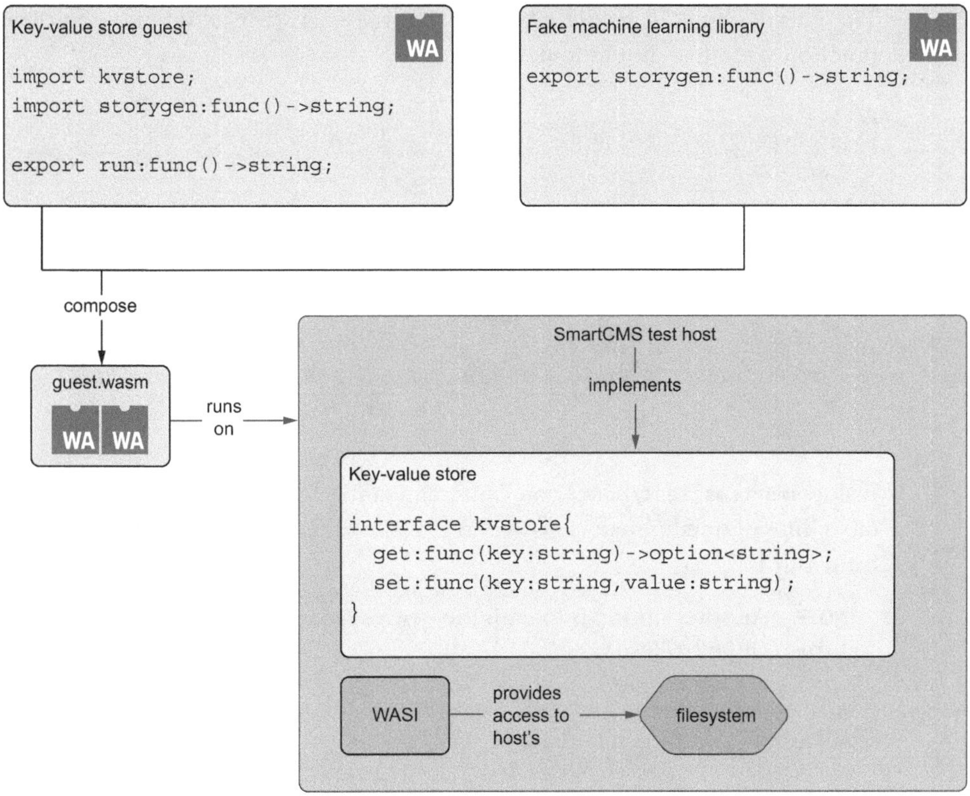

Figure 4.10 The architecture of our SmartCMS project with the addition of a machine learning component

Then modify its WIT file at `smartcms_ml_guest/wit/world.wit` to look like the following listing.

Listing 4.14 WIT file for our ML guest component (`world.wit`)

```
package component:smartcms-ml-guest;

world example {
    export storygen: func() -> string;
}
```

`storygen` will be the function doing all the heavy lifting. Next, for the random number generation, we will need to randomly select a story; we will be using the `rand` crate, which is possible because Rust's `rand` crate supports compiling to Wasm (meaning it can compile to targets like `wasm32-unknown-unknown`). Under `[dependencies]` in the `Cargo.toml` file, add

```
rand = "0.8.5"
```

Then modify the `lib.rs` file. First, rename the `hello_world` function to `storygen`. The function signature should look like this:

```
// ...
fn storygen() -> String {
    // ...
}
```

Inside it, we will be reading a file called `stories.txt` from the host's filesystem, like so:

```
// ...
fn storygen() -> String {
    let stories = std::fs::read_to_string("stories.txt").unwrap();
}
// ...
```

Inside `smartcms_test_host/` you can create a file called `stories.txt`. Inside it, add 10 or so lines of one-liner stories—feel free to be creative or, if not, just add the numbers from 1 to 10.

NOTE Another option is to grab the stories I made from the book's repository: https://mng.bz/Pwq8.

Then, back in `lib.rs`, under the creation of the `stories` variable, we can randomly select a story and return it like so:

```
// ...
fn storygen() -> String {
    let stories = std::fs::read_to_string("stories.txt").unwrap();
    let lines: Vec<&str> = stories.lines().collect();
    let random = rand::random::<usize>() % lines.len();
    lines[random].to_string()
}
// ...
```

Overall, the `lib.rs` file should look like the following listing.

Listing 4.15 Implementation of our ML guest component (`lib.rs`)

```
#[allow(warnings)]
mod bindings;

use bindings::Guest;

struct Component;

impl Guest for Component {
    fn storygen() -> String {
        let stories = std::fs::
            read_to_string("stories.txt").unwrap();    <-- Reads the stories.txt file
        let lines: Vec<&str> =
```

```
        ➥stories.lines().collect();
        let random = rand::random::
        ➥<usize>() % lines.len();
        lines[random].to_string()
    }
}

bindings::export!(Component with_types_in bindings);
```

- Collects the lines into a vector
- Generates a random number from 0 to the number of lines in the file to select a story
- Returns the selected story

With that done, from inside `smartcms_ml_guest/`, you can build the library component with

```
cargo component build --release
```

Next, let's make use of that in the `smartcms_kvstore_guest` component. Before, `smartcms_kvstore_guest` used the same WIT as `smartcms_test_host`, but because we are now bringing in an `import` from another component, we will need to split them up. So copy the `smart_cms.wit` file at `smartcms_test_host/` to `smartcms_kvstore_guest/`, and rename it to `kvstore_guest.wit`. Then modify the `kvstore_guest.wit` file to look like the following listing.

Listing 4.16 WIT for key-value store guest (`kvstore_guest.wit`)

```
package component:smartcms;

interface kvstore {
    get: func(key: string) -> option<string>;
    set: func(key: string, value: string);
}

world app {
    import kvstore;
    import storygen: func() -> string;
    export run: func() -> string;
}
```

- Imports the storygen function from the smartcms_ml_guest component

Note that if we had added this `import` to the same WIT utilized by the host, the host would think it should be the one providing the `storygen` function and would fail at the linking stage. Modify `guest.js` to look like the following listing.

Listing 4.17 Guest component for the SmartCMS (`guest.js`)

```
import { get, set } from "component:smartcms/kvstore";
import storygen from 'storygen';

export function run() {
    set('guest-hello', storygen());
    return get('guest-hello');
}
```

- Imports the storygen function
- Sets the story generated by the storygen function to the key guest-hello

You can then build the smartcms_kvstore_guest component (from within smartcms_kvstore_guest/) with

```
jco componentize guest.js --wit kvstore_guest.wit --world-name app -o
➥ ../smartcms_test_host/guest.wasm --disable stdio random clocks http
```

Now we can compose the two components together. From inside smartcms_ml_guest/, run

```
wac plug ../smartcms_test_host/guest.wasm --plug <path-
➥ to>/smartcms_ml_guest.wasm -o ../smartcms_test_host/guest_with_ml.wasm
```

Finally, all we are missing are some modifications to our smartcms_test_host to have it utilize WASI. First, let's add the following dependencies to the Cargo.toml file:

```
// ...
wasmtime-wasi = "30"
```

Then, in main.rs, let's modify our State variable to also contain WASI state as a tuple, like so:

```
// ...
struct State {
    key_value: KeyValue,
    wasi: (wasmtime_wasi::WasiCtx,
    ➥ wasmtime_wasi::ResourceTable)        ◄── Adds a tuple containing the WASI context and resource table
}
// ...
```

Because we are now using WASI, just like we did for hello_world_wasi02, we need to implement the WasiView and IoView traits for our State struct. Add the following to the impl blocks for State—note; we are accessing the tuple elements to get the specific struct properties:

```
impl wasmtime_wasi::WasiView for State {
    fn ctx(&mut self) -> &mut wasmtime_wasi::WasiCtx {
        &mut self.wasi.0        ◄── Returns the WASI context accessing the first element of the tuple
    }
}

impl wasmtime_wasi::IoView for State {
    fn table(&mut self) -> &mut wasmtime_wasi::ResourceTable {
        &mut self.wasi.1        ◄── Returns the resource table accessing the second element of the tuple
    }
}
```

Then let's modify the main function to utilize WASI. After creating the engine, modify the store creation to create a new WASI resource, pre-open the current directory in the host and map it to the guest with READ access, build the WASI context, and, finally, create a tuple containing the WASI context and resource table for State:

```
fn main() {
    // ...
    let wasi_table = wasmtime_wasi::
    ➥ ResourceTable::new();
    let wasi_ctx = wasmtime_wasi::WasiCtxBuilder::new()
        .preopened_dir(".", ".",
        ➥ wasmtime_wasi::DirPerms::READ,
        ➥ wasmtime_wasi::FilePerms::READ).unwrap()
        .build();
    let state = State {
        key_value: KeyValue { mem: std::collections::HashMap::new() },
        wasi: (wasi_ctx, wasi_table)
    };
    let mut store = wasmtime::Store::new(&engine, state);
    // ...
}
```

Creates a new WASI resource table

Pre-opens the current directory (i.e., ".") in the host and maps it to "." in the guest with READ permissions for files and directories

Builds the WASI context

Creates a tuple containing the WASI context and resource table for State

You'll be familiar with most of what we did in this bit from `hello_world_wasi02`. But, in particular, I want to highlight how WASI is giving the guest access to the host filesystem. WASI "pre-opens" the host directory (i.e., in this case `"."`) and maps it onto the guest's `"."` directory. This way, the guest only has access to a very limited view of the host's filesystem, and that view can be controlled with the permissions provided (i.e., `READ` for files and directories).

Then let's modify the `component` variable to load the `guest with guest_with_ml.wasm` instead of `guest.wasm`:

```
fn main() {
    // ...
    let component = wasmtime::component::
    ➥ Component::from_file(&engine,
    ➥ "guest_with_ml.wasm").unwrap();
    // ...
}
```

Loads the guest_with_ml.wasm file instead of the guest.wasm file

Finally, we can modify our linker setup to include WASI by adding this just after declaring the linker:

```
fn main() {
    // ...
    let mut linker = wasmtime::component::Linker::new(&engine);
    wasmtime_wasi::add_to_linker_sync(&mut linker).unwrap();
    // ...
}
```

Overall, the code should look like the following listing.

Listing 4.18 Final `main.rs` file for our SmartCMS test host

```
wasmtime::component::bindgen!({
    path: "./smart_cms.wit",
```

```
    world: "app",
});

struct KeyValue {
    mem: std::collections::HashMap<String, String>,
}

impl crate::component::smartcms::kvstore::Host for KeyValue {
    fn get(&mut self, key: String) -> Option<String> {
        self.mem.get(&key).cloned()
    }

    fn set(&mut self, key: String, value: String) {
        self.mem.insert(key, value);
    }
}

struct State {
    key_value: KeyValue,
    wasi: (wasmtime_wasi::WasiCtx,
    ➥wasmtime_wasi::ResourceTable)
}

impl wasmtime_wasi::WasiView for State {
    fn ctx(&mut self) -> &mut wasmtime_wasi::WasiCtx {
        &mut self.wasi.0
    }
}

impl wasmtime_wasi::IoView for State {
    fn table(&mut self) -> &mut wasmtime_wasi::ResourceTable {
        &mut self.wasi.1
    }
}

fn main() {
    let mut config = wasmtime::Config::default();
    config.wasm_component_model(true);

    let engine = wasmtime::Engine::new(&config).unwrap();

    let wasi_table = wasmtime_wasi::
    ➥ResourceTable::new();
    let wasi_ctx = wasmtime_wasi::WasiCtxBuilder::new()
        .preopened_dir(".", ".",
        ➥wasmtime_wasi::DirPerms::READ,
        ➥wasmtime_wasi::FilePerms::READ).unwrap()
        .build();
    let state = State {
        key_value: KeyValue { mem: std::collections::HashMap::new() },
        wasi: (wasi_ctx, wasi_table)
    };
    let mut store = wasmtime::Store::new(&engine, state);

    let component = wasmtime::component::
```

Adds a tuple containing the WASI context and resource table

Returns the WASI context accessing the first element of the tuple

Returns the resource table accessing the second element of the tuple

Creates a new WASI resource table

Pre-opens the current directory (i.e., ".") in the host and maps it to "." in the guest with READ permissions for files and directories

Builds the WASI context

Creates a tuple containing the WASI context and resource table for State

```
    ➥Component::from_file(&engine,
    ➥"guest_with_ml.wasm").unwrap();

    let mut linker = wasmtime::component::Linker::new(&engine);
    wasmtime_wasi::add_to_linker_sync(&mut linker).unwrap();
    component::smartcms::kvstore::add_to_linker
    ➥(&mut linker, |state: &mut State| &mut
    ➥state.key_value).unwrap();                  ◄── Loads the guest_with_ml.wasm
                                                      file instead of the guest.wasm file
    let app = App::instantiate(&mut store, &component, &linker).unwrap();

    println!("{:?}", app.call_run(&mut store).unwrap());
}
```

And that's it! You can run the `smartcms_test_host` with `cargo run --release`, and you should see a story added to the key-value store and then retrieved from it (which will get printed to the standard output).

Summary

- Wasm components have an established Canonical ABI that allows for easy interaction between two Wasms or a Wasm and a host.
- Wasm hosts implement WASI to provide a set of APIs for Wasm to interact with the host.
- WASI 0.1 defined a low-level POSIX-like set of APIs for Wasm to interact with the host. WASI 0.2 interfaces, on the other hand, provide higher-level interfaces for common application tasks, like databases and HTTP requests.
- WASI 0.2 defined two worlds: `wasi:cli/command` and `wasi:http/proxy`.
- Wasm's command components created with `cargo component new` export the `wasi:cli/run` function and can be run directly with `wasmtime`.
- Extracting a component's WIT with `wasm-tools component wit <path-to-wasm>` can be helpful for debugging.
- You can examine a component or module by seeing its metadata with `wasm-tools metadata show <path-to-wasm>`.
- Wasm modules can be converted to Wasm components with `wasm-tools component new <path-to-wasm>` to make use of WASI 0.2, higher-level types, and better composability.
- You can restrict the capabilities your Wasm component has access to with WASI-Virt.
- Aside from restricting capabilities, WASI-Virt can be used to set environment variables and mount virtual filesystem directories.
- You can use `wac plug <path-to-wasm1> --plug <path-to-wasm2> -o <path-to-output-wasm>` to compose two components together and match their imports/exports, allowing easy interaction between two distinct Wasms.

5 From machine learning to databases: Applications of Wasm

This chapter covers

- WASI as a collection of standardized interfaces
- Machine learning inference in Wasm
- Applying the ONNX format
- Running Wasm within databases

Up until now, we have undertaken much of the heavy lifting ourselves. We began the book without even using Wasm components, implementing our own lifting and lowering for the string type. Even after transitioning to Wasm components, we continued to create our own interfaces and hosts to serve as the backbone of our applications. This approach is not ideal for server-side development with Wasm. Instead, we should use out-of-the-box hosts and prewritten interfaces—unless, of course, we are developing a very specific application.

In this chapter, we will start utilizing standardized interfaces. Specifically, we will explore how to use the `wasi:nn` (for neural networks) interface to perform machine learning (ML) with Wasm, and we will discuss a separate use case for Wasm running inside a database to power user-defined functions.

5.1 WebAssembly Standard Interfaces

In chapter 4, you were introduced to WASI—the WebAssembly System Interface. Upon its release in 2019, WASI served as a subset of POSIX to enable Wasm to operate outside of the browser. Fast-forwarding to today, a more appropriate interpretation of WASI is perhaps "WebAssembly Standard Interfaces," as it encompasses a wide range of interfaces beyond POSIX and offers higher-level capabilities. As shown in figure 5.1, WASI serves as an umbrella for numerous interfaces, including WebGPU, threads, SQL, messaging, logging, distributed lock service, crypto, blob store, runtime config, ML, key-value store, HTTP, sockets, filesystem, I/O, and more.

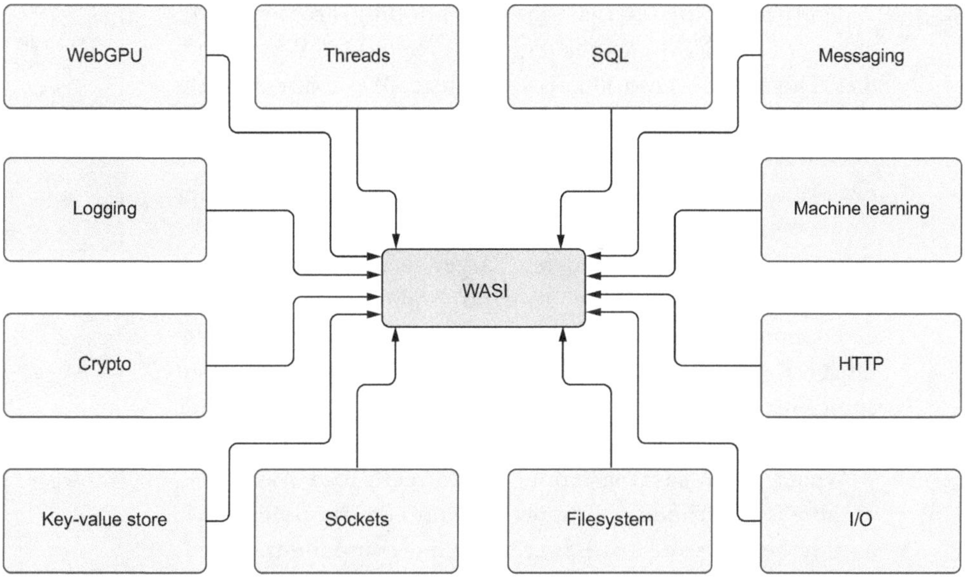

Figure 5.1 Some of WASI's interfaces

However, as of this writing, none of these interfaces are fully standardized. Instead, they are currently undergoing various phases of development. Specifically, for an interface to be considered fully standardized, among other criteria, it must have demonstrated general interest by the community, have precise and complete overview documents, possess a test suite, and have two or more implementers for the feature. You can verify the status of WASI interfaces here: https://mng.bz/rZ8x.

As we explored in chapter 4, when WASI 0.2 was released, it defined two worlds: the CLI command world (i.e., `wasi:cli/command`) and the HTTP proxy world (i.e., `wasi:http/proxy`). With each release of WASI, more of these worlds will be defined and become easily accessible. An example of a world that is not yet standardized but is in the works is `wasi:cloud-core`, which groups interfaces you'd likely need to create cloud applications. It includes interfaces such as `wasi:keyvalue`, `wasi:blobstore`, `wasi:messaging`, `wasi:sql`, `wasi:config`, and `wasi:http`. Aside from `wasi:cloud-core`, another interesting interface is `wasi:nn`, which is used for using ML. Let's try making use of it!

5.2 Machine learning with Wasm

If you are in a function-as-a-service system and using Wasm, `wasi:nn` is the go-to way of getting native performance for your ML workloads. In addition to native performance, you gain access to an ML SDK out of the box for your language of choice (provided it can be compiled or bundled into Wasm) and enjoy all of the security benefits of Wasm's sandboxed execution.

Alternatives to `wasi:nn` worth mentioning are some ML libraries (e.g., TVM and `tract`), which compile to Wasm modules. This allows ML workloads to run inside Wasm directly without relying on a host's implementation of `wasi:nn`. However, to conform to WASI 0.1's POSIX subset, these libraries make performance sacrifices, limiting their efficiency. On the other hand, `wasi:nn` uses the optimizations already implemented by existing ML frameworks, such as larger vector widths, specialized hardware instructions, threading, and accelerators like GPUs and neural processing units (NPUs). This results in significantly better performance, making `wasi:nn` the preferred choice for users who require high-performance ML workloads within a Wasm-based function-as-a-service system.

What's more, `wasi:nn` can be used directly with Wasmtime, as there is experimental support built into the runtime. All we have to be concerned with is creating our component, so let's do just that!

5.2.1 Understanding ML inference

For this example, we will be performing ML inference. Inference is the process of using ML to make predictions or decisions based on new, unseen data. In our use case, we'll apply inference to an image to classify what that image represents. Before we get started with the example, I want to mention that, while we can use ML as an example for server-side Wasm, ML is a vast field in itself, and I am by no means an ML expert. At best, I am a practitioner who has learned a great deal about it for the purpose of writing this section. If you find yourself in the same boat, see the following sidebar; it describes key concepts for the example we will be creating. Figure 5.2 shows a schematic for the application we will develop.

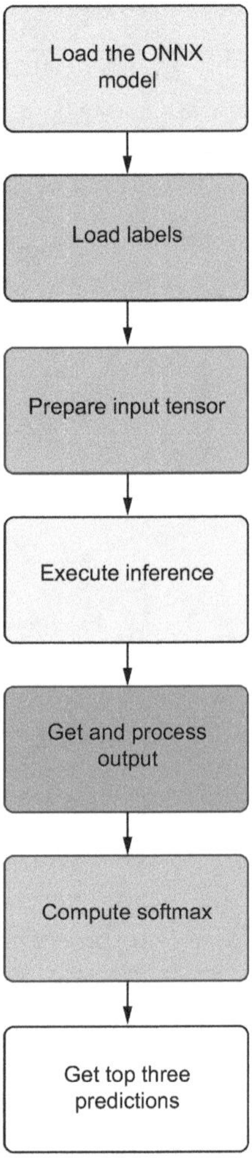

Figure 5.2 `wasi_nn_example` **application schematic**

ML 101: Essential concepts for server-side developers

Before we delve into the code example, it's important to understand some basic ML concepts that are relevant to the application. This sidebar provides a straightforward introduction to the key ideas you need to grasp to follow along.

ML models
An ML model is a program that has been trained to recognize patterns in data. In our case, we're using a model that can classify images—it can identify what objects are present in a picture. Also, we're using a pretrained model, which means that it has already been trained on large datasets and can be used out of the box for tasks like image classification, without the need to train it ourselves.

ONNX format
Open Neural Network Exchange (ONNX) is an open format for representing machine learning models. It allows models to be transferred between different frameworks and tools, making them more versatile.

Tensors
A tensor is essentially a multidimensional array used to store data. In the context of image processing, an image can be represented as a tensor with dimensions corresponding to width, height, and color channels (e.g., red, green, blue). Tensors are then used to feed data into the model and to receive outputs from the model.

Labels in classification
In classification tasks, labels are the categories that the model can predict. For image classification, labels might be objects the model can recognize in images, e.g., "cat," "dog," "car," etc. After the model processes an image, it outputs predictions associated with these labels.

Softmax function
The softmax function is a mathematical function that converts the raw output of the model (which can be any range of numbers) into probabilities that sum up to 1. It makes it easy to interpret the model's output by providing a probability for each possible label. Then the label with the highest probability is typically chosen as the model's prediction.

Putting it all together
In our example, we perform these steps:

1. *Load the model*—We load a pretrained image classification model in ONNX format.
2. *Prepare the input*—We process an input image and convert it into a tensor that the model can understand.
3. *Run inference*—We feed the tensor into the model to get predictions.
4. *Interpret results*—We apply the softmax function to the model's output to get probabilities for each label and identify the top predictions.

5.2.2 Using wasi-nn

To get started, inside our folder for chapter 5 projects, let's create a new project with `cargo component`:

```
cargo component new wasi_nn_example
```

As a reminder, this creates a command component, meaning it will export the `wasi:cli` `run` function. In theory, this allows us to run the component directly with Wasmtime. However, it's important to remember that we are also planning to use a specific interface (i.e., `wasi:nn`). If Wasmtime doesn't provide an implementation for this interface, we would be stuck having to create our own host implementation again. Fortunately, as we mentioned earlier, Wasmtime does provide experimental implementations for `wasi:nn` that can be enabled via command-line flags. At the time of writing, Wasmtime supports three different `wasi:nn` backends: OpenVINO (an open source toolkit that optimizes and deploys deep learning models for Intel hardware), ONNX (the format mentioned in the ML 101 sidebar), and WinML (a Windows-specific machine learning platform optimized for running ML models on Windows devices). All we have to do is create this component.

Next, we will need to add three dependencies inside our `Cargo.toml` file, as shown in listing 5.1. First, delete any dependencies that are already there. Then, we will add a dependency for `wit-bindgen` to allow us to generate code for the `wasi:nn` interface, the `image` crate, which is useful for processing our image to be inferred on, and `ndarray`, a crate that provides efficient numerical operations and matrix manipulation capabilities.

Listing 5.1 `Cargo.toml` file for the `wasi_nn_example`

```
[package]
name = "wasi_nn_example"
version = "0.1.0"
edition = "2021"

[dependencies]
wit-bindgen = { version = "0.33.0",
➥default-features = false, features =
➥["macros"] }
image = "0.25.2"
ndarray = "0.16.1"

[profile.release]
codegen-units = 1
opt-level = "s"
debug = false
strip = true
lto = true

[package.metadata.component]
package = "component:wasi-nn-example"

[package.metadata.component.dependencies]
```

The three added dependencies

Finally, to finish off our setup, we will need to download the `wasi:nn` interface. This step is currently a bit cumbersome, but it is being actively worked on upstream in the Wasm community. In particular, people are exploring ways to package Wasm components as Open Container Initiative (OCI) artifacts, but we'll cover that in more detail in later chapters. Currently, because `wasi:nn` isn't available as an OCI artifact, we have to handle it manually. For this particular demo, I have made `wasi:nn@0.2.0-rc-2024-08-19` available in this book's GitHub repository. You can access it here: https://mng.bz/V9WN. Copy the entire interface and paste it into a file called `wasi-nn.wit` inside the `wit/` folder at the same level as our component's `src/` folder.

CREATING OUR COMPONENT

Now that we are all set up, we are ready to start creating our component. First, delete all the autogenerated contents of our current `main.rs` file. Then, we can start by adding all dependencies that we need at the top of our file:

```
use image::{ImageReader, imageops::Triangle};
use ndarray::Array;
use std::{env, fs};
use std::io::BufRead;
```

Next, we will make a call to `wit_bindgen::generate!`. This is similar to `wasmtime::component::bindgen!`, which we've used in the past to generate interface glue code for the host side. However, in this case, `wit_bindgen::generate!` generates the glue code for the guest side:

```
wit_bindgen::generate!({
    path: "wit/wasi-nn.wit",
    world: "ml",
});
```

In particular, we are saying that we want to generate glue code for the `wit/wasi-nn.wit` interface and then use its `ml` world. This is an alternative to using WebAssembly Interface Types (WIT) files and `Cargo.toml` sections directly like we did in chapter 4 with our composability example. There, our setup involved writing a WIT file that contained our imports and using the `[package.metadata.component.target]` section to point to it. A similar approach is possible here by adding `wasi:nn` as a dependency in `[package.metadata.component.target.dependencies]`, but we are choosing to use `wit_bindgen` directly to highlight a different way of doing things and also because, for now, I have found it works a little bit better with code completion.

Next, we can add imports to structures and functions we will use from the generated code, like so:

```
use self::wasi::nn::{
    graph::{Graph, load, ExecutionTarget, GraphEncoding},
    tensor::{Tensor, TensorType},
};
```

With code generation done and the imports all in place, we are ready to start working on our `main` function. To start, we need to access the image path provided as a command-line argument to our application:

```
fn main() {
    let image_path = env::args().nth(1).expect("Usage: <image_path>");
}
```

Then, continuing inside our `main` function, we can read our pretrained ONNX ML model from the filesystem and load it into a graph representation, specifying that we want to use the CPU as the execution target. After that, we initialize an execution context for the graph, which prepares it to run inference operations. Of course, at this point you don't have the model in your own filesystem, but we'll get more details on that in a later section:

```
let model_data = fs::read("fixture/models/squeezenet1.1-
➥ 7.onnx").unwrap();
let graph = load(&[model_data], GraphEncoding::Onnx,
➥ ExecutionTarget::Cpu).unwrap();
let exec_context = Graph::init_execution_context(&graph).unwrap();
```

Then, equally, we can also read in our labels data and convert it into a vector of strings, where each string represents a label that corresponds to the classification categories our model can predict:

```
let labels_data = fs::read("fixture/labels/squeezenet1.1-
➥ 7.txt").unwrap();
let class_labels: Vec<String> = labels_data.lines().map(|line|
➥ line.unwrap()).collect();
```

We then convert our input image into a tensor format that the model can process using the `image_to_tensor` function, which we will code later. If you want a test image to use for the example, you can download the one I used from this link: https://mng.bz/xZ17. Next, we create a tensor with its dimensions (224 pixels, for both height and width), specifying the data type as 32-bit floating-point (`Fp32`). Finally, we set this tensor as the input to our execution context, preparing the model to perform inference with the provided image data:

```
let data = image_to_tensor(&image_path, 224, 224);
let dimensions = vec![1, 3, 224, 224];
let tensor = Tensor::new(&dimensions, TensorType::Fp32, &data);
exec_context.set_input("data", tensor).unwrap();
```

We are now finally ready to execute our inference. This is where the magic happens—our model processes the input data and generates predictions based on what it has learned during training. With just a single call, we trigger the computation that runs through the model's layers, performing the mathematical operations needed to interpret the image data. Here's how we do it:

```
exec_context.compute().unwrap();
```

This command initiates the inference process, transforming the input tensor into a set of predictions that we can analyze and interpret in the next steps.

Next, we retrieve the output from the model, which contains the raw prediction data in bytes. We then convert this byte data into a more usable format using the `bytes_to_f32_vec` function, which we'll code later. This function transforms the byte chunks into 32-bit floating-point numbers. Finally, we wrap this data into an array structure for easier manipulation and analysis in the subsequent steps:

```
let output_data = exec_context.get_output
➥("squeezenet0_flatten0_reshape0").unwrap().data();
let output_f32 = bytes_to_f32_vec(&output_data);
let output_array = Array::from_vec(output_f32);
```

Next, we apply a transformation to the model's output to make it easier to interpret as probabilities. We begin by taking the exponential of each value in the array, which amplifies the differences between the predicted scores. This is a common step in ML known as applying the softmax function. We then calculate the sum of all these exponential values. Finally, we divide each exponential value by this sum, normalizing the scores so that they represent probabilities that add up to 1. Here's the code:

```
let exp_output = output_array.mapv(f32::exp);
let sum_exp = exp_output.sum();
let softmax_output = exp_output / sum_exp;
```

This softmax operation converts the raw output into a probability distribution, where each value represents the likelihood of the input image belonging to a specific class.

Finally, we take the processed output probabilities and rank them to identify the most likely predictions. We start by pairing each probability with its corresponding class index and collecting these pairs into a list. Then, we sort this list in descending order to place the highest probabilities at the top. To finish, we display the top three predictions along with their associated class labels and probabilities, indicating the model's best guesses for the input image:

```
let mut probabilities: Vec<_> =
➥softmax_output.iter().enumerate().collect();
probabilities.sort_by(|a, b| b.1.partial_cmp(a.1).unwrap());

for &(index, &probability) in probabilities.iter().take(3) {
    println!("Class: {} - Probability: {}", class_labels[index],
    ➥probability);
}
```

This step reveals the classes that the model considers the most likely matches for the input image, along with the confidence level for each prediction, helping us interpret the results of the inference.

This wraps up our main function! The final tasks remaining are to code the bytes_to_f32_vec function and the image_to_tensor function, which will help us process the data for our model's inference.

Let's start with the bytes_to_f32_vec function. This function is responsible for converting a slice of byte data into a vector of 32-bit floating-point numbers (f32). It does this by iterating over the byte data in chunks of 4 (the size of an f32), converting each chunk into its corresponding floating-point value, and collecting these values into a vector:

```
pub fn bytes_to_f32_vec(data: &[u8]) -> Vec<f32> {
    data.chunks_exact(4)
        .map(|c| f32::from_le_bytes(c.try_into().unwrap()))
        .collect()
}
```

This function is crucial because it transforms the raw byte output from the model into a format we can use for numerical analysis, allowing us to perform operations like softmax to interpret the model's predictions.

Let's now tackle the image_to_tensor function to finish our example. The function starts by opening the image from the specified path, decoding it, and resizing it to the given dimensions. The resize_exact method ensures that the image is precisely adjusted to the required width and height. We're using the Triangle filter for resizing, which provides a good balance between speed and image quality. The resulting image data is then converted into a raw pixel array:

```
fn image_to_tensor(path: &str, height: u32, width: u32) -> Vec<u8> {
    let img = ImageReader::open(path).unwrap().decode().unwrap();
    let resized_img = img.resize_exact(width, height, Triangle).to_rgb8();
    let raw_pixels = resized_img.into_raw();
```

Next, we normalize the pixel values using predefined mean and standard deviation arrays. This normalization process is a common practice in ML to ensure that the input data is using the same scale the model expects. We iterate over each pixel, normalize its red, green, and blue values, and store the results in the data_f32 vector. The normalization helps the model process the input more effectively by standardizing the color values:

```
    let mean = [0.485, 0.456, 0.406];
    let std = [0.229, 0.224, 0.225];

    let num_pixels = (height * width) as usize;
    let mut data_f32 = vec![0f32; num_pixels * 3];

    for i in 0..num_pixels {
        let idx = i * 3;
        let r = raw_pixels[idx] as f32 / 255.0;
        let g = raw_pixels[idx + 1] as f32 / 255.0;
```

```
        let b = raw_pixels[idx + 2] as f32 / 255.0;

        data_f32[i] = (r - mean[0]) / std[0];
        data_f32[i + num_pixels] = (g - mean[1]) / std[1];
        data_f32[i + 2 * num_pixels] = (b - mean[2]) / std[2];
    }
```

Finally, we convert the normalized floating-point values into bytes, which are required for the tensor representation used by the model. Each floating-point value is transformed into its corresponding byte representation using the `to_ne_bytes` method, and these bytes are then stored in the `data_u8` vector:

```
    let mut data_u8 = Vec::with_capacity(data_f32.len() * 4);
    for &v in &data_f32 {
        data_u8.extend_from_slice(&v.to_ne_bytes());
    }

    data_u8
```

Overall, the code should come together as shown in the following listing.

Listing 5.2 `main.rs` file of our `wasi_nn_example` component

```
use image::{ImageReader, imageops::Triangle};
use ndarray::Array;
use std::{env, fs};
use std::io::BufRead;

wit_bindgen::generate!({
    path: "wit/wasi-nn.wit",
    world: "ml",
});

use self::wasi::nn::{
    graph::{Graph, load, ExecutionTarget, GraphEncoding},
    tensor::{Tensor, TensorType},
};

fn main() {
    let image_path = env::args().nth(1).expect("Usage: <image_path>");

    let model_data = fs::read("fixture/models
    ➥ /squeezenet1.1-7.onnx").unwrap();
    let graph = load(&[model_data], GraphEncoding::Onnx,
    ➥ ExecutionTarget::Cpu).unwrap();                          Loads the ONNX model
    let exec_context = Graph::init_execution_
    ➥ context(&graph).unwrap();

    let labels_data = fs::read("fixture/labels/
    ➥ squeezenet1.1-7.txt").unwrap();
    let class_labels: Vec<String> = labels_data.                Loads labels
    ➥ lines().map(|line| line.unwrap()).collect();
```

```
    let data = image_to_tensor
    ➥ (&image_path, 224, 224);
    let dimensions = vec![1, 3, 224, 224];
    let tensor = Tensor::new
    ➥ (&dimensions, TensorType::Fp32, &data);
    exec_context.set_input
    ➥ ("data", tensor).unwrap();
```

Prepares input tensor

```
    exec_context.compute().unwrap();
```

Executes inference

```
    let output_data =
    ➥  exec_context.get_output("squeezenet0_flatten0_
    ➥ reshape0").unwrap().data();
    let output_f32 = bytes_to_
    ➥ f32_vec(&output_data);
    let output_array = Array::from_vec(output_f32);
```

Gets and processes output

```
    let exp_output = output_array.mapv(f32::exp);
    let sum_exp = exp_output.sum();
    let softmax_output = exp_output / sum_exp;
```

Computes softmax

```
    let mut probabilities: Vec<_> = softmax_output.
    ➥ iter().enumerate().collect();
    probabilities.sort_by(|a, b| b.1.
    ➥ partial_cmp(a.1).unwrap());
```

Gets top three probabilities

```
    for &(index, &probability) in probabilities.iter().take(3) {
        println!("Class: {} - Probability: {}", class_labels[index],
        ➥ probability);
    }
}

pub fn bytes_to_f32_vec(data: &[u8]) -> Vec<f32> {
    data.chunks_exact(4)
        .map(|c| f32::from_le_bytes(c.try_into().unwrap()))
        .collect()
}

fn image_to_tensor(path: &str, height: u32, width: u32) -> Vec<u8> {
    let img = ImageReader::open(path).unwrap().decode().unwrap();
    let resized_img = img.resize_exact(width, height, Triangle).to_rgb8();
    let raw_pixels = resized_img.into_raw();

    let mean = [0.485, 0.456, 0.406];
    let std = [0.229, 0.224, 0.225];

    let num_pixels = (height * width) as usize;
    let mut data_f32 = vec![0f32; num_pixels * 3];

    for i in 0..num_pixels {
        let idx = i * 3;
        let r = raw_pixels[idx] as f32 / 255.0;
        let g = raw_pixels[idx + 1] as f32 / 255.0;
        let b = raw_pixels[idx + 2] as f32 / 255.0;
```

```
        data_f32[i] = (r - mean[0]) / std[0];
        data_f32[i + num_pixels] = (g - mean[1]) / std[1];
        data_f32[i + 2 * num_pixels] = (b - mean[2]) / std[2];
    }

    let mut data_u8 = Vec::with_capacity(data_f32.len() * 4);
    for &v in &data_f32 {
        data_u8.extend_from_slice(&v.to_ne_bytes());
    }

    data_u8
}
```

RUNNING THE COMPONENT

Now all that is left is to run the component! Like previously mentioned, we can do so directly with Wasmtime, as our component implements `wasi:cli run` thanks to `cargo component`'s behind-the-scenes scaffolding and because Wasmtime provides an implementation for `wasi:nn`. However, there's a small caveat: Wasmtime does not include its ONNX backend by default, which is what we rely on for this example.

To avoid having you build Wasmtime from source to include the ONNX backend, I've done so myself and packaged it as a Docker image that you can run. This image also contains our ONNX SqueezeNet model and labels baked in, which means we don't need them in our local filesystem. Just like we did in chapter 2, we'll be passing our Wasm component (and the image to run inference on) to the container by mounting a local directory containing our `.wasm` and `.jpg` files.

> **NOTE** To see how this image was built, check out its Dockerfile in the book's GitHub repo: https://mng.bz/AGme.

So, from inside `wasi_nn_example/`, run

```
cargo component build --release
```

Then, at the same level as the `src/` folder of `wasi_nn_example/`, create a folder called `data/` and copy the `.wasm` file there. If you haven't already, place the image you want to run inference on together with the `.wasm` file in this `data/` folder. Overall, the tree structure for our `wasi_nn_example` project should look somewhat like this:

```
wasi_nn_example/
├── data/
│   ├── cat.jpg
│   ├── wasi_nn_example.wasm
├── src/
│   ├── main.rs
│   ├── bindings.rs
├── wit/
│   ├── wasi-nn.wit
├── Cargo.toml
```

Finally, from inside our wasi_nn_example/ folder, we can run our component with the following command:

```
docker run --rm -v ./data:/data ghcr.io/danbugs/serverside-wasm-book-
➥ code/wasmtime-onnx:latest run -Snn --dir /fixture::fixture --dir
➥ /data::data /data/wasi_nn_example.wasm /data/cat.jpg
```

I've set up this Docker image to provide an entry point to Wasmtime directly. This way, all commands we pass to Docker after the image name ghcr.io/danbugs/serverside-wasm-book-code/wasmtime-onnx:latest are actually Wasmtime's CLI arguments. Let's walk through it:

- run—Wasmtime's command to run a Wasm module or component.
- -Snn—Enables Wasmtime's experimental support for wasi:nn.
- --dir /fixture::fixture --dir /data::data—Grants the Wasm guest access to the host's fixture/ and data/ directories, where our model, labels, Wasm component, and JPG image are located. This allows the guest to access these directories just as we do in the code.

Finally, we pass in our Wasm component and an argument specifying the path to our JPG image.

If you ran this example with the same cat image I used in figure 5.3, you should have gotten output from the Docker command similar to the following:

```
Class: n02123394 Persian cat - Probability: 0.9488756
Class: n02086079 Pekinese, Pekingese, Peke - Probability: 0.017302925
Class: n02112018 Pomeranian - Probability: 0.01678654
```

As a result, our inference correctly classified our image as a Persian cat!

But perhaps even more importantly, we've successfully used a standardized WASI interface for the first time, demonstrating the immense potential of using WASI to bring powerful capabilities to Wasm. We accomplished all of this from within the safety of Wasm's secure, sandboxed environment. This showcases not only the versatility of Wasm but also its ability to handle complex operations like ML inference without compromising on security or portability. By tapping into these standardized interfaces, we've taken a significant step toward building robust, server-side applications powered by Wasm.

Figure 5.3 Image of a Persian cat

ONNX vs. OpenVINO

Another option for running this example is to use another backend that Wasmtime provides for `wasi:nn`—OpenVINO. By making slight adjustments to our example and using a model suitable for OpenVINO, we could run this example directly with Wasmtime from the CLI. This is possible because the OpenVINO backend relies on runtime linking to the OpenVINO system library, meaning it does not require vendoring like the ONNX backend does.

However, for this example, we chose the ONNX backend to avoid the need to install additional dependencies on our system, prioritizing convenience.

Next, let's take a step back and see a different application of Wasm on the server side.

5.3 Running Wasm inside databases

Next up, we will talk about another application of Wasm—running it inside of a database. This has been a point of interest because it allows computations to be executed directly where the data resides, reducing latency and improving performance. By bringing the code close to the data, we minimize the amount of data we need to send between our database client and server, which is often a bottleneck in traditional architectures. Additionally, running Wasm inside a database uses Wasm's sandboxed execution environment, ensuring that the computations are performed securely and efficiently. This approach opens up possibilities for extending database functionalities with custom logic, enabling more complex operations and real-time data processing without compromising speed or security.

But how can we embed Wasm inside of a database? We achieve this by using *user-defined functions* (UDFs), which are custom functions that extend the capabilities of the database engine. UDFs allow developers to execute bespoke logic directly within the database, enabling more sophisticated data processing and operations without the overhead of transferring data between the database and external applications. Traditionally, UDFs are limited to specific programming languages like C or SQL, restricting flexibility and requiring developers to learn unfamiliar languages. However, with Wasm, we can write UDFs in any language that compiles to Wasm, offering greater language flexibility and enabling developers to use the tools they are most comfortable with.

We'll demonstrate this using libSQL, a popular SQLite fork with built-in Wasm support. It lets you embed Wasm functions directly into SQL queries, blending SQLite's lightweight reliability with Wasm's flexibility and performance.

5.3.1 Making Wasm UDFs

Wasm UDFs are an example of server-side Wasm applications where we currently use Wasm modules instead of Wasm components. There is ongoing work in the community around SQL embedding for Wasm components, notably the `wasi:sql-embed` proposal (https://github.com/WebAssembly/wasi-sql-embed), but this effort is still too nascent as of now. Therefore, because we'll be creating a Wasm module instead of a Wasm component, we'll create our project directly with `cargo` instead of `cargo component`. We'll use Rust because it provides excellent convenience for producing Wasm UDFs. In particular, the `libsql_bindgen` crate simplifies the process by generating bindings between Rust and libSQL, streamlining the creation of custom Wasm-based functions within the database. To start off, in your directory for chapter 5 projects, run

```
cargo new --lib wasm_udf_example
```

In this library, we will create two functions: `encrypt` and `decrypt`. The idea here is that we can implement custom encryption and decryption logic directly within the database, ensuring that sensitive data is securely handled without the need to transfer it outside the database environment. This minimizes the number of systems that can read the unencrypted data, reducing the chances that a bug in some other system could accidentally or maliciously leak private data. By using Wasm UDFs, we can perform these operations efficiently while maintaining data privacy, all within the database's sandboxed execution context. See figure 5.4 for an architecture diagram that illustrates how these functions integrate with the database system.

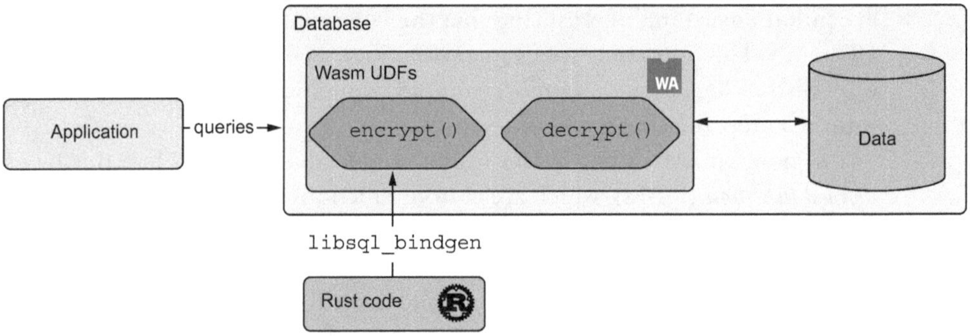

Figure 5.4 Architecture diagram displaying how an application relies on our database with Wasm UDFs

When developing UDFs in Rust for this example, we must navigate both Wasm's security restrictions and libSQL's type compatibility requirements. Wasm's sandboxed execution environment ensures that our functions cannot access system resources such as the network, filesystem, or system time/date, maintaining a secure and isolated runtime. Beyond these isolation rules, we need to limit our function parameters and return types to those compatible with both Wasm and libSQL. Specifically, for our Rust UDFs, we will use any primitive integer type for libSQL's `INTEGER` type, `f32` or `f64` for libSQL's `REAL` type, `String` or `&str` for libSQL's `TEXT` type, and `Vec<u8>` for libSQL's `BLOB` type. The `libsql_bindgen` crate plays a crucial role in this setup by enforcing these type constraints and automatically generating the necessary bindings between Rust and libSQL. This ensures that our custom Wasm-based functions are both type-safe and seamlessly integrated within the libSQL framework, simplifying development and reducing the potential for runtime errors.

With that said, let's now modify our `Cargo.toml` file, as shown in the following listing, to properly compile to Wasm (similar to how we did in chapter 2) and add the dependencies we need for the `encrypt` and `decrypt` functions, including `libsql_bindgen`.

Listing 5.3 `Cargo.toml` file for our `wasm_udf_example` project

```
[package]
name = "wasm_udf_example"
version = "0.1.0"
edition = "2021"

[dependencies]
libsql_bindgen = "0.3.1"
magic-crypt = "3.1"

[lib]
crate-type = ["cdylib"]
```

Provides encryption and decryption functionality for user-defined functions (annotation for `magic-crypt = "3.1"`)

With that done, we can move to our `lib.rs` file. Let's delete everything in the file and then bring in the imports we need:

```
use libsql_bindgen::*;
use magic_crypt::{new_magic_crypt, MagicCryptTrait};
```

We then move on to our first Wasm UDF: `encrypt`. We begin by applying the `libsql_bindgen` attribute to indicate that this function should be exposed as a user-defined function within libSQL. This attribute facilitates the generation of the necessary bindings, allowing our Rust function to be invoked directly from SQL queries. Notice that we are using standard Rust types—`String`—for both the input parameters and the return type, ensuring compatibility with libSQL's type system.

Inside the function, we utilize the `new_magic_crypt!` macro from the `magic_crypt` crate to create a new encryption instance with the provided key and a 256-bit encryption strength. This macro simplifies the setup process, enabling us to focus on implementing the core encryption logic. We then call the `encrypt_str_to_base64` method on our encryption instance, passing in the data we wish to encrypt. This method processes the input string and returns its encrypted form encoded in Base64, which is then returned by the function:

```
#[libsql_bindgen::libsql_bindgen]
pub fn encrypt(data: String, key: String) -> String {
    let mc = new_magic_crypt!(key, 256);
    mc.encrypt_str_to_base64(data)
}
```

How do encryption and decryption work?

Encryption is the process of converting readable data, known as *plaintext*, into an unreadable format called *ciphertext* using a specific key. This ensures that sensitive information remains secure and cannot be accessed by unauthorized parties. Decryption is the reverse process, where the ciphertext is transformed back into its original plaintext form using the same key. In our example, we use symmetric encryption, which means the same key is used for both encrypting and decrypting the data. This approach allows us to securely store and retrieve information directly within the database, ensuring that only those with the correct key can access the original data.

We then move on to our second Wasm UDF: `decrypt`. Similar to the `encrypt` function, we apply the `libsql_bindgen` attribute to designate this function as a user-defined function within libSQL. The `decrypt` function takes in the encrypted data and the encryption key as `String` parameters. Inside the function, we initialize a new encryption instance with the provided key using the `new_magic_crypt!` macro, maintaining the same 256-bit encryption strength. We then call the `decrypt_base64_to_string` method to convert the encrypted Base64 string back to its original plaintext form. If decryption fails—perhaps due to an incorrect key—we handle the error gracefully by returning a default message, such as `"[ACCESS DENIED]"`. This setup ensures that sensitive data can be securely retrieved and managed directly within the database environment using Wasm's secure execution model and libSQL's extensibility:

```
#[libsql_bindgen::libsql_bindgen]
pub fn decrypt(data: String, key: String) -> String {
    let mc = new_magic_crypt!(key, 256);
    mc.decrypt_base64_to_string(data)
        .unwrap_or("[ACCESS DENIED]".to_owned())
}
```

We have now finished writing all the code needed for our Wasm UDFs. For the full code, see the following listing.

Listing 5.4 `lib.rs` file of our `wasm_udf_example` project

```
use libsql_bindgen::*;
use magic_crypt::{new_magic_crypt, MagicCryptTrait};

#[libsql_bindgen::libsql_bindgen]
pub fn encrypt(data: String, key: String) -> String {
    let mc = new_magic_crypt!(key, 256);
    mc.encrypt_str_to_base64(data)
}

#[libsql_bindgen::libsql_bindgen]
pub fn decrypt(data: String, key: String) -> String {
```

```
    let mc = new_magic_crypt!(key, 256);
    mc.decrypt_base64_to_string(data)
        .unwrap_or("[ACCESS DENIED]".to_owned())
}
```

5.3.2 Getting Wasm into SQL

Now we are ready to compile our Rust code as a Wasm module. It's important to note that this is possible because the `magic_crypt` crate supports compilation to Wasm. To compile our project, from inside `wasm_udf_example/` run the following command:

```
cargo build --release --target wasm32-unknown-unknown
```

Then grab our compiled `wasm_udf_example.wasm` file and place it in the `wasm_udf_example/data/` directory. Our next step is to convert this Wasm module into a format that libSQL understands. There are two acceptable formats:

- *Literal blob*—In SQLite, a blob (binary large object) can be represented using a hexadecimal string prefixed with X. For example, `X'474F4F444341544348'` allows us to embed binary data directly within SQL statements. This format is suitable for storing the binary Wasm module as part of SQL queries or function definitions.
- *WebAssembly Text Format (WAT)*—WAT is a human-readable text representation of Wasm binary code. It enables easier inspection and editing of Wasm modules, which can be beneficial for debugging or manual adjustments. Converting our Wasm module to WAT allows us to define user-defined functions in a more transparent and editable format within libSQL.

For our purposes, we will use a literal blob. To create our blob from a Wasm binary, we will use a tool called `wasm_hex_dump`, which converts the binary data into a format that can be used directly in SQL statements. To install it, run `cargo install wasm_hex_dump@0.1.0 --locked`.

But before generating the hex dump for our Wasm binary, we need to create a `.sql` file—let's call it `create_wasm_udfs.sql`—inside the same `data/` folder within the `wasm_udf_example/` directory. This file will contain the necessary SQL statements to define our UDFs. As a preliminary step, add the following lines:

```
.init_wasm_func_table
DROP FUNCTION IF EXISTS encrypt;
DROP FUNCTION IF EXISTS decrypt;
```

This initializes the Wasm function table that libSQL uses to register Wasm-based UDFs. By dropping any existing `encrypt` and `decrypt` functions (if they exist), we ensure that we have a clean slate for adding these functions after their Wasm binaries have been converted and embedded as literal blobs. This avoids conflicts and ensures that the UDFs are defined properly when we recreate them.

Next, we are ready to get the hex dump for our Wasm binary. You can do this by running from the `data/` folder:

```
wasm_hex_dump -i wasm_udf_example.wasm
```

By default, `wasm_hex_dump` will output an `output.txt` file containing the hex dump for our input. We will use this hex dump to define our UDFs. Copy the generated hex and then, back in our SQL file, add the following:

```
CREATE FUNCTION encrypt LANGUAGE wasm AS X'<your hex text here>';
```

Next, using the same hex dump, add

```
CREATE FUNCTION decrypt LANGUAGE wasm AS X'<your hex text here>';
```

With the `CREATE FUNCTION` commands, we are defining our encrypt and decrypt UDFs within the database. Each function is associated with the Wasm binary we converted to hex and embedded as a literal blob. By specifying `LANGUAGE wasm`, we indicate that these functions are implemented in Wasm, allowing libSQL to run them in a sandboxed environment. The hex dump following the `AS X'...'` clause represents the Wasm binary code in hexadecimal format, which the database uses to execute the respective encryption and decryption logic.

Overall, your file should look like the following listing.

Listing 5.5 `data/create_wasm_udfs.sql` file

```
.init_wasm_func_table
DROP FUNCTION IF EXISTS encrypt;
DROP FUNCTION IF EXISTS decrypt;
CREATE FUNCTION encrypt LANGUAGE wasm AS X'0061736d01...';
CREATE FUNCTION decrypt LANGUAGE wasm AS X'0061736d01...';
```

Do pay special attention to ensure that both `CREATE FUNCTION` statements are properly closed with a closing single quote (`'`) and semicolon (`;`). This ensures that the functions are correctly defined within the SQL file and ready to be executed when importing the UDFs.

Optimizing Wasm UDFs with wasm-opt

When embedding Wasm binaries as UDFs in a database, it's worth considering optimization tools like `wasm-opt`. This tool is specifically designed to optimize Wasm binaries by reducing their size and improving performance. It applies a variety of optimizations, such as removing unused code, simplifying control flow, and making memory usage more efficient. For Wasm UDFs, running `wasm-opt` before embedding the binary as a literal blob in the database can lead to smaller file sizes and faster execution times, ensuring your UDF performs efficiently within the database environment.

5.3.3 Running Wasm UDFs in libSQL

Now we are ready to run our Wasm UDFs. For convenience, we will once again use a Docker image for this example. This is a Docker image I have prepared that comes with a prebuilt version of libSQL and provides an entry point to it. We will run the container while mounting the path to our `data/` folder where our SQL file and Wasm module reside. You can do so with the following command from the `wasm_udf_example/` folder:

```
docker run --rm -v ./data:/data -it ghcr.io/danbugs/
➥ serverside-wasm-book-code/libsql-wasmudf:latest
```

This command ensures that libSQL can access the `data/` directory, allowing it to locate the necessary SQL file and Wasm module to execute the UDFs defined within your project.

Next, you should be presented with a prompt like

```
libsql>
```

This indicates that you are inside the interactive libSQL shell, ready to execute SQL commands. Now run the following command to load and execute the SQL file that defines your Wasm UDFs:

```
.read /data/create_wasm_udfs.sql
```

This command reads and executes the SQL statements from the file, including the ones that initialize the Wasm function table and create your `encrypt` and `decrypt` functions. At this point, your functions should be fully defined and ready to use within the libSQL environment.

Now let's test our Wasm UDFs! Execute the following in your libSQL shell:

```
SELECT encrypt('Hello, I am a Wasm UDF!', 'dan');
```

In this command, we are encrypting the string `"Hello, I am a Wasm UDF!"` using the key `'dan'`. This should output the following:

```
YEBtLTvktUr2941iA0p0oY+Q6C0+ZfM8T1F+eqhzlKI=
```

There we go! We just successfully used the `encrypt` function we defined as a Wasm UDF. To conclude, we can then copy this encrypted result and provide it as the input to our `decrypt` function, like so:

```
SELECT decrypt('YEBtLTvktUr2941iA0p0oY+Q6C0+ZfM8T1F+eqhzlKI=', 'dan');
```

And we should get back

```
'Hello, I am a Wasm UDF!'
```

This confirms that both the encryption and decryption functions work as expected, with the data being securely processed within the database using our Wasm UDFs!

Using WAT to define Wasm UDFs

We can also use WAT to define UDFs directly in libSQL. Like previously mentioned, WAT is a human-readable format for Wasm that allows us to write and edit Wasm modules more easily. Here's an example of a simple `my_add` function written in WAT that adds two integers:

```
CREATE FUNCTION my_add LANGUAGE wasm AS '
(module
    (func $my_add (param i64 i64) (result i64)
        local.get 0
        local.get 1
        i64.add)
    (memory 16)
    (export "my_add" (func $my_add))
    (export "memory" (memory 0))
)';
```

This defines a Wasm function named `my_add` that takes two 64-bit integers as parameters and returns their sum. The memory export is necessary for managing memory, though in this case, it's not actively used.

Once you've defined the function, you can test it just like we did with the previous example. In your libSQL shell, run

```
SELECT my_add(1, 41);
```

This should output

```
42
```

With WAT, you can write and test simple Wasm functions like this, directly defining UDFs in a clear, readable format. It's a great alternative for small or custom logic without needing to precompile Wasm binaries.

With that, we've successfully created and executed Wasm UDFs within libSQL! Starting from writing the encryption and decryption logic in Rust, we compiled our code to Wasm, embedded it as a literal blob into SQL, and then tested our UDFs directly within the database. Along the way, we also explored how tools like `wasm_hex_dump` and `libsql_bindgen` help bridge the gap between Wasm and SQL, allowing us to extend the capabilities of the database with custom functions in a secure, sandboxed environment.

TIP To exit the libSQL shell, you can use the `.exit` command.

By embedding Wasm UDFs, we not only keep computations close to the data, minimizing latency and data movement, but we also take advantage of Wasm's language-agnostic nature and security features. Whether you need to encrypt data, perform complex calculations, or even run ML models directly in the database, Wasm UDFs provide a powerful, efficient way to extend database functionality with custom logic—all while ensuring performance, portability, and security and letting you use whatever programming language you already know.

5.4 Improving our example project with wasi-nn

In chapter 4, we introduced an ML component to our SmartCMS application. However, it wasn't truly an ML component at the time. Instead, it acted as a placeholder, simply querying a file of stories and selecting a line at random—a rudimentary stand-in for the real thing. But now that we've familiarized ourselves with `wasi:nn`, we can take things a step further. In this section, as shown in figure 5.5, we'll upgrade our `smartcms_ml_guest`

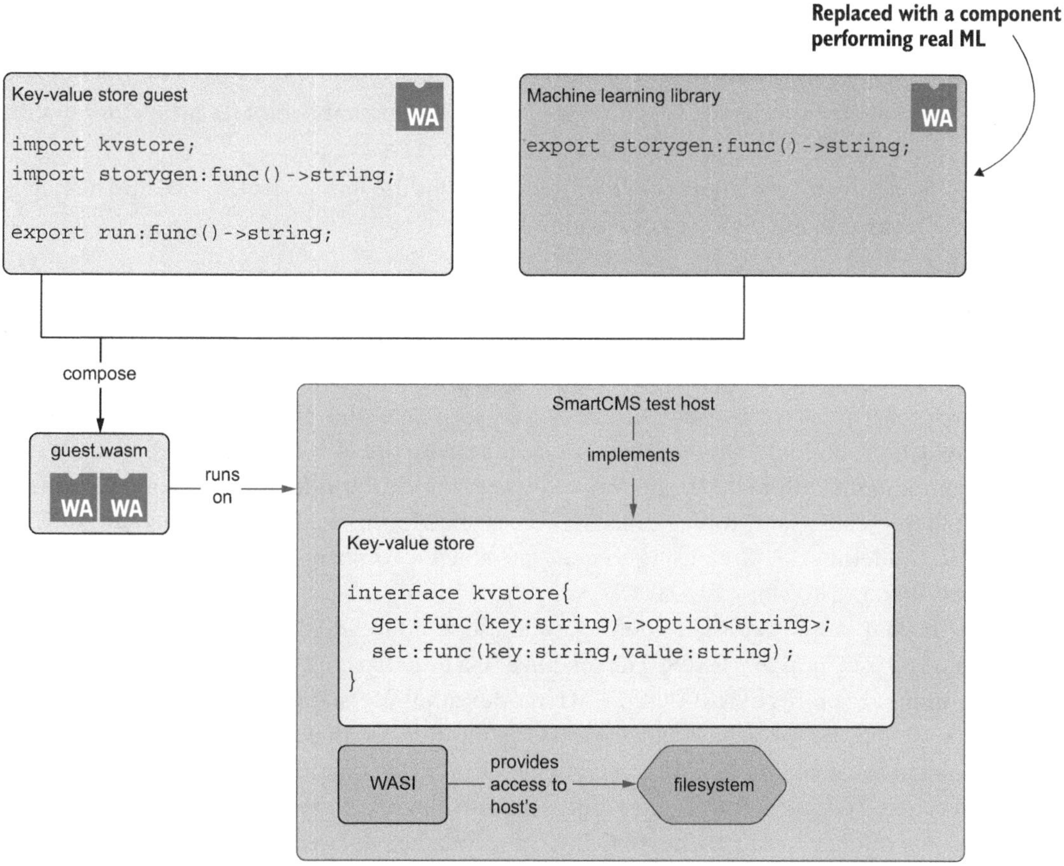

Figure 5.5 The architecture of our SmartCMS project with the addition of a real ML component

to use `wasi:nn` for actual ML functionality. With that change in place, we'll also need to modify our host implementation to incorporate Wasmtime's host support for `wasi:nn`, ensuring that the necessary backends (such as ONNX) are properly configured.

5.4.1 Setting up our project

We'll be continuing to work on our existing SmartCMS implementation from chapter 4. Feel free to work from the existing project, or copy your work from chapter 4 onto a new directory (i.e., `chapter05/`) if you want to keep each chapter's work separate.

> **TIP** If you're copying over your work from chapter 4 and have both the chapter 4 and chapter 5 SmartCMS projects in your workspace, it's a good idea to suffix each package's name (in their respective `Cargo.toml` files) with the chapter number. This helps avoid any naming clashes.

Inside the `smart_cms/` folder we worked on before, you should have three subfolders: `smartcms_kvstore_guest/`, `smartcms_ml_guest/`, and `smartcms_test_host/`. These represent the key components of our SmartCMS system:

- `smartcms_kvstore_guest/`—This folder contains the code for our key-value store guest component, which handles storage and retrieval of content for the CMS.
- `smartcms_ml_guest/`—This folder holds the logic for the ML guest component, which we'll be upgrading to use real ML with `wasi:nn`.
- `smartcms_test_host/`—This folder contains the host code that runs and manages the execution of the guest components.

Inside `smartcms_test_host/`, you should see two Wasm files from our previous work: `guest.wasm` and `guest_with_ml.wasm`. The `guest.wasm` file is the compiled Wasm version of our `smartcms_kvstore_guest` component, while `guest_with_ml.wasm` is the composition of `guest.wasm` along with the compiled version of our makeshift `smartcms_ml_guest` component. Feel free to delete the `guest_with_ml.wasm` file, as we'll be rebuilding the `smartcms_ml_guest` project and recomposing the two Wasm components with real ML support using `wasi:nn`. Still inside the `smartcms_test_host/` folder, create a new folder called `fixture/`. Inside this folder, we'll place the ONNX ML model that we'll be using to generate stories. You can download the model from this link: https://mng.bz/Z9DN.

In that same `fixture/` folder, you will also need to add the tokenizer file from this link: https://mng.bz/Rw0R. The tokenizer is a tool that converts text into tokens, which are smaller pieces of text that the ML model can understand and process. In our case, we will use the tokenizer to preprocess the input text and postprocess the output from the model, enabling the ML model to generate coherent stories based on the tokens it receives. To finish off with our configuration changes to `smartcms_test_host`, let's add a dependency to our `Cargo.toml` file. In particular, we are adding `wasmtime-wasi-nn`, which is Wasmtime's host implementation for the `wasi:nn` interface. This is similar to how we previously wrote our own implementation for the key-value store, except it's provided by Wasmtime. With the added dependency, the full `Cargo.toml` file should look like the following listing.

Listing 5.6 `Cargo.toml` file for the `smartcms_test_host` project

```
[package]
name = "smartcms_test_host"
version = "0.1.0"
edition = "2021"

[dependencies]
wasmtime = "30"
wasmtime-wasi = "30"
wasmtime-wasi-nn = { version = "30",
    features = ["onnx"] }
ort = { version = "=2.0.0-rc.6", default-features
    = false, features = ["copy-dylibs",
    "download-binaries"] }
ort-sys = { version = "=2.0.0-rc.6",
    default-features = false, features =
    ["copy-dylibs", "download-binaries"] }
```

Adds the wasmtime-wasi-nn dependency with the ONNX feature

Adds the ort and ort-sys dependencies (i.e., an ML inference in Rust library) at the specific version required by wasmtime-wasi-nn

Note that we are adding the dependency with the ONNX feature, which isn't enabled by default. This means we are opting to vendor (i.e., include and manage the ONNX backend directly within our project) the ONNX backend together with our host implementation, allowing Wasmtime to support ONNX-based ML models.

Now let's move our attention to the `smartcms_ml_guest` project. We'll be adding some dependencies to its `Cargo.toml` file—two in particular: `ndarray` (which we've seen before in the `wasm_nn_example` project) and `tokenizers`, a library used for tokenization (as introduced earlier). To use `tokenizers` with Wasm, we need to disable the default features and enable its `unstable_wasm` feature. Additionally, since we'll be including an extra WIT file (i.e., `wasi-nn.wit`, just like in `wasm_nn_example`), we need to add a `[package.metadata.component.target]` section to the `Cargo.toml` file. This section specifies our target world, which tells the build system what component we're targeting. We also need to specify the dependency on our target (i.e., `wasi:nn`) in the `[package.metadata.component.target.dependencies]` section. Overall, the updated `Cargo.toml` file looks like the following listing.

Listing 5.7 `Cargo.toml` file for the `smartcms_ml_guest` project

```
[package]
name = "smartcms_ml_guest"
version = "0.1.0"
edition = "2021"

[dependencies]
wit-bindgen-rt = { version = "0.41.0", features = ["bitflags"] }
rand = "0.8.5"
tokenizers = { version = "0.20.1",
```

```
➥default-features = false, features =
➥["unstable_wasm"] }
ndarray = "0.16.1"

[lib]
crate-type = ["cdylib"]

[profile.release]
codegen-units = 1
opt-level = "s"
debug = false
strip = true
lto = true

[package.metadata.component]
package = "component:smartcms-ml-guest"

[package.metadata.component.target]
path = "wit/world.wit"
world = "example"

[package.metadata.component.target.dependencies]
"wasi:nn" = { path = "wit/wasi-nn.wit" }
```

tokenizers is added with the Wasm-compatible unstable_wasm feature enabled.

ndarray is added to handle multidimensional arrays, a key tool for managing tensor data in ML applications.

In the [package.metadata.component.target] section, we specify the path to the WIT file and the world name.

The [package.metadata.component.target.dependencies] section includes the path to wasi-nn.wit.

For our `[package.metadata.component.target]` section, we specify the path to our WIT file and the world name, both of which are unaltered from chapter 4. This ensures that our guest component is properly connected to the correct world definition, as defined in `world.wit`.

In the `[package.metadata.component.target.dependencies]` section, we add the path to our `wasi-nn.wit`, which defines the ML interface that we will use. You can copy this `wasi-nn.wit` file from the `wit/` folder in the `wasi_nn_example/` project and place it in the `wit/` folder of your `smartcms_ml_guest/` directory. This step ensures that our component will have access to the `wasi:nn` functionality for performing ML tasks.

Finally, with everything in place, we can now modify our `smartcms_ml_guest/wit/world.wit` file to include the `wasi-nn.wit` dependency that we'll be utilizing. Note that this method of using `wasi:nn` is different from how we did it in the `wasi_nn_example` project, where we manually generated bindings via the `wit_bindgen` dependency. Here we're directly referencing the WIT dependency in the `world.wit` file. The updated `world.wit` file can be seen in the following listing.

Listing 5.8 Updated `world.wit` file for `smartcms_ml_guest`

```
package component:smartcms-ml-guest;

world example {
    include wasi:nn/ml@0.2.0-rc-2024-08-19;
    export storygen: func() -> string;
}
```

We include the wasi:nn/ml interface at the specified version.

Now we are ready to start working on our `smartcms_ml_guest` `lib.rs` file.

5.4.2 *Writing the ML Wasm component*

Let's begin by importing the necessary dependencies and setting up the foundation for our implementation:

```
#[allow(warnings)]
mod bindings;                  // Uses autogenerated glue code rather than wit_bindgen directly, unaltered from before

use tokenizers::Tokenizer;
use rand::prelude::*;
use ndarray::Array;
use std::fs;

use bindings::{Guest, wasi::nn::{      // Aside from bindings::Guest, also brings into scope needed wasi:nn structures and functions
    graph::{Graph, load, ExecutionTarget, GraphEncoding},
    tensor::{Tensor, TensorType},
}};
```

Now, luckily, we can breeze through much of this code since it's quite similar to what we worked on in the `wasi_nn_project`. However, one key difference is that here we're building a library rather than a binary. This means we'll be writing our business logic inside the `storygen` function that our component is expected to export.

To keep things simple, remove any existing code inside the `storygen` function so we can start fresh. After bringing in the necessary dependencies, your `lib.rs` should look like this:

```
struct Component;

impl Guest for Component {
    fn storygen() -> String {
        // ...
    }
}

bindings::export!(Component with_types_in bindings);
```

Now every subsequent piece of code in this section should be placed inside the `storygen` function, starting with loading the ONNX model:

```
let model_data = fs::read("fixture/modified_model.onnx").unwrap();
let graph = load(&[model_data], GraphEncoding::Onnx,
➥ExecutionTarget::Cpu).unwrap();
let exec_context = Graph::init_execution_context(&graph).unwrap();
```

We read the ONNX model from the filesystem, load it into a graph, and initialize an execution context to perform ML inference.

Next, we'll initialize the tokenizer, which we previously introduced. The tokenizer helps convert the input text into tokens that the model can process:

```
let tokenizer = Tokenizer::from_file("fixture/tokenizer.json").unwrap();
```

Here we'll load the tokenizer from the `tokenizer.json` file, preparing it to handle the text input for story generation. The tokenizer will break down the input into manageable pieces, which are then passed to the model for inference.

Next, we'll define the prompt and tokenize it, converting the text into a format the model can work with:

```
let prompt = "Once upon a time";
let encoding = tokenizer.encode(prompt, true).unwrap();
let mut input_ids = encoding.get_ids().to_vec();
```

We start by setting a simple text prompt, `"Once upon a time"`, which serves as the initial input for the story generation. The tokenizer then encodes this prompt, turning it into tokens. The encoded tokens are extracted as `input_ids`, which are numerical representations of the text that the model will use during inference.

Then we set up a random number generator (RNG) to introduce variability in the generated stories and define the end-of-sequence (EOS) token, which marks the conclusion of a generated story:

```
let mut rng = thread_rng();
let eos_token_id = tokenizer.token_to_id("<EOS>").unwrap_or(0);
```

The `rng` ensures that each story generated will be unique by adding randomness during inference. The `eos_token_id` retrieves the token ID for the `EOS` marker, which signals when the model should stop generating tokens, defaulting to 0 if the token isn't found. This fallback assumes that token 0 has a safe or meaningful interpretation (such as padding or an undefined token) and prevents runtime errors. However, if token 0 does not represent a valid stopping point, the generated output might not terminate as intended. To mitigate this, the code includes additional stopping criteria, such as checking for paragraph breaks.

Now we start a `for` loop that runs from 0 to 100, an arbitrary stopping point, to iteratively generate tokens for our story. Until noted otherwise, all subsequent code will be inside this `for` loop:

```
for _ in 0..100 {
    // ...
}
```

This loop serves to generate new tokens, which will eventually form the story. The number 100 acts as a safeguard to prevent the model from generating too many tokens, though the process may stop earlier if the end-of-sequence token is reached.

Inside the loop, we first prepare the input data by converting our token IDs into the format the model expects:

```
let sequence_length = input_ids.len();
let dimensions = vec![1, sequence_length as u32];
```

```
let input_f32: Vec<f32> = input_ids.iter().map(|&id| id as f32).collect();
let mut input_data = Vec::with_capacity(input_f32.len() * 4);
for &val in &input_f32 {
    input_data.extend_from_slice(&val.to_ne_bytes());
}
let tensor = Tensor::new(&dimensions, TensorType::Fp32, &input_data);
exec_context.set_input("input_ids", tensor).unwrap();
```

We start by calculating the length of the token sequence, then define the tensor dimensions based on this length. The token IDs are converted into 32-bit floating-point values (`f32`) since the model requires this format. Next, we create the byte representation of these values and store them in `input_data`. Finally, we wrap the data in a tensor and set it as the input for the model, using the key `"input_ids"` to ensure the model processes the correct data.

> **TIP** You can use Netron (https://netron.app/) to inspect your ML models and get a better understanding of their structure. It allows you to see details like tensor shapes, layer connections, and crucial information such as the tensor keys (e.g., `"input_ids"`).

Finally, we execute the model inference, just as we did before:

```
exec_context.compute().unwrap();
```

This runs the model on the provided input, processing the token sequence to generate the next output.

Next, we retrieve the model's output and convert it into a usable format:

```
let output_data = exec_context.get_output("logits").unwrap().data();
let output_f32 = bytes_to_f32_vec(&output_data);
```

We access the output tensor, which is stored under the key `"logits"` (i.e., the raw, unnormalized scores output by the neural network for each possible token in the vocabulary) and use the `bytes_to_f32_vec` function to convert the raw bytes into `f32` values that can be processed. This `bytes_to_f32_vec` function is identical to the one from the `wasi_nn_example` project, so you can copy it from there and paste it at the end of this file.

Next, we process the model's output to isolate the logits for the last generated token:

```
let vocab_size = output_f32.len() / sequence_length;
let start = (sequence_length - 1) * vocab_size;
let end = sequence_length * vocab_size;
let last_token_logits = &output_f32[start..end];
```

Here we calculate the size of the vocabulary (i.e., the full set of tokens, such as words or subwords, that the model recognizes and can generate as output) by dividing the total length of the output by the `sequence_length`. We then determine the start and end positions for the logits of the last token in the sequence. The last_token_logits slice represents the predicted probabilities for each possible next token based on the input sequence, which will be used to generate the next token in our story.

Next, we apply the softmax function to the logits to convert them into probabilities:

```
let probabilities = softmax(last_token_logits);
```

This step is essentially the same as what we did in the wasi_nn_example project, but now the softmax operation has been split into its own function for reusability. You can define the softmax function at the end of the file, together with bytes_to_f32_vec:

```
fn softmax(logits: &[f32]) -> Vec<f32> {
    let logits_array = Array::from_vec(logits.to_vec());
    let exp_logits = logits_array.mapv(f32::exp);
    let sum_exp = exp_logits.sum();
    (exp_logits / sum_exp).to_vec()
}
```

By applying softmax, we convert the logits into a probability distribution over the possible next tokens. This will help us sample the next token based on the model's predictions.

Next, we sample the next token based on the probability distribution generated by the softmax function:

```
let dist = rand::distributions::WeightedIndex::new(&probabilities).unwrap();
let next_token = dist.sample(&mut rng);
input_ids.push(next_token as u32);
let generated_text = tokenizer.decode(&input_ids, true).unwrap();
```

Here we use a weighted distribution (WeightedIndex) to sample the next token. The probabilities vector is passed to the distribution, and a token is sampled based on those probabilities using the random number generator (rng). This ensures that the model picks the next token based on the predicted likelihood while still introducing some randomness to the output. The sampled token is then appended to the input_ids, representing the sequence generated so far. Finally, the tokenizer.decode function is used to convert the sequence of token IDs in input_ids back into a human-readable string (generated_text), updating the generated text output with the newly sampled token.

Next, we add checks to determine when to terminate the story generation loop. Specifically, we break the loop if the generated text ends with two newline characters ("\n\n") or if the next token matches the EOS token. I decided to include the "\n\n" check in addition to the EOS token because, empirically, it helped our code run quicker and reduced the likelihood of stories being cut short by the 100-token limit:

```
if generated_text.ends_with("\n\n") {
    break;
```

```
}

if next_token as u32 == eos_token_id {
    break;
}
```

This ensures that story generation stops appropriately, either when a natural ending is detected or when the predefined token limit is reached.

Finally, outside the loop, we decode the generated tokens back into a human-readable story and return the result:

```
tokenizer.decode(&input_ids, true).unwrap().trim().to_string()
```

Here the `tokenizer.decode` function takes the `input_ids` (which now contain the generated tokens) and converts them back into a readable string. We use `trim()` to remove any extra whitespace and then convert it to a `String`, which will be returned as the final generated story. Overall, the full code can be seen in the following listing.

Listing 5.9 `lib.rs` file from `smartcms_ml_guest`

```
#[allow(warnings)]
mod bindings;

use tokenizers::Tokenizer;
use rand::prelude::*;
use ndarray::Array;
use std::fs;

use bindings::{Guest, wasi::nn::{
    graph::{Graph, load, ExecutionTarget, GraphEncoding},
    tensor::{Tensor, TensorType},
}};

struct Component;

impl Guest for Component {
    fn storygen() -> String {
        let model_data = fs::read("fixture
        ➥/modified_model.onnx").unwrap();
        let graph = load(&[model_data],
        ➥GraphEncoding::Onnx, ExecutionTarget
        ➥::Cpu).unwrap();
        let exec_context = Graph::init_execution_
        ➥context(&graph).unwrap();

        let tokenizer =
        ➥Tokenizer::from_file("fixture/
        ➥tokenizer.json").unwrap();

        let prompt = "Once upon a time";
        let encoding = tokenizer.
```

Loads the ONNX model and sets up the graph and execution context

Loads the tokenizer from the provided file

Defines the prompt and encodes it into token IDs

```
➥ encode(prompt, true).unwrap();
let mut input_ids =
➥ encoding.get_ids().to_vec();

let mut rng = thread_rng();
let eos_token_id = tokenizer.token_
➥ to_id("<EOS>").unwrap_or(0);

for _ in 0..100 {
    let sequence_length = input_ids.len();
    let dimensions = vec!
    ➥ [1, sequence_length as u32];
    let input_f32: Vec<f32> = input_
    ➥ ids.iter().map(|&id| id as f32).collect();
    let mut input_data = Vec::
    ➥ with_capacity(input_f32.len() * 4);
    for &val in &input_f32 {
        input_data.extend_from_slice
    ➥ (&val.to_ne_bytes());
    }
    let tensor = Tensor::new
    ➥ (&dimensions, TensorType::Fp32, &input_data);
    exec_context.set_input
    ➥ ("input_ids", tensor).unwrap();

    exec_context.compute().unwrap();

    let output_data = exec_context.
    ➥ get_output("logits").unwrap().data();
    let output_f32 = bytes_to_f32_vec
    ➥ (&output_data);

    let vocab_size = output_f32.
    ➥ len() / sequence_length;
    let start = (sequence_length - 1)
    ➥ * vocab_size;
    let end = sequence_length * vocab_size;
    let last_token_logits =
    ➥ &output_f32[start..end];

    let probabilities = softmax
    ➥ (last_token_logits);

    let dist = rand::distributions::
    ➥ WeightedIndex::new(&probabilities).unwrap();
    let next_token = dist.sample(&mut rng);
    input_ids.push(next_token as u32);

    let generated_text =
    ➥ tokenizer.decode(&input_ids, true).unwrap();

    if generated_text.ends_with("\n\n") {
        break;
    }
```

Annotations:
- Defines the prompt and encodes it into token IDs
- Initializes the random number generator and sets the EOS token
- Loops up to 100 iterations to generate tokens
- Prepares and sets the input tensor
- Runs the model inference
- Retrieves and converts the model's output
- Extracts the logits for the last token in the sequence
- Applies softmax to calculate token probabilities
- Samples the next token based on probabilities and appends it to the sequence
- Decodes the generated text
- Breaks the loop if a natural end to the story is detected

```
            if next_token as u32 == eos_token_id {
                break;
            }
        }

        tokenizer.decode(&input_ids, true)
        ➥ .unwrap().trim().to_string()
    }
}

pub fn bytes_to_f32_vec(data: &[u8]) -> Vec<f32> {
    data.chunks_exact(4)
        .map(|c| f32::from_le_bytes(c.try_into().unwrap()))
        .collect()
}

fn softmax(logits: &[f32]) -> Vec<f32> {
    let logits_array = Array::from_vec(logits.to_vec());
    let exp_logits = logits_array.mapv(f32::exp);
    let sum_exp = exp_logits.sum();
    (exp_logits / sum_exp).to_vec()
}

bindings::export!(Component with_types_in bindings);
```

Breaks the loop if a natural end to the story is detected

Returns the final generated story

The function to convert bytes to f32 values

The softmax function to compute the probability distribution

Finally, inside the `smartcms_ml_guest/` folder, we can compile our component by running

```
cargo component build --release
```

With this done, from the `smartcms_ml_guest/` folder, we can then once again compose it with the `guest.wasm` (our key-value store component) like we did prior:

```
wac plug ../smartcms_test_host/guest.wasm --plug <path-
➥ to>/smartcms_ml_guest.wasm -o ../smartcms_test_host/guest_with_ml.wasm
```

This step creates the `guest_with_ml.wasm` file, which is the composition of the two components: the SmartCMS key-value store and the newly generated ML component.

5.4.3 Updating our host to use ONNX for wasi:nn

Now we are ready to update our host at `smartcms_test_host/`. Our changes are straightforward because we don't have to implement `wasi:nn` manually—there's already an implementation provided by Wasmtime, which we included via the `wasmtime-wasi-nn` dependency.

First, we need to modify our `State` structure to include the `WasiNnCtx`. This is similar to when we added WASI support to our host by including the `WasiCtx` in the store. In `smartcms_test_host/src/main.rs`, add

```
struct State {
    key_value: KeyValue,
```

```
    wasi: (wasmtime_wasi::WasiCtx, wasmtime_wasi::ResourceTable),
    wasi_nn: wasmtime_wasi_nn::wit::WasiNnCtx
}
```

This setup prepares our host to manage both key-value storage and ML functionality, the latter using Wasmtime's `wasi:nn` implementation. Then we can act on the updated `State` struct in our `main` function by preloading the ML backends, initializing the `WasiNnCtx`, and setting up the store:

```
let (backends, registry) = wasmtime_wasi_nn::preload(&[]).unwrap();
let wasi_nn_ctx = wasmtime_wasi_nn::wit::WasiNnCtx::new(backends, registry);

let state = State {
    key_value: KeyValue { mem: std::collections::HashMap::new() },
    wasi: (wasi_ctx, wasi_table),
    wasi_nn: wasi_nn_ctx,
};

let mut store = wasmtime::Store::new(&engine, state);
```

Here the `preload` function loads the available ML backends and creates a registry (i.e., a container for graphs). We then create a new `WasiNnCtx` using these values. Finally, we initialize the `Store` with the engine and updated `State`, which now includes both the `WasiCtx` for general WASI functionality and the `WasiNnCtx` for ML support.

Finally, we can complete the setup by adding the `wasi:nn` context to the linker so that it can be accessed during the component's execution, alongside the key-value store functionality:

```
wasmtime_wasi_nn::wit::add_to_linker(&mut linker, |state: &mut State| {
    wasmtime_wasi_nn::wit::WasiNnView::new(&mut state.wasi.1, &mut
    ➥ state.wasi_nn)
}).unwrap();
component::smartcms::kvstore::add_to_linker(&mut linker, |state: &mut
➥ State| &mut state.key_value).unwrap();
let app = App::instantiate(&mut store, &component, &linker).unwrap();
```

Here we add the `wasi:nn` context to the linker with `add_to_linker` to ensure that the neural network functionality can be invoked by the Wasm component. We also link the key-value store as before. Finally, the component is instantiated using the `App::instantiate` method, with the fully set-up `store` and `linker`. This allows our host to handle both key-value store operations and ML inference using `wasi:nn`. Overall, the code should look like the following listing.

Listing 5.10 `main.rs` file for the `smartcms_test_host` project

```
wasmtime::component::bindgen!({
    path: "./smart_cms.wit",
    world: "app",
});
```

```
struct KeyValue {
    mem: std::collections::HashMap<String, String>,
}

impl component::smartcms::kvstore::Host for KeyValue {
    fn get(&mut self, key: String) -> Option<String> {
        self.mem.get(&key).cloned()
    }

    fn set(&mut self, key: String, value: String) {
        self.mem.insert(key, value);
    }
}

struct State {
    key_value: KeyValue,
    wasi: (wasmtime_wasi::WasiCtx, wasmtime_wasi::ResourceTable),
    wasi_nn: wasmtime_wasi_nn::wit::WasiNnCtx
}

impl wasmtime_wasi::WasiView for State {
    fn ctx(&mut self) -> &mut wasmtime_wasi::WasiCtx {
        &mut self.wasi.0
    }
}

impl wasmtime_wasi::IoView for State {
    fn table(&mut self) -> &mut wasmtime_wasi::ResourceTable {
        &mut self.wasi.1
    }
}

fn main() {
    let mut config = wasmtime::Config::default();
    config.wasm_component_model(true);

    let engine = wasmtime::Engine::new(&config).unwrap();

    let wasi_table = wasmtime_wasi::ResourceTable::new();
    let wasi_ctx = wasmtime_wasi::WasiCtxBuilder::new()
        .preopened_dir(".", ".", wasmtime_wasi::DirPerms::READ,
        ➥wasmtime_wasi::FilePerms::READ).unwrap()
        .build();

    let (backends, registry) = wasmtime_wasi_nn
    ➥::preload(&[]).unwrap(); #B
    let wasi_nn_ctx = wasmtime_wasi_nn::
    ➥wit::WasiNnCtx::new(backends, registry);

    let state = State {
        key_value: KeyValue { mem: std::collections::HashMap::new() },
        wasi: (wasi_ctx, wasi_table),
        wasi_nn: wasi_nn_ctx,
    };
```

Adds the wasi_nn context to the state for handling ML tasks (annotation on `wasi_nn: wasmtime_wasi_nn::wit::WasiNnCtx`)

Preloads ML backends and creates a new WasiNnCtx to handle the wasi:nn interface for neural network execution (annotation on `wit::WasiNnCtx::new(backends, registry);`)

Adds the wasi_nn context to the state for handling ML tasks (annotation on `wasi_nn: wasi_nn_ctx,`)

```
    let mut store = wasmtime::Store::new(&engine, state);

    let component = wasmtime::component::Component::from_file(&engine,
    ➥"guest_with_ml.wasm").unwrap();

    let mut linker = wasmtime::component::Linker::new(&engine);
    wasmtime_wasi::add_to_linker_sync(&mut linker).unwrap();
    wasmtime_wasi_nn::wit::add_to_linker
    ➥(&mut linker, |state: &mut State| {
        wasmtime_wasi_nn::wit::WasiNnView::new
    ➥(&mut state.wasi.1, &mut state.wasi_nn)
    }).unwrap();
    component::smartcms::kvstore::add_to_linker
    ➥(&mut linker, |state: &mut State| &mut state.key_value).unwrap();

    let app = App::instantiate(&mut store, &component, &linker).unwrap();

    println!("{:?}", app.call_run(&mut store).unwrap());
}
```

Links the wasi_nn functionality to the component by adding wasi:nn to the linker, enabling the SmartCMS component to use Wasmtime's ML capabilities

Finally, we are ready to run our host over the updated component. From the `smartcms_test_host/` folder, run

```
cargo run --release
```

This should generate and output a story. For example, when I ran it, I got the following:

```
"Once upon a time, there was a little girl named Lily. She loved playing
➥with her toys and running around outside. One day, Lily's aunt came to
➥visit. She brought a big present for Lily. Lily was very excited to see
➥what was inside."
```

At this point, our setup is complete, and our ML component is now fully integrated with the SmartCMS host using `wasi:nn`!

Summary

- WASI has expanded beyond POSIX and now serves as a collection of standardized interfaces offering higher-level capabilities, including WebGPU, ML, and SQL interfaces.
- The `wasi:nn` interface allows native performance for ML workloads within Wasm, using optimizations from existing ML frameworks like GPUs and NPUs. Alternatives like TVM and `tract` can run ML within Wasm but often sacrifice performance to conform to WASI 0.1's POSIX subset.
- Running Wasm within databases is achieved by using UDFs, which allow secure, efficient data processing within a sandboxed environment.
- By integrating Wasm into databases, UDFs can be written in any language that compiles to Wasm, enabling flexible and secure database extensions.

- The libSQL database can embed Wasm UDFs, providing a reliable environment for running secure, sandboxed Wasm functions directly in SQL queries.
- The WAT provides a human-readable representation of Wasm binaries, enabling easier inspection, debugging, and manual adjustments.
- Optimizing Wasm UDFs with tools like `wasm-opt` ensures performance and reduces the size of Wasm binaries embedded in SQL databases.

Part 2

WebAssembly for developers

Armed with a deep understanding of WebAssembly's architecture, you're ready to put that knowledge into practice. This part of the book shifts from theory to implementation, guiding you through building production-ready WebAssembly applications using modern tools and best practices. You'll move beyond handcrafting hosts and interfaces to using the standardized tooling and prebuilt environments that make WebAssembly development practical and efficient.

The transition from architect to developer mirrors the evolution of WebAssembly itself—from low-level primitives to high-level productivity. Whereas part 1 taught you to understand the machinery, part 2 teaches you to operate it effectively in real-world scenarios. You'll discover how familiar tools like Docker and Kubernetes have evolved to support WebAssembly workloads, making deployment as straightforward as traditional containers while delivering WebAssembly's unique benefits.

Chapter 6 demonstrates creating production-grade applications using standardized interfaces and generic hosts, freeing you from the complexity of custom implementations. Chapter 7 introduces WebAssembly containers, showing how to package and deploy WebAssembly workloads using the containerization workflows you already know. Chapter 8 explores Kubernetes integration, teaching you to orchestrate and scale WebAssembly applications in cloud environments with the same tools used for traditional workloads. Finally, chapter 9 examines the future of WebAssembly, from emerging proposals to its potential effects on cloud computing paradigms.

6 Creating production-grade Wasm applications

This chapter covers

- wasmCloud as an off-the-shelf host
- Integrating persistent storage
- Scaling Wasm applications
- Distributing applications using NATS
- Embedding machine learning capabilities in wasmCloud

We've been steadily expanding our toolbox. We started with Wasm modules, where all we had were four basic types, linear memory, and a dream. Then we introduced WebAssembly Interface Types (WIT) and Wasm components, which brought higher-level types and a canonical ABI for lifting and lowering constructs like `String` values, enabling composability between components across languages. Next, we explored interacting with the underlying system via WebAssembly System Interface (WASI), applying it to scenarios like executing machine learning workloads with wasi-nn (using WASI 0.2) and running Wasm user-defined functions in a database (using WASI 0.1).

Yet, in nearly all our examples, we've written custom hosts to run our applications. For instance, our SmartCMS host is currently bootstrapped to set up WASI and wasi-nn, which diverts us from focusing on business logic and is not ideal for server-side Wasm development. In this chapter, I'll introduce you to wasmCloud and Spin, two off-the-shelf hosts designed to streamline the development of Wasm microservices.

These off-the-shelf hosts function similarly to the `HelloWorldHost` from chapter 2 or the SmartCMS host we've been building in recent chapters, as they also embed Wasmtime to run Wasm. However, unlike our custom hosts, off-the-shelf ones are designed to be generic and versatile for any application. Beyond that, they also provide software development kits (SDKs) and developer toolchains to simplify using Wasm. Let's dive deeper by creating a "Hello, World" application, beginning with wasmCloud.

6.1 *Creating a wasmCloud "Hello, World" application*

Begin by installing wasmCloud's developer tooling:

```
cargo install --locked wash-cli --version "^0.37"
```

Specifically, you are installing `wash`, the wasmCloud Shell—a comprehensive command-line interface that facilitates various development tasks within the wasmCloud ecosystem. With `wash`, you can generate new projects, manage cryptographic keys, interact with Open Container Initiative (OCI)–compliant registries, and more.

> **WARNING** wasmCloud's support for Windows is not at the same tier as its support for Linux and macOS. If you are using Windows, I recommend that you run the examples in this chapter within Windows Subsystem for Linux.

Once installed, inside your `chapter06/` folder, run

```
wash new component hello-world-wasmcloud --template-name hello-world-rust
```

This command initializes a new wasmCloud component named `hello-world-wasmcloud` using the `hello-world-rust` template. This template provides a foundational Rust project configured for wasmCloud, including necessary files and directory structures.

> **TIP** While this example utilizes the `hello-world-rust` template, wasmCloud offers a variety of templates in different languages. Visit https://mng.bz/Jwqz for more templates in languages such as C, Go, Python, and TypeScript.

To use this with Rust, you'll need to install a new target for Wasm compilation using the following command:

```
rustup target add wasm32-wasip2
```

With that done, inside this template, you'll notice a `wit/` folder, which contains the following structure:

```
.
├── deps
│   ├── wasi-cli-0.2.2
│   ├── wasi-clocks-0.2.2
│   ├── wasi-http-0.2.2
│   ├── wasi-io-0.2.2
│   └── wasi-random-0.2.2
└── world.wit
```

Our application's world definition (i.e., `world.wit`), as shown in the following listing, exports an incoming handler—a mechanism for handling HTTP requests routed to this application.

Listing 6.1 `hello-world-wasmcloud`'s `wit/world.wit`

```
package wasmcloud:hello;

world hello {
   export wasi:http/incoming-handler@0.2.2;
}
```

This incoming handler relies on several other WASI interfaces, which are listed as dependencies in the `wit/deps` folder.

We also have a `wasmcloud.toml` file, shown in the following listing, which serves as the manifest for configuring the wasmCloud component.

Listing 6.2 `hello-world-wasmcloud`'s `wasmcloud.toml` file

```
name = "http-hello-world"
version = "0.1.0"
language = "rust"
type = "component"

[component]
wit_world = "hello"
wasm_target = "wasm32-wasip2"
```

This manifest specifies key details about the application, such as its name, version, language, and type. Under the `[component]` section, it links the `wit_world` to the `hello` world definition and defines the Wasm compilation target as `wasm32-wasip2`, which corresponds to WASI 0.2. This setup ensures compatibility with the interfaces and features provided by the WASI 0.2 standard.

Let's now take a look at the implementation of the incoming handler in `src/lib.rs`.

Listing 6.3 `src/lib.rs` `incoming-handler` implementation

```
use wasmcloud_component::http;

struct Component;
```

```
http::export!(Component);

impl http::Server for Component {
    fn handle(
        _request: http::IncomingRequest,
    ) -> http::Result<http::Response<impl http::OutgoingBody>> {
        Ok(http::Response::new("Hello from Rust!\n"))
    }
}
```

This incoming handler is designed to work alongside an HTTP server, routing requests to the root route (i.e., /) to this Wasm component. When invoked, it responds to HTTP requests with a plain text message: `"Hello from Rust!"`. This routing functionality is defined in another file included with our template—`wadm.yaml`—partially shown in the following listing.

Listing 6.4 `wadm.yaml` file (template comments/annotations hidden)

```
apiVersion: core.oam.dev/v1beta1
kind: Application
metadata:
  name: rust-hello-world
  # ...
spec:
  components:
    - name: http-component
      type: component
      properties:
        image: file://./build/http_hello_world_s.wasm
      traits:
        - type: spreadscaler
          properties:
            instances: 1

    - name: httpserver
      type: capability
      properties:
        image: ghcr.io/wasmcloud/http-server:0.23.2
      traits:
        - type: link
          properties:
            target: http-component
            namespace: wasi
            package: http
            interfaces: [incoming-handler]
            source_config:
              - name: default-http
                properties:
                  address: 127.0.0.1:8000
```

The spreadscaler trait configures the number of instances to deploy, in this case, setting it to 1.

Capabilities define reusable components for specific functions, such as the HTTP server in this example.

Links HTTP server capability to our defined incoming handler implementation

This *wasmCloud Application Deployment Manager* (`wadm`) file outlines the deployment configuration for our application. It specifies the application's components, including the `http-component` and the HTTP server capability, as well as the link between the two via the `incoming-handler` implementation. Additionally, it uses the `spreadscaler` trait to configure the number of instances to deploy, allowing you to scale the application by adjusting this value—in this example, it's set to a single instance.

Now, we are ready to run our application. Start by executing

```
wash up -d
```

You will see output similar to the following:

```
>>> Starting NATS ...
NATS server successfully started, using config @ [<your path>\nats.conf]
NATS server logs written to [<your path>\nats.log]
>>> Starting wadm ...
Found wadm version on the disk: wadm-cli 0.18.0
Using wadm version [v0.18.0]

wash up completed successfully
NATS is running in the background at 127.0.0.1:4222
Logs for the host are being written to <your path>\wasmcloud.log

To stop wasmCloud, run "wash down"
```

> **TIP** Make a note of the path where logs are being written to (it's useful when things go wrong!) and remember to execute the `wash down` command to stop the wasmCloud platform once we are done with this exercise.

This command bootstraps the essential processes for a wasmCloud application:

- *wasmCloud Host*—Embeds the Wasmtime runtime to execute Wasm components and provides capabilities such as the HTTP server. Like in previous chapters, Wasmtime runs locally on your machine.
- *NATS lattice*—Sets up a NATS (https://nats.io/) server to facilitate communication between application components within the lattice, which is a distributed network that allows multiple wasmCloud hosts to communicate and coordinate seamlessly, even if they are running on different physical machines or environments—similar to how a Kubernetes cluster orchestrates containers across nodes.
- `wadm` *monitor*—Oversees the lattice and manages the state of deployments, ensuring that components are correctly deployed and linked.

What is NATS?

NATS is a lightweight, high-performance messaging system designed for cloud-native applications. It acts as a message broker that enables communication between distributed components in a system.

TIP You can inspect the wasmCloud host we just started by running `wash get hosts`.

In chapter 4, when we learned about composability, we looked at examples where two Wasm components were combined into a single Wasm binary at build time, before running our application. While you can still use composed Wasm binaries in wasmCloud, it goes a step further by enabling runtime linking through `wadm` and NATS.

In wasmCloud, components can either run on the same host or be distributed across multiple hosts within the NATS lattice. By defining links between components in the `wadm` manifest, wasmCloud ensures these connections are dynamically established and managed during run time. This approach allows components to communicate over NATS, regardless of their physical location, using the component-native remote procedure call (wRPC) protocol facilitated by the wasmCloud host. Overall, the architecture of our application looks like figure 6.1.

What is RPC?

Remote procedure call (RPC) is a communication protocol that allows programs to execute functions or procedures on another system, making it easier to build distributed systems by enabling interaction between components running on different machines or environments.

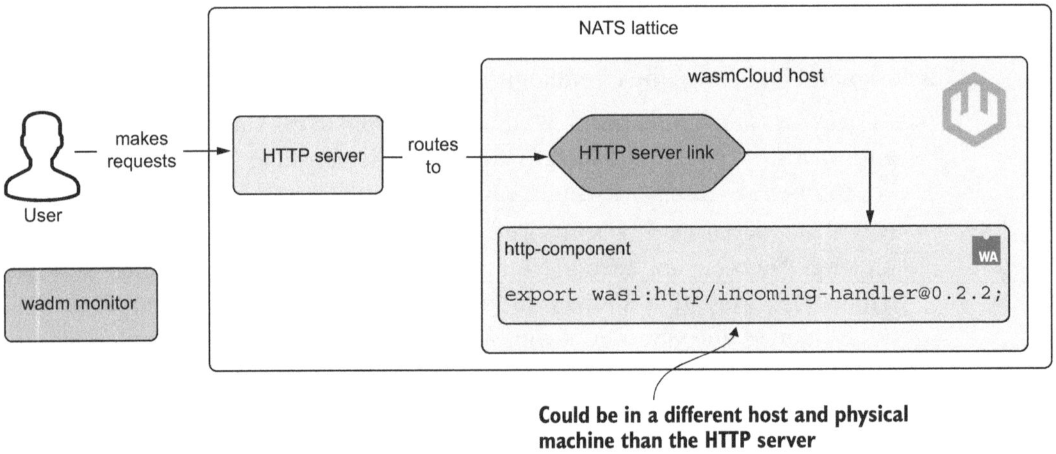

Figure 6.1 The architecture of our "Hello, World" wasmCloud application

Now that we better understand what happens when we execute the `wash up -d` command and how wasmCloud applications operate, let's build our Wasm component. From the `hello-world-wasmcloud/` folder, you can do so with the following:

```
wash build
```

This command will build our Wasm component inside of the `build/` directory. Upon inspecting this directory, you'll see

```
.
├── http_hello_world.wasm
└── http_hello_world_s.wasm
```

NOTE Even though we're building Rust applications, I didn't add any of the wasmCloud apps from this chapter to our Cargo workspace. As you can see in listing 6.4, our `wadm.yaml` file directly points to the path of our built Wasm. Since adding the project to the workspace would change that, I decided it's better not to bother.

Why do we have two build artifacts? wasmCloud produces two files because it not only builds the Wasm component (`http_hello_world.wasm`) but also signs it, creating a signed artifact (`http_hello_world_s.wasm`) for secure deployment.

What is cryptographic signing?

Cryptographic signing is the process of generating a unique digital signature for a file or message using a private key. This signature can be verified with the corresponding public key, ensuring the file's integrity (it hasn't been tampered with) and authenticity (it comes from a trusted source). Signing often includes metadata, such as the signer's identity and claims about the file's purpose or permissions.

Inspecting the `wadm` manifest from listing 6.4 once again, you'll notice it refers to the signed component. Now, with the wasmCloud host up and the component built, we can run our application by executing

```
wash app deploy ./wadm.yaml
```

This command deploys the application to the lattice, registering its components and linking them as specified in the manifest. It ensures that all dependencies, such as capabilities and routes, are properly configured for the application to function.

We can verify that the deployment succeeded by running

```
wash app list
```

This command displays information about your deployment, similar to what is shown in table 6.1.

Table 6.1 Currently deployed applications

Name	Deployed version	Status
`rust-hello-world`	01JDR8HJYJWCV1AJM559R72KE8	Deployed

From the status column, you can see our application is marked as deployed.

> **TIP** You can also verify we properly linked the HTTP server capability with our HTTP component incoming handler by running `wash get links`.

The app's deployed HTTP server is running and should be accessible at the address specified in our `wadm` manifest (i.e., `http://127.0.0.1:8000`). To confirm, you can test it by running

```
curl http://127.0.0.1:8000
```

This should produce the following output:

```
Hello from Rust!
```

Awesome! We set up a wasmCloud host, built and signed a Wasm component, explored the `wadm` manifest, and deployed our application to the lattice—all with just a few commands and without having to write any nonbusiness logic, such as the HTTP server capability itself. Next up, let's explore how we can provide even more capabilities to our wasmCloud apps.

6.2 Adding persistent storage to our Wasm app

So far, in our SmartCMS application, we've been using a custom WIT interface for a key-value store. While this approach has been effective and allowed us to explore WIT, we'll now shift to using a standardized interface. For persistent storage, one such choice is the `wasi:keyvalue` interface, which provides a consistent way to handle key-value operations across various providers.

The `wasi:keyvalue` interface provides basic operations like `get` and `set`, similar to our custom interface. However, it also introduces additional interface capabilities, such as

- *Atomics* for operations like increment and compare-and-swap, enabling safe concurrent updates
- *Batch* for eventually consistent batch operations, reducing the number of network roundtrips and improving performance in distributed systems

By adopting `wasi:keyvalue`, we align with best practices and ensure greater interoperability. Beyond its additional capabilities, `wasi:keyvalue` is designed as a portable interface that works across various key-value store providers, such as Redis, Memcached, Etcd, AWS DynamoDB, Azure CosmosDB, Google Cloud Firestore, and so on. It serves as the standard for providing persistent storage capabilities in hosts like Wasmtime and wasmCloud. So let's see how we can use `wasi:keyvalue` in wasmCloud.

6.2.1 Modifying our WIT and wadm manifest

Let's start by removing our current application from the lattice. You can do so with

```
wash app delete rust-hello-world
```

With that done, we can begin working on the new version of our application, which will include persistent storage. First, we need to add an import for the `wasi:keyvalue` interfaces in our WIT file.

Listing 6.5 `hello-world-wasmcloud/wit/world.wit`

```
package wasmcloud:hello;

world hello {
   import wasi:keyvalue/atomics@0.2.0-draft;
   import wasi:keyvalue/store@0.2.0-draft;
   export wasi:http/incoming-handler@0.2.2;
}
```

Adds wasi:keyvalue interfaces for atomics and store

By importing these interfaces, we grant our Wasm component permission to access the `wasi:keyvalue` capability (recall the only-what-you-need security principle from chapter 3). Specifically, we're importing the `store` and `atomics` interfaces:

- The *store* interface provides access to a bucket resource—a collection of key-value pairs. Using the `open` function, we can connect to a bucket by passing a string identifier for the resource provided by the host.
- The *atomics* interface is included because, for this example, we'll increment a counter from multiple requests concurrently.

Next, let's modify our `wadm.yaml` file to support persistent storage. First, we'll add a new capability for the key-value provider. Then, we'll link this capability to the `wasi:keyvalue` interfaces we imported in our WIT.

Listing 6.6 `wadm.yaml` **(template comments/annotations hidden)**

```
apiVersion: core.oam.dev/v1beta1
kind: Application
metadata:
  name: rust-hello-world
  # ...
spec:
  components:
    - name: http-component
      type: component
      properties:
        image: file://./build/http_hello_world_s.wasm
      traits:
        - type: spreadscaler
          properties:
            instances: 1
        - type: link
          properties:
            namespace: wasi
            package: keyvalue
```

Links the wasi:keyvalue interfaces (store and atomics) to the kvnats capability

```
            interfaces: [store, atomics]
            target:
              name: kvnats
              config:
                - name: wasi-keyvalue-config
                  properties:
                    bucket: default
                    enable_bucket_auto_create:
                    ➥ 'true'

    - name: httpserver
      type: capability
      properties:
        image: ghcr.io/wasmcloud/http-server:0.23.2
      traits:
        - type: link
          properties:
            target: http-component
            namespace: wasi
            package: http
            interfaces: [incoming-handler]
            source_config:
              - name: default-http
                properties:
                  address: 127.0.0.1:8000

    - name: kvnats
      type: capability
      properties:
        image: ghcr.io/wasmcloud/keyvalue-nats:0.3.1
```

Links the wasi:keyvalue interfaces (store and atomics) to the kvnats capability

Configuration to use a default bucket and enable automatic bucket creation if it doesn't exist

Defines the key-value store provider, named kvnats

In this updated manifest, we added a NATS-based key-value provider (`kvnats`). While NATS is primarily known as a high-performance messaging system, it also offers key-value storage as part of its feature set. This allows our application to use NATS for storing and managing key-value pairs. Additionally, wasmCloud officially supports other key-value providers, such as Redis and HashiCorp Vault. Since these providers all implement the `wasi:keyvalue` interface, you can switch between them with minor configuration changes and no code modifications.

Finally, we link the `kvnats` provider to the specific `wasi:keyvalue` interfaces (`store` and `atomics`) we gave our component access to and provide some basic configuration. This includes setting the default bucket name and enabling the automatic creation of buckets as needed. With these changes, our updated architecture is illustrated in figure 6.2.

6.2.2 Modifying our application and redeploying it

Now it's time to update our application code to utilize persistent storage. The changes, as shown in listing 6.7, are straightforward.

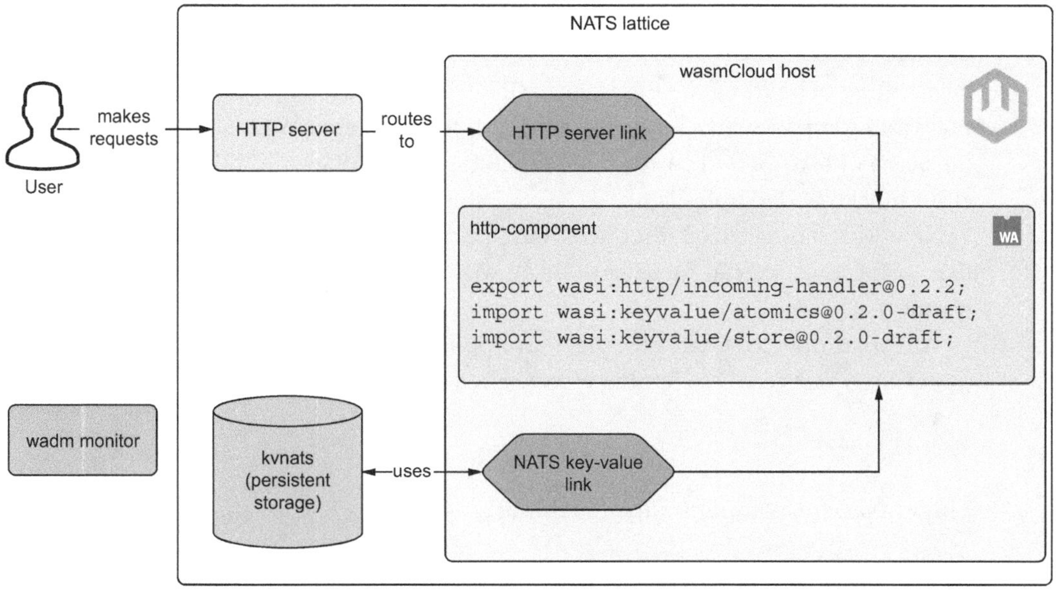

Figure 6.2 Updated architecture diagram for "Hello, World" wasmCloud app with persistent storage

Listing 6.7 Updated `hello-world-wasmcloud/src/lib.rs`

```
use wasmcloud_component::http;
use wasmcloud_component::wasi::keyvalue::*;

struct Component;

http::export!(Component);

impl http::Server for Component {
    fn handle(
        _request: http::IncomingRequest,
    ) -> http::Result<http::Response<impl http::OutgoingBody>> {
        let bucket = store::open
        ➥("default").unwrap();
        let count = atomics::increment
        ➥(&bucket, "counter", 1).unwrap();

        Ok(http::Response::new(format!
        ➥("Hello! I was called {count} times\n")))
    }
}
```

Imports the wasi:keyvalue bindings for storage operations

Opens the default bucket, automatically creating it if it doesn't exist

Increments the counter key in the bucket by 1

Returns a response indicating how many times the endpoint has been accessed

Here we updated the application to interact with the `wasi:keyvalue` interfaces. The key steps involve opening a persistent bucket (named `default`), accessing a key called "counter," incrementing the value stored within it, and returning its value in the HTTP response.

This marks a significant departure from the work we did in prior chapters. When we implemented our own key-value store interface, the process required not only the heavy lifting of building the interface itself but also substantial operational setup to run the Wasm component. From configuring and creating a raw Wasm engine to setting up the `Store` with WASI and custom contexts and programmatically linking interfaces, the effort quickly added up.

Now, with standardized interfaces like `wasi:keyvalue` and a robust off-the-shelf host like wasmCloud, we can focus entirely on writing business logic—like incrementing a counter!

With that done, we can redeploy our application. Since we never terminated our wasmCloud host (e.g., by running `wash down`), it should still be running. To confirm, run

```
wash get hosts
```

This will produce output similar to table 6.2.

Table 6.2 Currently active wasmCloud hosts

Host ID	Friendly name	Uptime (seconds)
NCJXH5...	`silent-dew-9876`	7461

If no hosts are listed or you encounter any problems, you may need to restart the host with

```
wash up -d
```

> **TIP** If you prefer a graphical interface for managing wasmCloud, you can open a separate terminal window and run `wash ui`. This UI provides information on hosts, components, capabilities, and links.

Next, let's ensure no old versions of our component are running. You can check this by running

```
wash app list
```

If the table isn't empty and shows the old component, you can remove it by running

```
wash app delete rust-hello-world
```

Now, with a running wasmCloud host and no old versions of our component deployed, we can rebuild and redeploy the new version of our application:

```
wash build
wash app deploy ./wadm.yaml
```

After deployment, you can verify the new component is running by checking

```
wash app list
```

You should see your newly deployed component listed. To confirm all links are working as expected, you can run

```
wash get links
```

That should show you something similar to table 6.3.

Table 6.3 Currently active links between components and capabilities

Source ID	Target	Interface(s)	...
...-http_component	...-kvnats	wasi:keyvalue/store,atomics	...
...-httpserver	...-http_component	wasi:http/incoming-handler	...

Finally, test the application by making a few calls to the endpoint:

```
curl http://127.0.0.1:8000
```

You should see the counter increment with each call. To test the persistence of the application, shut down the host with

```
wash down
```

Then restart it with

```
wash up -d
```

Rerun

```
curl http://127.0.0.1:8000
```

The counter should continue from where it left off, rather than resetting to 1.

Awesome! We've successfully created a wasmCloud application that uses the standard `wasi:keyvalue` interface and relies on the capability provided by the wasmCloud host to implement persistent storage. Up next: exploring the scalability of our application.

6.3 Scaling our wasmCloud application

When we first created our application, recall that in our `wadm` manifest, we defined a `spreadscaler` trait with just one instance:

```
- type: spreadscaler
  properties:
    instances: 1
```

This configuration limits our application to handling only a single request at a time. For short-lived applications like our current implementation that quickly increments a counter and returns a response, this limitation might not seem significant. However, for longer-running operations, it means that concurrent requests must wait for the previous ones to finish, potentially leading to poor average response times under load.

Let's test this limitation by updating our application to simulate a longer-running operation by sleeping for 2 seconds after incrementing the counter. The updated code is shown in the following listing.

Listing 6.8 Updated `hello-world-wasmcloud/src/lib.rs`

```
use wasmcloud_component::http;
use wasmcloud_component::wasi::keyvalue::*;

struct Component;

http::export!(Component);

impl http::Server for Component {
    fn handle(
        _request: http::IncomingRequest,
    ) -> http::Result<http::Response<impl http::OutgoingBody>> {
        let bucket = store::open("default").unwrap();
        let count = atomics::increment(&bucket, "counter", 1).unwrap();
        std::thread::sleep(std::time::
        ➥ Duration::from_secs(2));      ◄── Simulates a long-running operation
                                             by sleeping for 2 seconds

        Ok(http::Response::new(format!("Hello! I was called {count}
        ➥ times\n")))
    }
}
```

With this change, rebuild and redeploy the application:

```
wash build
wash app delete rust-hello-world
wash app deploy ./wadm.yaml
```

Now let's benchmark the application. We can use `oha`, a lightweight HTTP benchmarking tool written in Rust.

> **TIP** If you'd like to try this yourself, you can install `oha` with: `cargo install oha@1.4.7 --locked`.

To benchmark, run

```
oha -n 10 -c 5 http://127.0.0.1:8000
```

This command sends 10 requests, 5 of them concurrently. Given our single-instance setup, we expect to see poor response times due to the bottleneck. The results are shown in the following listing.

Listing 6.9 Benchmarks from wasmCloud application with one replica

```
Summary:
  Success rate: 100.00%
  Total:        20.0729 secs
  Slowest:      10.0551 secs
  Fastest:      2.0055 secs
  Average:      8.0334 secs
  Requests/sec: 0.4982
# …

Response time histogram:
   2.006 [1] |■■■■■
   2.810 [0] |
   3.615 [0] |
   4.420 [1] |■■■■■
   5.225 [0] |
   6.030 [1] |■■■■■
   6.835 [0] |
   7.640 [0] |
   8.445 [1] |■■■■■
   9.250 [0] |
  10.055 [6] |■■■■■■■■■■■■■■■■■■■■■■■■■■■■■■■■
# …
```

As you can see, the first response takes 2 seconds, the second takes 4 seconds, the third takes 6 seconds, and so on. This sequential processing results in an average response time of 8 seconds, which is far from ideal.

To address this, we can update our `spreadscaler` configuration to deploy 10 replicas of our `http-component`, allowing our application to handle requests in parallel:

```
- type: spreadscaler
  properties:
    instances: 10
```

Redeploy the application with the updated configuration:

```
wash app delete rust-hello-world
wash app deploy ./wadm.yaml
```

Finally, rerun the benchmark:

```
oha -n 10 -c 5 http://127.0.0.1:8000
```

The results, shown in the following listing, demonstrate significant improvement.

Listing 6.10 Benchmarks from wasmCloud app with 10 replicas

```
Summary:
  Success rate: 100.00%
  Total:        4.0910 secs
  Slowest:      2.0471 secs
  Fastest:      2.0055 secs
  Average:      2.0315 secs
  Requests/sec: 2.4444
# ...

Response time histogram:
  2.005 [1] |■■■■■
  2.010 [1] |■■■■■
  2.014 [1] |■■■■■
  2.018 [0] |
  2.022 [0] |
  2.026 [1] |■■■■■
  2.030 [0] |
  2.035 [0] |
  2.039 [0] |
  2.043 [0] |
  2.047 [6] |■■■■■■■■■■■■■■■■■■■■■■■■■■■■■■
# ...
```

With 10 replicas, each request is handled in parallel, resulting in an average response time of just over 2 seconds—exactly what we expect given the simulated application processing. The wasmCloud host manages these 10 replicas as separate component instances within the host process, with the NATS lattice distributing incoming requests across them. As we saw in chapter 1, components are internally single threaded, which is why this external load balancing is necessary—it allows multiple requests to be processed concurrently by running multiple instances of the component. The updated architecture reflecting this scaled deployment is shown in figure 6.3.

By scaling our application to multiple instances, we've effectively improved its ability to handle concurrent requests, significantly reducing response times and increasing throughput. Up next: exploring how to distribute our application.

6.4 Distributing our wasmCloud application

We've learned how to increase the number of replicas of our Wasm components, but we can take it a step further. These replicas can be distributed across different hosts, which, in principle, could run on separate machines or data centers, or even across different geographic regions. This architecture is displayed in figure 6.4.

This image illustrates how requests are routed through the NATS lattice to replicas spread across multiple wasmCloud hosts. The `spreadscaler` load balances incoming requests across all available replicas, regardless of their physical or geographic location. Each replica links to the `kvnats` key-value store provider, ensuring consistent access to shared, persistent storage.

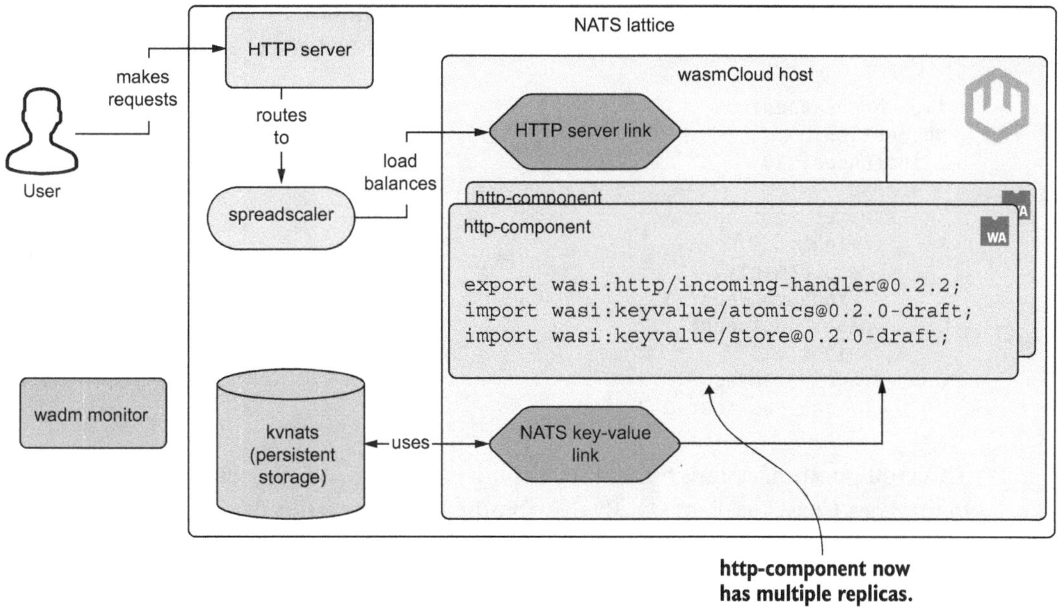

Figure 6.3 Updated architecture diagram for "Hello, World" wasmCloud app with 10 replicas of the `http-component`

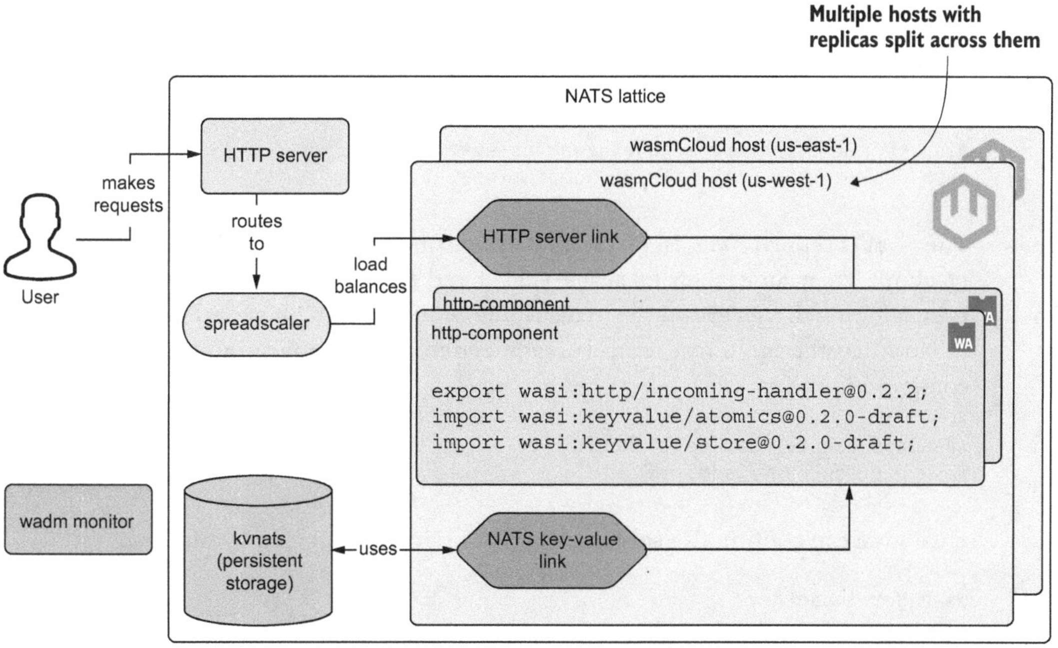

Figure 6.4 Updated architecture diagram for "Hello, World" wasmCloud app with 10 replicas of the `http-component` split across different hosts and regions (i.e., us-east-1 and us-west-1)

To demonstrate this, we can modify our `spreadscaler` configuration to distribute our 10 replicas across two different hosts—simulating East and West Coasts:

```
- type: spreadscaler
  properties:
    instances: 10
    spread:
      - name: eastcoast
        weight: 80
        requirements:
          zone: us-east-1
      - name: westcoast
        weight: 20
        requirements:
          zone: us-west-1
```

This configuration assigns 80% of the instances to the East Coast (`us-east-1`) and 20% to the West Coast (`us-west-1`). By distributing components in this way, we achieve not only better fault tolerance but also reduced latency for users in different regions, as requests can be routed to the closest available host.

Before we can deploy the updated manifest, we need to run multiple hosts on our machine to simulate this multiregion setup. Start by shutting down any currently running host:

```
wash down
```

Then spin up two separate hosts with distinct zone labels using the `--multi-local` flag:

```
wash up --multi-local --label zone=us-east-1 -d
wash up --multi-local --label zone=us-west-1 -d
```

The `--multi-local` flag is what enables starting independent hosts on the same machine. Then zone labels (`zone=us-east-1` and `zone=us-west-1`) are assigned to each host, allowing the `spreadscaler` to distribute replicas based on geographic zones.

Now that the multihost setup is ready, redeploy the application with the updated configuration:

```
wash app delete rust-hello-world
wash app deploy ./wadm.yaml
```

Finally, we can confirm the `spreadscaler` is working as expected by running

```
wash get inventory
```

This command provides detailed information about each host, as shown in the following listing.

Listing 6.11 Partial output of `wash get inventory`

```
  Host ID                      Friendly name
  NAKHN5...                    divine-emoji-6927

  Host labels
  hostcore.arch                x86_64
  hostcore.os                  linux
  hostcore.osfamily            unix
  zone                         us-west-1

  Component ID                 Name              Max count
  ...-http_component           http-hello-world    2

  Provider ID                  Name
  rust_hello_world-kvnats      keyvalue-nats-provider

  Host ID                      Friendly name
  NBIYLP...                    solitary-wildflower-2472

  Host labels
  hostcore.arch                x86_64
  hostcore.os                  linux
  hostcore.osfamily            unix
  zone                         us-east-1

  Component ID                 Name              Max count
...-http_component             http-hello-world    8

  Provider ID                  Name
  ...-httpserver               http-server-provider
```

Two replicas (20% weight) were assigned to the us-west-1 host.

Eight replicas (80% weight) were assigned to the us-east-1 host.

This demonstrates that the `spreadscaler` successfully distributed our application across multiple hosts based on the defined weights and zone labels.

Now let's simulate an outage by shutting down one of our hosts. Select one of the two host IDs from the inventory and run

```
wash down --host-id <your-host-id>
```

Next, try calling the endpoint again:

```
curl http://127.0.0.1:8000
```

You should still receive a "`Hello! …`" message, demonstrating that the remaining host continues handling requests. Verify the inventory again with

```
wash get inventory
```

It will now show only one active host.

Awesome! Not only did we learn how to create multiple instances of our Wasm components to handle concurrent requests better, but we also demonstrated how to

- Simulate a globally distributed deployment with lower latency by spreading components across multiple hosts in different regions.
- Achieve fault tolerance, where application availability is maintained even when one of the hosts goes offline.

With that, we've concluded our "Hello, World" wasmCloud application that incorporates persistent storage using the standardized `wasi:keyvalue` interface, scales effortlessly with `spreadscaler`, and supports global distribution for enhanced performance and reliability.

> **TIP** To clean up your environment, remember to run `wash app delete rust -hello-world` (or `wash app delete ./wadm.yaml`) and `wash down --all`.

If you've worked with Kubernetes in the past, you may notice that much of what we've done here mirrors concepts like scaling workloads, managing deployments, and ensuring high availability. However, it's important to note that wasmCloud is not a replacement for Kubernetes. Instead, it complements Kubernetes, making it easier to run Wasm workloads in production while using existing infrastructure. We'll explore these integrations in upcoming chapters.

> **Upcoming changes to wasmCloud**
>
> wasmCloud is actively evolving. This chapter reflects the architecture and tooling available as of wasmCloud version 1.4.2. The wasmCloud team has announced significant architectural changes for Q3 2025 and beyond (detailed at https://mng.bz/qRvN), including simplifying the host model, transitioning capability providers to "wRPC servers," and moving away from the application-centric deployment model.
>
> While the core concepts covered here—such as component scaling, distributed networking via the NATS lattice, and the separation of business logic from capabilities—will remain foundational to wasmCloud, specific implementation details may change substantially. In particular, `wadm` manifests, the Open Application Model (OAM)–based application model, and how capability providers are configured and deployed are all subject to revision. For the latest updates, visit https://wasmcloud.com/blog/.

6.5 Another off-the-shelf host: Spin

wasmCloud isn't the only off-the-shelf host available—another popular option is Spin. To demonstrate the differences between the two, let's create a simple "Hello, World" application with Spin.

6.5.1 Creating a Spin "Hello, World" application

First things first: you'll need to install Spin. You can do so following the instructions from https://developer.fermyon.com/spin/v3/install.

NOTE For the Spin examples in this book, I'll be using `spin 3.2.0 (c9be6d8 2025-03-24)`. To keep things consistent, it's best to install the same version when following along.

IMPORTANT Spin requires Rust 1.85.0 or later because some of its dependencies use Rust edition 2024. If you've been following along with Rust 1.84.0 (as recommended earlier in the book), you'll need to upgrade for this section. Install Rust 1.85.0 and its required components with `rustup install 1.85.0`, `rustup default 1.85.0`, and `rustup target add wasm32-wasip1`. You can verify the change with `rustc --version`.

With that done, in your `chapter06/` folder, run

```
spin new
```

This will give you an option to choose from a few Spin templates:

```
> http-c (HTTP request handler using C and the Zig toolchain)
  http-empty (HTTP application with no components)
  http-go (HTTP request handler using (Tiny)Go)
  http-grain (HTTP request handler using Grain)
  http-js (HTTP request handler using JavaScript)
  http-php (HTTP request handler using PHP)
  http-py (HTTP request handler using Python)
  http-rust (HTTP request handler using Rust)
  http-ts (HTTP request handler using TypeScript)
  http-zig (HTTP request handler using Zig)
  redirect (Redirects a HTTP route)
  redis-go (Redis message handler using (Tiny)Go)
  redis-js (Redis message handler using JavaScript)
  redis-rust (Redis message handler using Rust)
  redis-ts (Redis message handler using TypeScript)
  static-fileserver (Serves static files from an asset directory)
```

NOTE Spin's SDK is also available in various languages, including JavaScript/TypeScript, Python, .NET, Rust, Go, Java, and more—feel free to choose the language you are most comfortable with!

For this example, I'll select the `http-rust` template, which generates a Rust-based HTTP request handler with the necessary setup.

After selecting the template, you'll be prompted to name your application—let's call it `hello-world-spin`. Next, it will ask for a description and an HTTP path; you can accept the defaults by pressing Enter. Once completed, your project will be created in the `hello-world-spin` directory. Inside, you'll find the following:

```
.
├── Cargo.toml
├── spin.toml
└── src
```

This structure resembles a typical Rust project, with the addition of spin.toml. The spin.toml file serves as the application manifest, defining the configuration for your Spin application. It specifies details such as the application name, version, components, and their respective triggers. In Spin, a trigger maps an event—like an HTTP request or a Redis message—to a component that handles that event. For instance, an HTTP trigger routes incoming HTTP requests to the appropriate Wasm component based on the specified route. This setup enables Spin to efficiently manage event-driven applications by directing events to their corresponding handlers as defined in the manifest. You can see the spin.toml for our hello-world-spin application in the following listing.

Listing 6.12 spin.toml file for the hello-world-spin project

```
spin_manifest_version = 2

[application]
name = "hello-world-spin"
version = "0.1.0"
authors = ["your-name-here <your-email-here@email.com>"]
description = ""

[[trigger.http]]
route = "/..."
component = "hello-world-spin"

[component.hello-world-spin]
source = "target/wasm32-wasip1/release/hello_world_spin.wasm"
allowed_outbound_hosts = []
[component.hello-world-spin.build]
command = "cargo build --target
➥ wasm32-wasip1 --release"
watch = ["src/**/*.rs", "Cargo.toml"]
```

All incoming HTTP requests, regardless of their path, are directed to the hello-world-spin component.

Defines the command to compile the component's source code into a Wasm module

Spin's goal is to make developing Wasm microservices straightforward. Part of that, as shown in figure 6.5, is achieved through its trigger-based, event-driven setup.

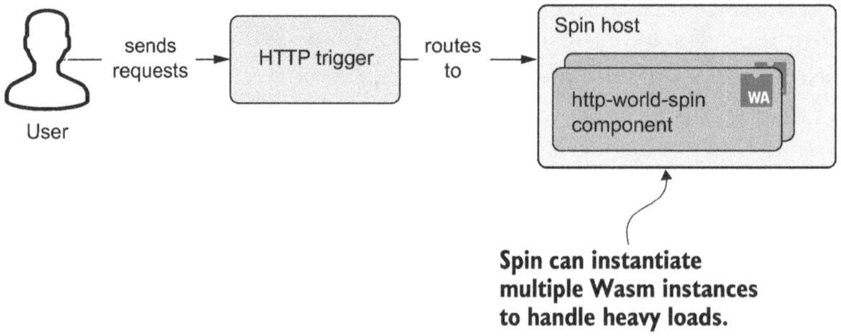

Figure 6.5 Spin's event-driven setup for Wasm microservices

Inside `src/lib.rs` (shown in listing 6.13), you'll find the default application generated by Spin's `http-rust` template. This code, compiled to Wasm, serves as the event handler and executes whenever the defined trigger—in our case, an HTTP request—is activated.

Listing 6.13 `src/lib.rs` file for the `hello-world-spin` project

```
use spin_sdk::http::{IntoResponse, Request, Response};
use spin_sdk::http_component;

/// A simple Spin HTTP component.
#[http_component]
fn handle_hello_world_spin(req: Request) -> anyhow::Result<impl
➥ IntoResponse> {
    println!("Handling request to {:?}", req.header("spin-full-url"));
    Ok(Response::builder()
        .status(200)
        .header("content-type", "text/plain")
        .body("Hello World!")
        .build())
}
```

This code uses Spin's SDK to define a handler for incoming HTTP requests. The handler logs the request URL and responds with `"Hello, World!"` alongside an HTTP status of 200.

Next, from `hello-world-spin/`, compile the Spin application with

```
spin build
```

And run it using

```
spin up
```

Upon running the command, you'll see output similar to this:

```
Logging component stdio to ".spin/logs/"

Serving http://127.0.0.1:3000
Available Routes:
  hello-world-spin: http://127.0.0.1:3000 (wildcard)
```

From another terminal, test the application by running

```
curl http://127.0.0.1:3000
```

You should see the response: `"Hello World!"`. Awesome! With that, we've successfully created our simple `"Hello, World!"` application using Spin!

IMPORTANT Now that you've completed the Spin example, you should revert to Rust 1.84.0 to maintain consistency with the rest of the book. Run `rustup default 1.84.0`. You can verify the change with `rustc --version`.

6.5.2 Comparing wasmCloud and Spin

While we didn't dive as deeply with Spin as we did with wasmCloud (e.g., scaling the application or simulating global distribution), it's clear that Spin and wasmCloud have fundamentally different designs. The following is a breakdown of the key distinctions and considerations:

- *Scaling and concurrency*
  - wasmCloud exposes scalability details, such as the `spreadscaler`, allowing users to configure instances and scaling behavior directly in the manifest.
  - Spin handles concurrency by default, creating new instances to handle requests out of the gate without requiring explicit configuration. For example, you can test this by benchmarking the Spin app with `oha -n 10 -c 5 http://127.0.0.1:3000`. However, scaling Spin applications beyond a single host typically requires an orchestrator like Kubernetes (via SpinKube).
- *Language support*
  - Spin offers templates in a broader range of languages, including C#, Grain, Swift, and Zig, in addition to Rust.
  - wasmCloud has more limited language support but focuses on extensibility and native integration with its ecosystem.
- *Extensibility and capabilities*
  - wasmCloud shines in extensibility. It allows users to easily integrate third-party capabilities by pointing to OCI artifacts in the manifest. For instance, while neither wasmCloud nor Spin officially supports `wasi:nn`, wasmCloud lets you integrate a third-party implementation.
  - Spin, on the other hand, relies solely on the capabilities provided by the host or external microservices accessed via HTTP.

No host is inherently "better" than the other—it all comes down to your specific use case. Each host shines in different scenarios, and understanding their strengths can help you make an informed decision:

- If you value language support and prefer a simple setup, Spin may be the better choice. For instance, if your team uses a mix of languages like Go, Python, or TypeScript, Spin's extensive template and SDK support make it a versatile option. The ability to get started with minimal configuration means it's ideal for teams looking to quickly prototype event-driven applications without delving deeply into custom configurations.
- If extensibility and fine-grained configurability are critical for your application, wasmCloud offers significant advantages. For example, if your application needs

to integrate with a specific machine learning capability or a proprietary system that doesn't conform to standardized WASI interfaces, wasmCloud's support for third-party providers—using WIT interfaces and custom capability providers—lets you extend its functionality to fit your needs.

For our SmartCMS host application, I chose wasmCloud due to its extensibility and the ease of integrating third-party capabilities.

6.6 *Implementing the example project as a wasmCloud app*

For this iteration of improvements to our SmartCMS, rather than migrating our existing code, we'll start fresh with a new wasmCloud application. Since we'll be retiring our custom host, this approach simplifies the transition. To create the application, use the following command in the `chapter06/` folder:

```
wash new component smart_cms --template-name hello-world-rust
```

Then we need to update the name of the application to reflect our SmartCMS project. This requires changes in two locations: `Cargo.toml` and `wasmcloud.toml`. The updated `Cargo.toml` file is shown in the following listings.

Listing 6.14 Updated application name in `Cargo.toml`

```
[package]
name = "smart-cms"
edition = "2021"
version = "0.1.0"

[workspace]

[lib]
crate-type = ["cdylib"]

[dependencies]
wasmcloud-component = "0.2.0"
```

Next, we modify our `wasmcloud.toml`.

Listing 6.15 Updated application name in `wasmcloud.toml`

```
name = "smart-cms"
version = "0.1.0"
language = "rust"
type = "component"

[component]
wit_world = "backend"        <- Also updated the wit_world name, which we'll align with our WIT file later in the process
wasm_target = "wasm32-wasip2"
```

With the template set up, let's consider the architecture of our application, as illustrated in figure 6.6.

We want it to include the following functionalities:

- A `wasi:keyvalue`-backed key-value store linked to a NATS key-value store for ease of setup
- A machine learning component to generate children's stories

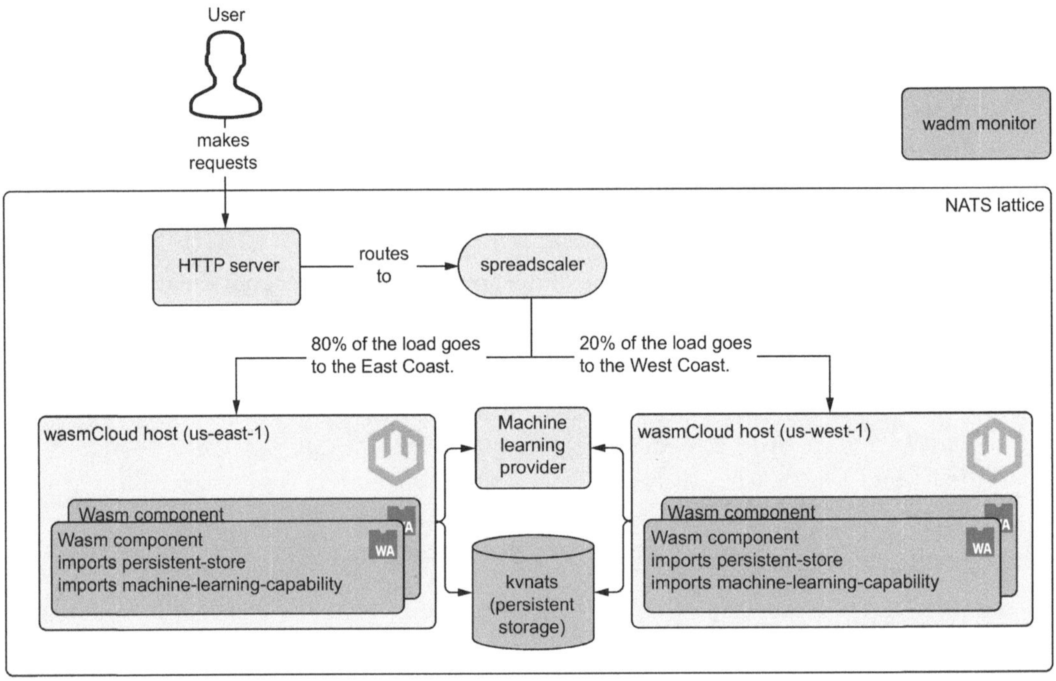

Figure 6.6 The architecture of our SmartCMS application

For simplicity, these functionalities can be bundled into a single `http-component`. This approach enables the component to inspect incoming requests and handle them appropriately. Specifically, the application will expose three routes:

- `/api/create`—Accepts a story name and content in the request body and persists them to the key-value store.
- `/api/generate`—Triggers the machine learning backend to generate a story, persists the story (e.g., using names like generate-x to maintain a counter), and returns it to the client.
- `/api/retrieve`—Accepts a story name in the request body and fetches the corresponding story from the key-value store. If the story doesn't exist, it returns an appropriate error message.

Now let's make some small configuration changes to our `wadm.yaml`. Specifically, we'll update the application name from `rust-hello-world` to `smart-cms` and clean up our app's annotations. Additionally, we'll modify the `spreadscaler` trait to deploy 100 instances of our component, distributed across two hosts with an 80:20 weight ratio between East Coast and West Coast zones. You can see the updated `wadm.yaml` in the following listing.

Listing 6.16 Updated `wadm.yaml` file for the SmartCMS

```
apiVersion: core.oam.dev/v1beta1
kind: Application
metadata:
  name: smart-cms
  annotations:
    description: "A smart CMS!"
spec:
  components:
    - name: http-component
      type: component
      properties:
        image: file://./build/smart_cms_s.wasm
      traits:
        - type: spreadscaler
          properties:
            instances: 100
            spread:
              - name: eastcoast
                weight: 80
                requirements:
                  zone: us-east-1
              - name: westcoast
                weight: 20
                requirements:
                  zone: us-west-1

    - name: httpserver
      type: capability
      properties:
        image: ghcr.io/wasmcloud/http-server:0.23.2
      traits:
        - type: link
          properties:
            target: http-component
            namespace: wasi
            package: http
            interfaces: [incoming-handler]
            source_config:
              - name: default-http
                properties:
                  address: 127.0.0.1:8000
```

Changes the application name to smart-cms

Cleans up application annotations

Changes Wasm artifact name to smart_cms_s.wasm

Updates the spreadscaler to deploy 100 instances, distributing them between East Coast (80%) and West Coast (20%)

We're now ready to spin up our hosts. Use the following commands to set up two local wasmCloud hosts, each labeled with its respective zone:

```
wash up --multi-local --label zone=us-east-1 -d
wash up --multi-local --label zone=us-west-1 -d
```

With that set, let's get started by adding persistent storage to our application and creating the first two routes: `/api/create` and `/api/retrieve`.

6.6.1 Adding persistent storage to the SmartCMS

Like we did for our "Hello, World" application, the first step is to update our WIT file to import `wasi:keyvalue`. While we're at it, we'll also update the namespace, package, and world name. The updated WIT is shown in the following listing.

Listing 6.17 Updated SmartCMS `world.wit` file

```
package smartcms:store-and-ai-story-generator;     ← Updates namespace and package name

world backend {                                    ← Updates world name to backend
    import wasi:keyvalue/atomics@0.2.0-draft;      ⎤ Imports wasi:keyvalue interfaces
    import wasi:keyvalue/store@0.2.0-draft;        ⎦ for atomic and store operations
    export wasi:http/incoming-handler@0.2.2;
}
```

With the WIT updated, the next step is to add the capability provider and create a link to it in our `wadm.yaml` file. The updated configuration is shown in the following listing.

Listing 6.18 Updated `wadm.yaml` file with key-value provider and link

```
apiVersion: core.oam.dev/v1beta1
kind: Application
metadata:
  name: smart-cms
  annotations:
    description: "A smart CMS!"
spec:
  components:
    - name: http-component
      type: component
      properties:
        image: file://./build/smart_cms_s.wasm
      traits:
        - type: spreadscaler
          properties:
            instances: 100
            spread:
              - name: eastcoast
                weight: 80
                requirements:
                  zone: us-east-1
              - name: westcoast
                weight: 20
```

```
          requirements:
            zone: us-west-1
    - type: link
      properties:
        namespace: wasi
        package: keyvalue
        interfaces: [store, atomics]
        target:
          name: kvnats
          config:
            - name: wasi-keyvalue-config
              properties:
                bucket: default
                enable_bucket_auto_create:
                ➥ 'true'

- name: httpserver
  type: capability
  properties:
    image: ghcr.io/wasmcloud/http-server:0.23.2
  traits:
    - type: link
      properties:
        target: http-component
        namespace: wasi
        package: http
        interfaces: [incoming-handler]
        source_config:
          - name: default-http
            properties:
              address: 127.0.0.1:8000

- name: kvnats
  type: capability
  properties:
    image: ghcr.io/wasmcloud/keyvalue-nats:0.3.1
```

Adds the key-value capability link to the wasi:keyvalue interface

Adds the key-value provider from OCI image

With the updated `wadm.yaml` in place, we can now move to the application code in `src/lib.rs`. First, update the imports at the top of your file to include

```
use std::io::Read;
use wasmcloud_component::http;
use wasmcloud_component::wasi::keyvalue::*;
```

These imports bring in two new dependencies. The `std::io::Read` one will allow us to process the body of incoming HTTP requests, while the `wasi::keyvalue::*` one provides the interfaces to interact with our persistent storage.

Next, delete the body of the existing `handle` function and replace it with the following skeleton:

```
fn handle(
    request: http::IncomingRequest,
```

Renames the variable to request as we are now actively using it

```
) -> http::Result<http::Response<impl http::OutgoingBody>> {
    let (parts, mut body) = request.into_parts();

    match parts.uri.path() {
        "/api/create" => {
            // ...
        }
        "/api/retrieve" => {
            // ...
        }
        _ => {
            Ok(http::Response::new("Invalid route!\n".to_string()))
        }
    }
}
```

In this updated function, the request is split into `parts` and `body`. The `parts` allow us to determine which route is being accessed, while the `body` gives us the data needed for specific routes. Using a `match` statement, we handle requests for the `/api/create` and `/api/retrieve` routes, while returning an error message for invalid paths.

> **NOTE** We're only matching against the URI (e.g., `"/api/create"`, `"/api/retrieve"`, etc.) of the request. This means we're not considering the request's method (e.g., `GET`, `POST`, etc.). If you want to check the method, you can inspect `parts.method`.

With this skeleton in place, we can now implement the logic for each route.

CREATING THE /API/CREATE ROUTE

Inside the `/api/create` `match` arm, add the following code:

```
let bucket = store::open("default").unwrap();

let mut buf = Vec::new();
body.read_to_end(&mut buf).unwrap();
let body = String::from_utf8(buf).unwrap();
```

This code opens the default key-value bucket and reads the body of the incoming HTTP request into a buffer. The buffer is then converted to a UTF-8 string for processing. Note that this code includes minimal error handling—many of the unwrap statements could be replaced with more robust error-handling strategies to ensure resilience in production.

Next, add the following:

```
let mut lines = body.lines();
let story_name = lines.next().unwrap_or("Unnamed Story").trim();
let story_content = lines.collect::<Vec<&str>>().join("\n");
```

Here we define how the backend expects information to be passed in the request body. The first line of the body is treated as the story name, defaulting to "Unnamed Story" if no name is provided. The remaining lines are joined to form the story content. In a more robust implementation, the request body would likely be formatted in a structured way, such as JSON, and parsed using serialization/deserialization techniques for better clarity and error handling.

Finally, add the logic to persist the data:

```
bucket.set(story_name, story_content.as_bytes()).unwrap();
Ok(http::Response::new(format!("Stored {}\n", story_name)))
```

This code stores the story in the key-value bucket using the name as the key and the content as the value. The HTTP response confirms the operation by returning the story name.

Next, let's implement the `/api/retrieve` route.

CREATING THE /API/RETRIEVE ROUTE

Just like with the `/api/create` route, the first step for the `/api/retrieve` route is to open the default key-value bucket and extract the request body. Here's how:

```
let bucket = store::open("default").unwrap();

let mut buf = Vec::new();
body.read_to_end(&mut buf).unwrap();
let story_name = String::from_utf8(buf).unwrap().trim().to_string();
```

This code opens the key-value store bucket and processes the incoming HTTP request body. The body is read into a buffer, converted to a UTF-8 string, and trimmed to extract the story name.

Next, we attempt to retrieve the story:

```
match bucket.get(&story_name).unwrap() {
    Some(content) => {
        let story_content = String::from_utf8(content).unwrap();
        Ok(http::Response::new(format!("{story_content}\n")))
    }
    None => {
        Ok(http::Response::new("Story not found\n".to_string()))
    }
}
```

Here the code checks if the requested story exists in the key-value store. If found, the content is retrieved, converted to a UTF-8 string, and returned as the HTTP response. Otherwise, the response indicates that the story was not found. Overall, the updated `lib.rs` file for our application should look like the following listing.

Listing 6.19 Updated `smart-cms/src/lib.rs`

```
use std::io::Read;
use wasmcloud_component::http;
```

```
use wasmcloud_component::wasi::keyvalue::*;

struct Component;

http::export!(Component);

impl http::Server for Component {
    fn handle(
        request: http::IncomingRequest,
    ) -> http::Result<http::Response<impl http::OutgoingBody>> {
        let (parts, mut body) = request.into_parts();

        match parts.uri.path() {
            "/api/create" => {
                let bucket = store::open
                ➥ ("default").unwrap();

                let mut buf = Vec::new();
                body.read_to_end(&mut buf).unwrap();
                let body = String::from_utf8(buf).unwrap();

                let mut lines = body.lines();
                let story_name = lines.next()
                ➥ .unwrap_or("Unnamed Story").trim();
                let story_content =
                ➥ lines.collect::<Vec<&str>>().join("\n");

                bucket.set(story_name,
                ➥ story_content.as_bytes()).unwrap();

                Ok(http::Response::new
                ➥ (format!("Stored {}\n", story_name)))
            }
            "/api/retrieve" => {
                let bucket = store::open("default").unwrap();

                let mut buf = Vec::new();
                body.read_to_end(&mut buf).unwrap();
                let story_name =
                ➥ String::from_utf8(buf).unwrap().trim().to_string();

                match bucket.get
                ➥ (&story_name).unwrap() {
                    Some(content) => {
                        let story_content =
                        ➥ String::from_utf8(content).unwrap();

                        ➥ Ok(http::Response::new(format!("{story_content}\n")))
                    }
                    None => {
                        Ok(http::
                        ➥ Response::new("Story not found\n".to_string()))
                    }
                }
            }
```

- **Matches on endpoints to route requests** (`match parts.uri.path() {`)
- **Opens the default bucket of our NATS key-value persistent storage** (`let bucket = store::open("default").unwrap();`)
- **Reads HTTP request body lines, where the first line is the story title and the rest is the story content**
- **Stores the story in the bucket** (`bucket.set(...)`)
- **Returns a success response for storing the story** (`Ok(http::Response::new(format!("Stored {}\n", story_name)))`)
- **Retrieves the story from the bucket, returning the content if found** (`match bucket.get(&story_name).unwrap() {`)

```
            _ => {
                Ok(http::Response::new
                ➥ ("Invalid route!\n".to_string()))
            }
        }
    }
}
```

Handles other routes by returning an "Invalid route!" message

Now let's test our work so far.

TESTING OUR APPLICATION

At the beginning of section 6.6, we started our hosts. By now, you should be working in a clean environment with no applications deployed. If you're unsure, verify using `wash app list` and delete any outdated applications with `wash app delete <application_name>`.

Once your environment is ready, build and deploy the application:

```
wash build
wash app deploy ./wadm.yaml
```

After deployment, check the application status to confirm it was successfully deployed:

```
wash app list
```

Once you see a Deployed status, you're ready to test your API.

To test the `/api/create` route, run

```
curl -X POST -H "Content-Type: text/plain"
➥  -d $'MyStory\nOnce upon a time, in a land far, far away...'
➥  http://127.0.0.1:8000/api/create
```

This command sends a POST request to the `/api/create` route with the `Content-Type` set to `text/plain`. The body of the request contains a new story, where the first line specifies the story's title (`MyStory`) and the remaining lines provide the story content (`Once upon a time, in a land far, far away...`).

NOTE The key-value provider does not support spaces in keys, so use `MyStory` instead of `My Story`.

The response should confirm:

```
Stored MyStory
```

Next, test the `/api/retrieve` route with

```
curl -X POST -H "Content-Type: text/plain"
➥  -d 'MyStory'
➥  http://127.0.0.1:8000/api/retrieve
```

This retrieves the content of the story `MyStory`, returning

```
Once upon a time, in a land far, far away...
```

Awesome! You've successfully created and retrieved a story using your SmartCMS application!

6.6.2 Adding machine learning to the SmartCMS

wasmCloud does not officially support the `wasi:nn` interface. This means there isn't an out-of-the-box solution, such as a prebuilt OCI artifact for a provider or a simple dependency to integrate machine learning capabilities. However, wasmCloud's extensible architecture allows us to use third-party providers to achieve similar functionality.

To demonstrate this, we'll integrate a third-party provider for the Ollama interface. Unlike `wasi:nn`, the Ollama interface is not part of an ongoing standardization process. This makes it a valuable example to show how custom WIT interfaces can be embedded into your wasmCloud applications.

> **What is Ollama?**
>
> Ollama is a lightweight machine learning runtime that allows you to locally run large language models. It simplifies inference by offering an easy-to-use CLI for downloading and interacting with models, enabling developers to run large language models without needing specialized server infrastructure.

To proceed with this integration, you'll need to install Ollama on your local machine. You can find installation instructions at https://ollama.com/.

Once installed, pull the model we'll use for this example with the following command:

```
ollama pull gurubot/tinystories-656k-q8
```

This model, similar to the one used in chapter 5, generates stories based on a given prompt containing the beginning of a story. While the generated stories may not always be perfectly coherent, this lightweight model (less than 1 MB) is ideal for demonstrating the integration due to its simplicity and minimal resource requirements.

With Ollama installed and the model ready, let's move on to embedding the custom interface into our SmartCMS.

BUILDING THE CUSTOM PROVIDER

While we could create our own custom provider embedding ONNX for `wasi:nn`, we'll simplify things by utilizing a third-party provider.

To include the provider in our project, we'll add it as a Git submodule. A Git submodule allows us to track an external repository within our project's directory. From inside the `smart-cms/` directory, add the submodule with the following command:

```
git submodule add https://github.com/danbugs/ollama-provider.git
```

Inside the `ollama-provider/` directory, two key components are relevant for our application:

- The source code for the Ollama provider
- The WIT interface for the custom Ollama interface, located in the `wit/` directory

The Ollama WIT interface is shown in the following listing.

Listing 6.20 `ollama.wit` interface (comments/documentation omitted)

```
interface generate {
    record request {
        prompt: string,
        images: option<list<string>>
    }

    record response {
        model: string,
        created-at: string,
        response: string,
        done: bool,
        context: option<list<s32>>,
        total-duration: option<u64>,
        load-duration: option<u64>,
        prompt-eval-count: option<u16>,
        prompt-eval-duration: option<u64>,
        eval-count: option<u16>,
        eval-duration: option<u64>,
    }

    generate: func(req: request) -> result<response, string>;
}
```

This interface defines

- *Request record*—Contains input parameters for the Ollama API, such as a `prompt` or `images` (e.g., PNG or JPEG files)
- *Response record*—The output of the model, which includes properties like `response` (the generated text), `done` (indicating process completion), and additional metadata for evaluation and performance
- *Generate function*—The primary function that takes a `request` and returns either a `response` or an error message

Additionally, the provider includes another WIT file, `provider.wit`, as shown in the following listing.

Listing 6.21 `provider.wit` file for the `ollama-provider`

```
package thomastaylor312:ollama;

world provider-ollama {
    export generate;
}
```

This WIT defines the `provider-ollama` world, where the provider implements the `generate` function. The provider interacts with the Ollama API, which is accessible locally by default at `http://127.0.0.1:11434`.

Ensure the Ollama API is running by either starting the Ollama application or executing `ollama serve`. At the root of the `ollama-provider/` directory, you'll find a `wasmcloud.toml` file.

Listing 6.22 `wasmcloud.toml` file for the `ollama-provider`

```
name = "Ollama"
language = "rust"
type = "provider"

[provider]
vendor = "thomastaylor312"
```

This file declares the provider type with the line `type = "provider"`. Similar to building Wasm components, you can use `wash` to build providers. In the `ollama-provider/` directory, build the Ollama provider with

```
wash build
```

This will generate `ollama-provider.par.gz` in the `build/` directory, which is a provider archive.

> **TIP** wasmCloud offers tools to interact with provider archives using `wash par`. To inspect the archive, run `wash par inspect <path to ollama-provider.par.gz>`.

With the provider built, add it to the `wadm.yaml` file, placing it below the `kvnats` provider:

```
# ...

    - name: ollama
      type: capability
      properties:
        image: file://./ollama-provider/build/ollama-provider.par.gz
```

Before linking it to our application, we need to add the WIT dependency. Let's handle that next.

USING CUSTOM WIT INTERFACES WITH WASMCLOUD

To integrate custom WIT interfaces in wasmCloud, the first step is to define the namespace and package in the application's `wasmcloud.toml` file. This is done by adding an override. See the following listing for the updated `smart-cms/wasmcloud.toml` file with the necessary changes.

Listing 6.23 Updated `wasmcloud.toml` file with custom interface override

```
name = "smart-cms"
version = "0.1.0"
language = "rust"
type = "component"

[component]
wit_world = "backend"
wasm_target = "wasm32-wasip2"

[overrides]
"thomastaylor312:ollama" =
➥{ path = "./ollama-provider/wit/" }
```

Adds override to link the thomastaylor312:ollama interface

Here the override links the `thomastaylor312:ollama` namespace and package combination to the local path of the Ollama provider's WIT directory. This ensures that the interface is resolvable within our application.

With the override in place, we can now import the Ollama interface in our `smart-cms` WIT file. The updated `smart-cms/wit/world.wit` file is shown in the following listing.

Listing 6.24 Updated `world.wit` file with import to custom ollama interface

```
package smartcms:store-and-ai-story-generator;

world backend {
    import wasi:keyvalue/atomics@0.2.0-draft;
    import wasi:keyvalue/store@0.2.0-draft;
    import thomastaylor312:ollama/generate;
    export wasi:http/incoming-handler@0.2.2;
}
```

Imports thomastaylor312:ollama/generate interface

This import makes the `generate` interface from the Ollama package accessible to our application, allowing us to use its machine learning functionality.

The next step is to link the Ollama capability provider to the WIT interface in the `wadm.yaml` file. The following listing shows the updated `wadm.yaml` manifest with this addition.

Listing 6.25 Updated `wadm.yaml` file

```
apiVersion: core.oam.dev/v1beta1
kind: Application
metadata:
```

```
  name: smart-cms
  annotations:
    description: "A smart CMS!"
spec:
  components:
    - name: http-component
      type: component
      properties:
        image: file://./build/smart_cms_s.wasm
      traits:
        - type: spreadscaler
          properties:
            instances: 100
            spread:
              - name: eastcoast
                weight: 80
                requirements:
                  zone: us-east-1
              - name: westcoast
                weight: 20
                requirements:
                  zone: us-west-1
        - type: link
          properties:
            namespace: wasi
            package: keyvalue
            interfaces: [store, atomics]
            target:
              name: kvnats
              config:
                - name: wasi-keyvalue-config
                  properties:
                    bucket: default
                    enable_bucket_auto_create: 'true'
        - type: link
          properties:
            target: ollama
            namespace: thomastaylor312
            package: ollama
            interfaces: [generate]
            target_config:
              - name: ollama-conf
                properties:
                  model_name: gurubot/
                  ➥tinystories-656k-q8

    - name: httpserver
      type: capability
      properties:
        image: ghcr.io/wasmcloud/http-server:0.23.2
      traits:
        - type: link
          properties:
            target: http-component
            namespace: wasi
```

Links capability provider (ollama) to WIT interface (thomastaylor312:ollama/generate)

```
          package: http
          interfaces: [incoming-handler]
          source_config:
            - name: default-http
              properties:
                address: 127.0.0.1:8000

    - name: kvnats
      type: capability
      properties:
        image: ghcr.io/wasmcloud/keyvalue-nats:0.3.1

    - name: ollama
      type: capability
      properties:
        image: file://./ollama-provider/build/ollama-provider.par.gz
```

In this configuration,

- The `ollama` provider is linked to the `generate` interface.
- The `target_config` specifies the model name `gurubot/tinystories-656k-q8`, which we downloaded earlier.

Finally, since the Ollama interface isn't officially supported by wasmCloud, we need to use `wit-bindgen` to generate bindings for the WIT interface. Add the following dependency to your `Cargo.toml` file:

```
wit-bindgen = "0.36.0"
```

With that, we've prepared everything needed to integrate the Ollama functionality. Next, we'll add the `/api/generate` route to our SmartCMS application.

CREATING THE /API/GENERATE ROUTE

To enable interaction with our custom WIT interface in the SmartCMS application, we use `wit-bindgen` to generate the necessary glue code. At the top of your `smart-cms/src/lib.rs` file, add

```
wit_bindgen::generate!({ generate_all });
```

This generates all required glue code for our custom interface. With that, next, we can bring in the specific bindings for the `generate` function and its `Request` struct:

```
use thomastaylor312::ollama::generate::{generate, Request};
```

With the setup complete, add a `/api/generate` route to the `match` statement in your component's `handle` function:

```
match parts.uri.path() {
    "/api/create" => {
        // ...
```

```
        }
        "/api/retrieve" => {
            // ...
        }
        "/api/generate" => {
            // ...
        }
        _ => {
            Ok(http::Response::new("Invalid route!\n".to_string()))
        }
    }
}
```

Adds the /api/generate route

All the new logic will be inside the /api/generate match arm. Start by generating a story:

```
let prompt = "Once upon a time".to_string();
let generated_story = generate(&Request {
    prompt: prompt.clone(),
    images: None,
}).unwrap();
let story = format!("{}{}", prompt, generated_story.response);
```

Here a static prompt, "Once upon a time", is passed to the generate function. Then the response is concatenated with the prompt to create the final story.

Next, store the generated story in the key-value bucket:

```
let bucket = store::open("default").unwrap();
let count = atomics::increment(&bucket, "counter", 1).unwrap();
let story_name = format!("generated{}", count);
bucket.set(&story_name, story.clone().as_bytes()).unwrap();
```

Here again, the bucket is opened using the default namespace. Then a counter is incremented to create a unique story title, generatedX, and the story is stored in the key-value bucket.

Finally, structure the HTTP response:

```
Ok(http::Response::new(format!("{}\n{}\n", story_name, story)))
```

The response follows the format established in the /api/create route, where the first line is the title, and the subsequent lines are the content of the story.

See the following listing for the overall updated smart-cms/src/lib.rs file.

Listing 6.26 Final smart-cms/src/lib.rs file

```
use std::io::Read;
use wasmcloud_component::http;
use wasmcloud_component::wasi::keyvalue::*;

wit_bindgen::generate!({ generate_all });
```

```
use thomastaylor312::ollama::generate::{generate, Request};

struct Component;

http::export!(Component);

impl http::Server for Component {
    fn handle(
        request: http::IncomingRequest,
    ) -> http::Result<http::Response<impl http::OutgoingBody>> {
        let (parts, mut body) = request.into_parts();

        match parts.uri.path() {
            "/api/create" => {
                let bucket = store::open("default").unwrap();

                let mut buf = Vec::new();
                body.read_to_end(&mut buf).unwrap();
                let body = String::from_utf8(buf).unwrap();

                let mut lines = body.lines();
                let story_name = lines.next().unwrap_or("Unnamed
➥Story").trim();
                let story_content = lines.collect::<Vec<&str>>().join("\n");

                bucket.set(story_name, story_content.as_bytes()).unwrap();

                Ok(http::Response::new(format!("Stored {}\n", story_name)))
            }
            "/api/retrieve" => {
                let bucket = store::open("default").unwrap();

                let mut buf = Vec::new();
                body.read_to_end(&mut buf).unwrap();
                let story_name =
➥String::from_utf8(buf).unwrap().trim().to_string();

                match bucket.get(&story_name).unwrap() {
                    Some(content) => {
                        let story_content =
➥String::from_utf8(content).unwrap();

➥Ok(http::Response::new(format!("{story_content}\n")))
                    }
                    None => {
                        Ok(http::Response::new
➥("Story not found\n".to_string()))
                    }
                }
            }
            "/api/generate" => {
                let prompt = "Once upon a time".to_string();
                let generated_story = generate(&Request {
                    prompt: prompt.clone(),
                    images: None,
```

Annotations:
- `impl http::Server for Component {` — **Implements http::Server to expose the component via HTTP**
- `"/api/create" => {` — **/api/create handles story creation and stores it in the key-value bucket.**
- `"/api/retrieve" => {` — **/api/retrieve retrieves stories from the bucket based on a provided key.**
- `"/api/generate" => {` — **/api/generate generates a story, stores it, and returns the title and content.**

```
                }).unwrap();
                let story = format!("{}{}", prompt,
                ➥ generated_story.response);

                let bucket = store::open("default").unwrap();
                let count = atomics::increment(&bucket, "counter",
                ➥ 1).unwrap();
                let story_name = format!("generated{}", count);
                bucket.set(&story_name, story.clone().as_bytes()).unwrap();

                Ok(http::Response::new(format!("{}\n{}\n", story_name,
                ➥ story)))
            }
            _ => {
                Ok(http::Response::new("Invalid route!\n".to_string()))
            }
        }
    }
}
```

Finally, in the `smart-cms/` folder, build and deploy your application:

```
wash build
wash app deploy ./wadm.yaml
```

Verify the deployment status with `wash app list`. If everything is configured correctly, the app will show a Deployed status. Up next: testing the functionality of our `/api/generate` route.

TESTING OUR APPLICATION

With our application running via an HTTP endpoint, we can now connect it to a frontend interface. You're welcome to build your own, or you can use the one I've created. You can find it at https://mng.bz/7QqV.

To use this frontend:

1. Copy the raw file content from the link.
2. Save it locally as `index.html` in the `smart-cms/` directory.
3. Open the file in a browser.

NOTE If you want, instead of opening in your browser directly, you can use a tool like `http-server` (installable with `cargo install http-server`). From the `smart-cms/` folder, run `http-server ./index.html`, then navigate to the appropriate localhost URL (shown in the terminal output) in your browser.

The interface should look like figure 6.7.

Using this frontend, you can

- Create new stories.
- Retrieve existing stories by name.
- Generate AI stories.

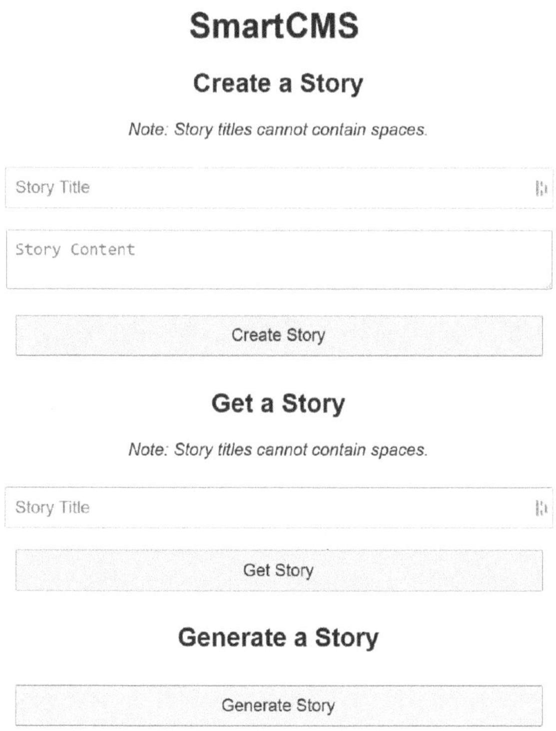

Figure 6.7 Interface of our SmartCMS frontend

When you click the "Generate Story" button, the application will call the `/api/generate` route, and you should see a response pop up.

Awesome! We've successfully rebuilt our SmartCMS application using wasmCloud. This time, we avoided writing any host-related code while gaining the benefits of a robust hosting environment. wasmCloud handles

- Load balancing across instances of our component
- Spreading those instances across multiple hosts, which could be on entirely different physical machines

We only had to focus on implementing the business logic for our application. Additionally, we've enhanced the SmartCMS by making it accessible via an HTTP interface, ensuring smooth integration with frontend tools like the one demonstrated here.

Summary

- wasmCloud and Spin provide robust platforms for running Wasm microservices, significantly reducing the need for custom host development.
- Standardized interfaces, like `wasi:keyvalue`, streamline the process of integrating capabilities such as persistent storage into applications while ensuring interoperability with various providers.

- Applications in wasmCloud can be scaled dynamically with the `spreadscaler` trait, allowing efficient handling of concurrent requests by deploying multiple component instances.
- The NATS lattice enables seamless communication between components distributed across multiple hosts, ensuring resilience and fault tolerance.
- Machine learning functionalities can be added to wasmCloud applications using custom WIT interfaces and third-party providers, showcasing wasmCloud's extensibility.
- wasmCloud's architecture eliminates the need for developers to write nonbusiness logic, focusing solely on application features and functionality.
- By using off-the-shelf Wasm hosts, developers can achieve faster development cycles while maintaining robust and scalable architectures.

7 Introducing Wasm containers

This chapter covers

- The differences between containers and Wasm
- Wasm containers
- Distributing Wasm as Open Container Initiative images
- Containerizing wasmCloud applications
- Converting containers to Wasm

We've come a long way from manually handling `String` objects by storing their UTF-8 encoded characters in a Wasm module's linear memory and passing them across the host-to-module boundary using integer parameters for the `String`'s length and memory location. In the previous chapter, we explored wasmCloud—a high-level Wasm runtime—and saw how it enables the use of standard and nonstandard WebAssembly Interface Types (WIT) interfaces to bring higher-level capabilities such as key-value stores and machine learning models to our Wasm applications.

However, one important aspect we've yet to explore—aside from briefly mentioning it in chapter 1—is Wasm's distribution story. Traditionally, developers distribute and deploy their applications using containers, which package code and its dependencies into a single unit, allowing applications to run consistently across environments, from local machines to cloud platforms. At first glance, Wasm, as a hardware abstraction layer, may sound similar to containers—and if you think so, you're not wrong!

In this chapter, we'll dive deeper into how containers work and highlight the parallels between containers and Wasm. We'll also examine Wasm containers—the concept we teased in chapter 1. Finally, we'll explore how to convert traditional containers to Wasm, bridging the gap between these two powerful paradigms for application deployment and distribution.

7.1 Containers vs. Wasm

If you've ever developed an application, chances are you've reached a point where you wanted to share it with others. But what if your application requires other software (e.g., Ubuntu 22.04 and Python 3.8) that other people don't have installed? You'd like your app to behave consistently, even if its users are running it in a very different environment, like Windows using Python 3.10. Today, the most common way to do that is by using containers, which package your application so it runs consistently across any two computers with the same CPU architecture.

This consistency is achieved by using operating system mechanisms such as control groups (cgroups) and namespaces (or their equivalents on platforms like Windows). These mechanisms provide the isolation and resource control needed for containers to function. As illustrated in figure 7.1, containers bundle your application together with everything it needs to run—such as a userspace environment (including system libraries and utilities), binaries, and other dependencies—on top of the container runtime (e.g., the Docker engine). Importantly, containers share the host's kernel rather than including their own, which distinguishes them from virtual machines.

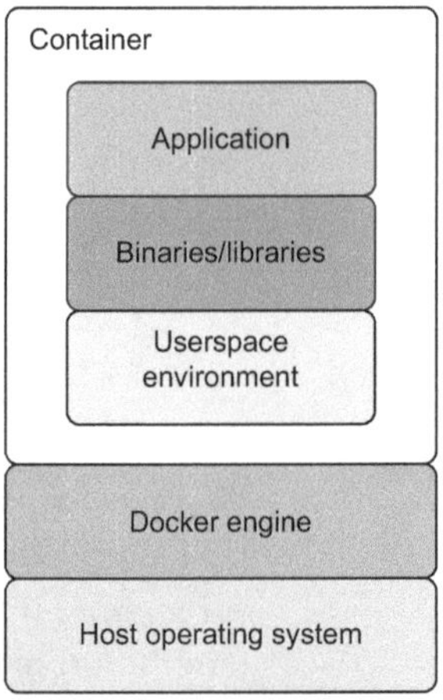

Figure 7.1 The typical architecture of a containerized system, illustrating how applications are packaged with their dependencies and userspace environment, all managed by the Docker engine on top of the host operating system

By packaging your application this way, you ensure that it behaves identically on two different computers running different operating systems. This consistency is guaranteed because the application always runs in the same userspace environment and with the same dependencies, regardless of the underlying host. For example, your application might require Ubuntu userspace utilities and libraries, but it could be deployed to a machine running either Ubuntu or a different Linux, or even Windows.

Wasm, as we know, is also a method for packaging applications, and its execution model shares many similarities with Docker's approach. As shown in figure 7.2,

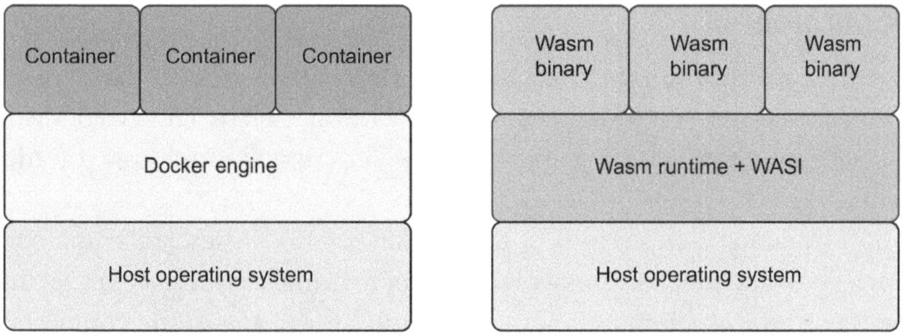

Figure 7.2 A side-by-side comparison of the execution models for containers and Wasm, showing how both systems provide an abstraction layer between applications and the host operating system

the Wasm runtime, when combined with WebAssembly System Interface (WASI), occupies an architectural layer similar to the Docker engine, providing the interface between your application binaries and the host operating system.

However, to understand the differences between containers and Wasm, we need to zoom in and examine what exactly is being distributed. When you distribute your app via containers, you often package a userspace environment with system libraries and utilities. But when you distribute via Wasm, you only package your application logic. This distinction brings two key benefits:

- *Smaller binaries*—Wasm binaries are typically much smaller than container images, making them easier to distribute and faster to download. For comparison, even minimal "distroless" container images are typically a few megabytes, while Wasm binaries are often measured in kilobytes.
- *Faster startup times*—Wasm binaries can start almost instantaneously, whereas containers often have higher overhead due to initializing their userspace environment and its resources.

These advantages are achieved without sacrificing portability, because Wasm doesn't make assumptions about its hosting environment. Instead, it relies on WASI—our standardized, portable system interface—to communicate with any host operating system.

However, it's worth noting that WASI itself must be implemented by Wasm runtimes (e.g., Wasmtime). This means the responsibility of ensuring portability shifts from application developers to runtime developers, simplifying the process for those building Wasm applications while maintaining flexibility and cross-platform compatibility.

Wasm is actually even more portable than traditional containers. As mentioned earlier, Docker ensures an application runs the same on two computers, provided they share the *same CPU architecture*. This means that a container image (i.e., what you build containers from) created for, say, AMD will not work on ARM without creating a multiarchitecture image. Wasm, on the other hand, eliminates this requirement. Wasm is entirely hardware agnostic, meaning a Wasm binary built on AMD will run the same on an ARM machine.

7.2 Wasm containers

What do people mean when they talk about Wasm containers? Is it Wasm inside a traditional Linux container? Is it just a rebranding of Wasm itself as a means of distribution? Or is it something entirely new? To answer that, let's first explore how traditional containers work.

We'll start by taking a closer look at the Docker engine. When you run a container, a series of processes and mechanisms work together to bring it to life. At its core, the Docker engine relies on *runC*—a low-level container runtime—to spawn the container process. Once the container is up and running, runC hands off control to the *containerd-shim*.

Think of a shim like a physical shim: it fits between two things and fills the gap so they can work together smoothly. In this case, the containerd-shim sits between the runtime and the container, acting as a kind of spacer and helper. It allows the container to continue running even after the parent process exits, redirects the container's logs, and manages lifecycle events like pause and restart.

Sitting above these shims is the *containerd process*, which acts as the central manager for all containers on a host system. It interfaces with the Docker engine and orchestrates interactions between the containerd-shims, the underlying host system, and any external resources required by the containers. Both containerd and containerd-shim are integral components of the Cloud Native Computing Foundation (CNCF) ecosystem. This layered architecture is illustrated in figure 7.3.

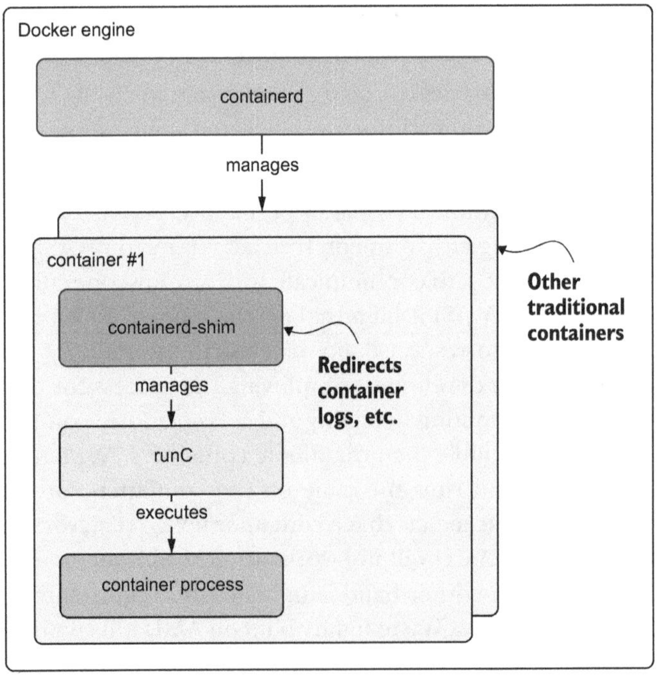

Figure 7.3 A detailed view inside the Docker engine, showcasing the key components and mechanisms (e.g., containerd, runC, and containerd-shim) responsible for managing and starting container processes

Back in 2022, Docker introduced the *Docker+Wasm Technical Preview*, enabling developers to use their familiar Docker tooling for Wasm workloads. While this feature has moved from technical preview to beta, support remains experimental and can be unstable across different environments and Docker versions. For learning purposes, we'll focus on running Wasm containers directly with containerd—the underlying container runtime that Docker itself uses.

What do the inner workings of the Docker engine look like when running Wasm? Let's take a look at figure 7.4 and compare it to figure 7.3.

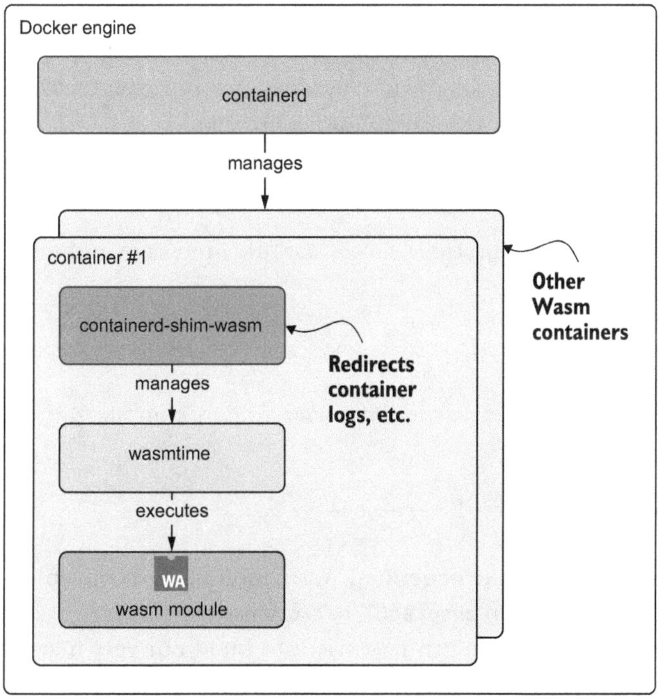

Figure 7.4 A closer look inside the Docker engine when executing a Wasm module, showing the key components, including containerd-shim-wasm and the Wasm runtime

As you can see, there are very few differences. First, instead of having a container process, we now have the Wasm module. The Wasm module is executed by a runtime we're already familiar with (e.g., Wasmtime) and is managed by a new type of shim—the *containerd-shim-wasm*, which, again, handles tasks such as redirecting logs, etc.

> **TIP** If you want to check out which other runtimes are supported aside from Wasmtime, visit the `runwasi` project: https://mng.bz/64qR. `runwasi` is the umbrella name for container runtime extensions for containerd that support running Wasm workloads.

Running Wasm inside traditional containers

Using containerd-shims isn't the only way to run Wasm modules or components within containers. Another option is to embed a Wasm runtime inside a traditional Docker container, effectively allowing you to run Wasm on top of it.

This approach is particularly useful for projects that require more than just a standalone Wasm binary—such as those that rely on additional infrastructure components. For example, wasmCloud projects often depend on an ecosystem that includes a NATS server. We'll explore this approach in more detail later in the chapter.

7.3 Running a Wasm container

Let's walk through running a simple Wasm container. In your `chapter07/` directory, create a standard Rust application with the following command:

```
cargo new hello-wasm-container
```

Feel free to update the default `println!("Hello, World!")` message in the `main.rs` file to something like

```
println!("Hello, Wasm containers!");
```

Once that's done, from the `hello-wasm-container/` folder, compile the application into a Wasm module by running

```
cargo build --target wasm32-wasip1 --release
```

After the build completes, locate the generated Wasm module. For convenience, move it to a new folder called `bin/` within `chapter07/hello-wasm-container/`.

With the Wasm module ready, we can now use it to build our very first Wasm container. To do this, we'll use a Dockerfile. Dockerfiles are configuration files that define how a container image is built, specifying the base image, copying application files, and setting the execution command.

Next, we should create a file called `Dockerfile` at the root of `hello-wasm-container/` and populate it as shown in the following listing.

Listing 7.1 The Dockerfile for our first Wasm container

```
FROM scratch
COPY /bin/hello-wasm-container.wasm /hello-wasm-container.wasm

ENTRYPOINT ["hello-wasm-container.wasm"]
```

In this listing, we are doing the following:

- `FROM scratch`—Specifies an empty base image, as Wasm binaries don't require an operating system
- `COPY`—Copies our compiled Wasm module (`hello-wasm-container.wasm`) into the container at the specified path (`/hello-wasm-container.wasm`)
- `ENTRYPOINT`—Defines the Wasm module as the main executable to run when the container starts

7.3.1 Setting up containerd and Wasm support

Before building our Wasm container, we need to install containerd, `ctr` (i.e., a command-line client for containerd), and the Wasmtime shim. The setup script we'll use is designed for Linux systems. If you're on Windows, Windows Subsystem for Linux (WSL) is recommended. Mac users should note that `ctr` doesn't currently run natively on macOS (see https://mng.bz/oZoD), so a Linux VM is recommended.

Run the following command to download and execute the installation script:

```
curl -sSL https://raw.githubusercontent.com/danbugs/serverside-wasm-book-
➥ code/refs/heads/main/chapter07/hello-wasm-container/install-containerd-
➥ wasm.sh | bash
```

The script will

- Download and install containerd
- Configure containerd to run as a systemd service
- Download and install the containerd-shim-wasmtime binary
- Verify the installation

After the script completes, verify that containerd is running:

```
sudo systemctl status containerd
```

You should see output indicating that containerd is active and running.

Verify the Wasmtime shim is installed:

```
which containerd-shim-wasmtime-v1
```

This should output `/usr/local/bin/containerd-shim-wasmtime-v1`.

7.3.2 Building and running the Wasm container

Now that we have containerd and the Wasmtime shim installed, we can build our Wasm container image. We'll use Docker's `buildx` tool to create the image, then run it with containerd's `ctr` command.

First, create a builder that supports the Wasm platform:

```
docker buildx create --name wasm-builder --driver docker-container --use
```

The `buildx` plugin extends Docker with advanced build capabilities powered by BuildKit. We name it `wasm-builder` and set it as the active builder with the `--use` flag. This builder will allow us to build images for the `wasi/wasm32` platform. Now, from inside `hello-wasm-container/`, build the Wasm container image and export it as an OCI archive:

```
docker buildx build --platform wasi/wasm32 -t
➥hello-wasm-container --output type=oci,dest=hello-wasm-container.oci .
```

In this command,

- The `--platform wasi/wasm32` flag specifies that we are building a Wasm container targeting the `wasi/wasm32` platform. This ensures the image metadata correctly identifies the binary as Wasm.
- The `--output type=oci,dest=hello-wasm-container.oci` flag exports the image as an OCI archive instead of loading it into Docker's image store. We'll dive deeper into OCI and its role in Wasm distribution in the next section.
- The `-t` flag (short for "tag") assigns a name and optional tag to the container image (e.g., `hello-wasm-container`).
- The final `.` indicates the current directory, where the Dockerfile and build context are located.

Import the OCI image into containerd:

```
sudo ctr -n default images import --platform=wasi/wasm32 hello-wasm-
➥container.oci
```

The `-n default` flag specifies the namespace (`default` is the standard namespace for containerd), and the `--platform` flag tells containerd which platform variant to import.

Verify the image was imported successfully:

```
sudo ctr -n default images ls | grep hello-wasm
```

Now run the Wasm container:

```
sudo ctr run --rm --runtime io.containerd.wasmtime.v1 --platform
➥wasi/wasm32 docker.io/library/hello-wasm-container:latest hello-wasm-
➥instance
```

The `--runtime io.containerd.wasmtime.v1` flag specifies we want to use the Wasmtime runtime via its containerd-shim, and `hello-wasm-instance` is a unique identifier we assign to this running container instance. This should output

```
Hello, Wasm containers!
```

Congratulations! You just ran your very first Wasm container! This is significant because, as we discussed in chapter 1, Wasm containers offer several advantages over traditional Docker containers.

One of the biggest benefits is faster cold starts. Unlike Docker containers, which require initializing their userspace environment, Wasm containers only load the application itself. This significantly reduces startup times—often making Wasm containers up to 160% faster to boot compared to their Docker counterparts.

Another key advantage is smaller binary sizes. Traditional Docker container images include not just the application but often also a userspace environment with system libraries and utilities, resulting in large image sizes that need to be downloaded and deployed. In contrast, Wasm binaries contain only the application logic and any necessary dependencies, often making them 80% smaller than equivalent Docker container images. This reduction in size speeds up distribution and deployment while minimizing storage and bandwidth requirements.

These benefits make Wasm containers an excellent choice for resource-constrained environments, such as IoT devices or edge-computing platforms, where traditional containers may struggle due to their size and initialization overhead.

7.4 Wasm and the OCI

The OCI is an open governance structure maintained by the Linux Foundation, focused on defining industry standards for container runtimes, images, and distribution. It ensures interoperability between container technologies, allowing developers to build and run applications across different platforms without being locked into vendor-specific solutions.

In early 2024, OCI released version 1.1 of its specification (https://mng.bz/4n7Q). One of the most significant additions in this update was support for OCI artifacts, which allows metadata and noncontainer objects to be stored and distributed using OCI registries. This extends OCI's scope beyond just containers, enabling it to package and manage arbitrary content, including Wasm components and WIT definitions.

With this expanded capability, the Wasm artifact format (https://mng.bz/Qw54) was introduced, defining a standardized way to package Wasm components and their required WIT dependencies as OCI artifacts. This means that both Wasm components and WIT definitions can now be stored, distributed, and deployed using OCI registries—just like traditional container images. As a result, Wasm workloads can integrate with existing cloud and container infrastructure, making it easier to deploy and manage Wasm applications across major cloud providers. Let's see an example of packaging and publishing a Wasm component as an OCI image!

7.4.1 Packaging and publishing Wasm components as OCI images

We'll be publishing our image to our personal GitHub accounts using the GitHub Container Registry (GHCR). Before we begin, if you'd like to follow along, you'll first need to log in to GHCR.

To do so, you'll need a personal access token (PAT) for your GitHub account. You can generate one by following these instructions: https://mng.bz/X7XE. Make sure to grant the token the following permissions:

- `write:packages` allows pushing images to GHCR
- `read:packages` allows pulling images from GHCR
- `delete:packages` (optional) allows deleting images from GHCR

Once you have your token, you're ready to log in. Run the following command in your terminal:

```
echo "<your PAT>" | docker login ghcr.io -u <your GH username> --password-
➥ stdin
```

NOTE While testing this example, I encountered mixed results on Windows. If you're using Windows, it's recommended to run this inside WSL for better compatibility.

Now that we're all set up, we need a Wasm component to publish. To keep our focus on OCI packaging, let's reuse the component we built in chapter 4, section 4.2.1. If you don't have that component handy, you can create a new one using

```
cargo component new --bin <your component name>
cd <you component name>
cargo component build --release
```

Once you have a component, place it in a new directory inside `chapter07/`—for example, `chapter07/wasm-oci/<component name>.wasm`.

Now, in your terminal, run

```
wkg oci push ghcr.io/<your GH username>/<your oci image name>:latest <path
➥ to your wasm component>
```

NOTE `wkg` is a tool for managing Wasm OCI artifacts, making it easy to package and distribute Wasm components. You can install it locally by running `cargo install wkg@0.10.0 --locked`.

If everything went as expected, you should now see your package listed under the Packages tab of your GitHub profile. However, keep in mind that, by default, packages published to GHCR are private. If you want to share your Wasm component with others, you'll need to update its visibility settings.

Awesome! We've just packaged a Wasm component as an OCI image! Now, what can we do with it?

7.4.2 Inspecting Wasm component OCI images

Let's take a moment to understand what's happening under the hood. To do that, we'll inspect our published image using `regctl`, a command-line tool for interacting with OCI registries.

NOTE If you'd like to follow along, you can install `regctl` on Ubuntu using snap with `sudo snap install regclient`. At the time of writing, this installs `regctl` version 0.8.0. For other operating systems, follow https://regclient.org/install.

To start, let's take a look at our application's manifest by running

```
regctl manifest get ghcr.io/<your GH username>/<your oci image name>:latest
```

NOTE If your package is not public, you'll need to log in to the registry first using your GH PAT: `echo "<your PAT> " | regctl registry login ghcr.io -u "<your GH username>" --pass-stdin`.

You should get output like the following listing.

Listing 7.2 Partial manifest for a Wasm OCI image

```
...
Config:
  Digest:    sha256:2ef427...
  MediaType: application/vnd.wasm.config.v0+json
  Size:      520B
Layers:
  Digest:    sha256:0223cb...
  MediaType: application/wasm
  Size:      82583B
```

Here we can see that `Config.MediaType` and `Layers.MediaType` indicate that this is a Wasm OCI image. These fields follow the Wasm artifact format we mentioned earlier, ensuring compatibility across different tools and platforms. By adhering to these standards, the ecosystem can build tooling around Wasm OCI images just like it does for traditional container images, enabling distribution and integration across registries, cloud environments, and runtimes.

Next up, we can further inspect our `Config.MediaType` by referencing its digest—a unique identifier derived from the content of a file or object, ensuring integrity and preventing accidental modifications. We do this using the following command:

```
regctl blob get ghcr.io/<your GH username>/
➥<your oci image name>:latest sha256:2ef427... | jq
```

Here we are fetching the config blob associated with our OCI image using `regctl blob get` and then piping (`|`) the output to `jq`, a command-line JSON processor that helps format and analyze JSON data.

NOTE To install `jq`, visit https://jqlang.org/download/.

This command produces output similar to the following listing.

Listing 7.3 Result from inspecting a Wasm `Config.MediaType`

```
{
  "created": "<some date>",
  "author": null,
  "architecture": "wasm",
  "os": "wasip2",
  "layerDigests": [
    "sha256:0223cb..."
  ],
  "component": {
    "exports": [
      "wasi:cli/run@0.2.0"
    ],
    "imports": [
      "wasi:cli/environment@0.2.0",
      "wasi:cli/exit@0.2.0",
      "wasi:io/error@0.2.0",
      "wasi:io/streams@0.2.0",
      "wasi:cli/stdin@0.2.0",
      "wasi:cli/stdout@0.2.0",
      "wasi:cli/stderr@0.2.0",
      "wasi:clocks/wall-clock@0.2.0",
      "wasi:filesystem/types@0.2.0",
      "wasi:filesystem/preopens@0.2.0"
    ],
    "target": null
  }
}
```

In this output, we can see that our Wasm OCI image is explicitly marked as targeting the `wasm` architecture with `wasip2` as the operating system. Additionally, we get a full breakdown of the component's WIT imports and exports, showing exactly what capabilities our Wasm module expects from the host and what it provides.

This standardized approach to packaging Wasm components within OCI artifacts establishes a foundation for distributing and discovering Wasm components at scale. Instead of manually copying WIT interfaces as we did in previous chapters, we can now pull them directly as OCI artifacts using familiar tooling.

To see some examples of standard WIT interfaces being distributed as OCI artifacts, check out the Bytecode Alliance's published packages: https://github.com/orgs/bytecodealliance/packages.

7.4.3 Pulling and running Wasm OCI images

Now that we've successfully published our Wasm component as an OCI image, let's pull it back down and run it to complete the cycle.

From inside the `wasm-oci/` folder, run the following command:

```
wkg oci pull ghcr.io/<your GH username>/
➥ <your oci image name>:latest -o ./pulled.wasm
```

This command fetches the Wasm OCI image from GHCR and outputs it as a standalone Wasm module, ready to be executed by a Wasm runtime.

To run it using Wasmtime, do

```
wasmtime run ./pulled.wasm
```

If everything works correctly, you should see the following output:

```
Hello, World!
```

And that's it! We've pushed, inspected, pulled, and executed a Wasm OCI image.

Overall, Wasm OCI images provide a standardized way to distribute Wasm components, integrating seamlessly into existing OCI-based tooling. This enables

- *Discoverability*—Developers can store and retrieve Wasm components from registries just like container images.
- *Integration with cloud-native workflows*—By using OCI, Wasm components can be managed alongside traditional containers, making them easier to adopt in existing infrastructure.

7.5 wasmCloud and Wasm containers

Earlier, when running our Wasm container, we used the following command:

```
sudo ctr run --rm --runtime io.containerd.wasmtime.v1 --platform
➥ wasi/wasm32 docker.io/library/hello-wasm-container:latest hello-wasm-
➥ instance
```

This let us run a Wasm module inside a container using Wasmtime as the execution runtime. But, as we've seen earlier, there are other options—different `--runtime` values or shims, like `io.containerd.spin.v2`, let you run Spin applications in a similar way.

So does wasmCloud work the same way? Can we just swap in a wasmCloud shim and pass a different `--runtime` flag to containerd?

The answer is no. Unlike the containerd-shim-based approach we've used so far, wasmCloud doesn't just wrap a single Wasm binary in a container—it packages the entire wasmCloud ecosystem. This ensures that wasmCloud retains its full feature set, including `wadm` and the NATS lattice, even when running in a containerized environment.

Rather than using a lightweight shim to start individual Wasm binaries, wasmCloud provides a complete, self-contained runtime that runs inside a container. Figure 7.5 illustrates how this setup works.

On the left, we see the approach we've explored throughout this chapter—the native method of running Wasm in containers. This involves using containerd with a containerd-shim that provides a Wasm runtime, such as Wasmtime or a higher-level runtime like Spin. On the right, we have wasmCloud's approach, which takes a different route. Instead of relying on a shim, wasmCloud packages its entire host environment inside

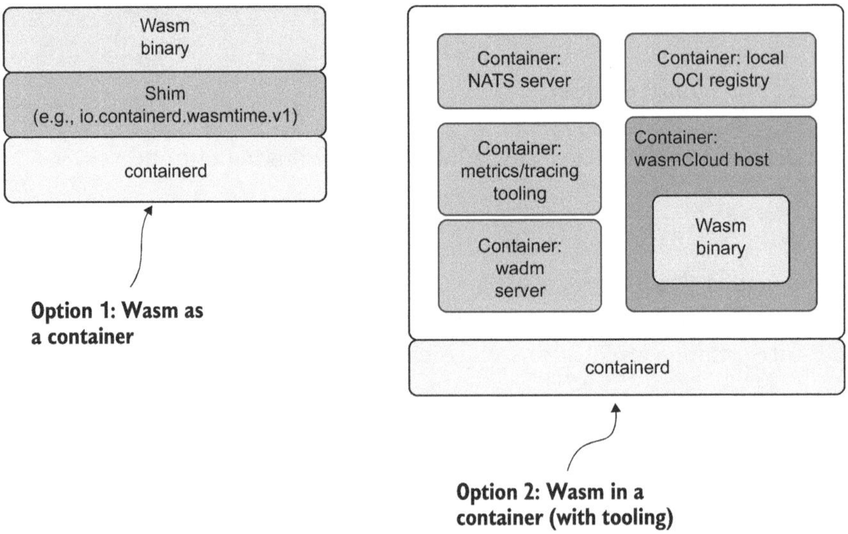

Figure 7.5 A comparison of two approaches to running Wasm in containers. On the left, Wasm runs directly inside a container using a lightweight shim. On the right, Wasm is packaged within a container alongside supporting infrastructure, as seen in wasmCloud's approach, which includes components like the NATS server, a local OCI registry, and metrics/tracing tools.

the container, running it as a self-contained unit. This approach is more opinionated. It packages more tools, resulting in larger containers but ensuring that developers can still take full advantage of wasmCloud's ecosystem, including features like linking Wasm components to specific implementations that satisfy their imports and so on.

Let's take a look at an example. To demonstrate, we'll use *Docker Compose*, which allows us to define and manage multicontainer applications using a single configuration file. One of its key benefits is that it sets up a virtual network, enabling communication between the containers it orchestrates.

In figure 7.5, we illustrated a Docker Compose setup with multiple components (available here: https://mng.bz/Mwq8). This setup includes not only the core wasmCloud infrastructure—such as the required NATS server, `wadm` server, and wasmCloud host—but also additional services like a local OCI registry (for storing Wasm artifacts) and metrics/tracing tooling to monitor performance. For our example, we'll be using a streamlined version of that setup, shown in the following listing.

Listing 7.4 `docker-compose.yaml` for wasmCloud ecosystem

```
version: "3"
services:
  nats:
    image: nats:2.10-alpine
```

Defines the NATS service, pulling the nats:2.10-alpine image and exposing port 4222. The -js flag enables JetStream.

```
    ports:
      - "4222:4222"
    command: ["-js"]
  wasmcloud:
    depends_on:
      - "nats"
    image: wasmcloud/wasmcloud:latest
    environment:
      RUST_LOG: debug,hyper=info,async_nats=info,oci_client=
      ➥ info,cranelift_codegen=warn
      WASMCLOUD_LOG_LEVEL: debug
      WASMCLOUD_RPC_HOST: nats
      WASMCLOUD_CTL_HOST: nats
    ports:
      - "8000:8000"
  wadm:
    depends_on:
      - "nats"
    image: ghcr.io/wasmcloud/wadm:latest
    environment:
      - WADM_NATS_SERVER=nats
```

Defines the NATS service, pulling the nats:2.10-alpine image and exposing port 4222. The -js flag enables JetStream.

Defines the wasmCloud host service, which depends on NATS. It runs the wasmcloud/wasmcloud image and sets environment variables for logging and RPC communication.

Defines the wadm server service, which also depends on NATS and runs the ghcr.io/wasmcloud/wadm image

This Docker Compose file sets up a minimal wasmCloud ecosystem, ensuring that the necessary services—NATS, the wasmCloud host, and the `wadm` server—are correctly orchestrated within separate containers. Now place this `docker-compose.yaml` file inside a new directory under your `chapter07/` projects folder, naming the subdirectory `hello-wasmcloud-container/`.

With this done, let's quickly put together a `wadm.yaml` file for our application. This file defines how our wasmCloud components will be deployed and connected within our Docker Compose setup. Overall, it should look like the following listing.

Listing 7.5 `wadm.yaml` file for our Docker Compose example

```
apiVersion: core.oam.dev/v1beta1
kind: Application
metadata:
  name: hello-wasmcloud-container
  annotations:
    description: ''
spec:
  components:
    - name: http-component
      type: component
      properties:
        image: ghcr.io/wasmcloud/
        ➥ components/http-hello-world-rust:0.1.0
      traits:
        - type: spreadscaler
          properties:
            instances: 1

    - name: httpserver
```

Defines the http-component, which is sourced from a prebuilt Wasm OCI image stored in GHCR.

```
      type: capability
      properties:
        image: ghcr.io/wasmcloud/http-server:0.25.0
      traits:
        - type: link
          properties:
            target:
              name: http-component
            namespace: wasi
            package: http
            interfaces: [incoming-handler]
            source:
              config:
                - name: default-http
                  properties:
                    address: 0.0.0.0:8000
```

This `wadm.yaml` file specifies how our Wasm components will be orchestrated inside the wasmCloud runtime. Unlike previous examples where we referenced a locally built Wasm component, here, for ease of setup, we are using a prepackaged `http-component` stored in GHCR. With this in place, we're ready to run the example!

On one terminal, from inside our `hello-wasmcloud-container/` directory, run

```
docker compose up
```

This command will start all the services defined in our `docker-compose.yaml` file, bringing up the NATS server, wasmCloud host, and `wadm` server as separate containers. Note that since Docker Compose creates a dedicated network for these containers, they can communicate without additional configuration.

Once the services are up and running, in another terminal, we can verify that our wasmCloud host is active by running

```
wash get hosts
```

If everything is set up correctly, the host should appear in the output, confirming that wasmCloud is successfully running inside the container.

With our host verified, we can proceed with deploying our `wadm.yaml` application definition. Now run

```
wash app deploy ./wadm.yaml
```

After deploying, we can check that the application is running by listing active applications with

```
wash app list
```

If everything is working correctly, we should see our `hello-wasmcloud-container` application in the output with confirmation that it has been deployed successfully.

To further verify that our deployed component is handling requests, we can send a request to the exposed HTTP server by running

```
curl http://127.0.0.1:8000/
```

If the application is running properly, this should return

```
Hello from Rust!
```

Awesome—with that, we just deployed our Wasm component onto the host running inside the `wasmcloud` Docker Compose service! To stop Docker Compose, press Ctrl-C, and then run `docker compose down` to clean up our resources.

Now, while this setup demonstrates how to run a wasmCloud application inside a container, it is by no means production ready. Docker Compose is primarily designed for local development and lacks key features required for production-grade orchestration in a real-world deployment. In the next chapter, we'll take this a step further by learning how to use Kubernetes to orchestrate and manage our wasmCloud-based applications in a production-ready manner.

7.6 Converting Linux containers to Wasm

Unlike previous chapters, we won't be modifying our SmartCMS in this one—we're saving that for the next chapter, where we'll explore Wasm in Kubernetes. Instead, we'll focus on a different hands-on demo: converting a Linux container to Wasm. Let's get started!

7.6.1 Introducing container2wasm

If you are not familiar with QEMU (https://www.qemu.org/), it is an open source machine emulator and virtualizer that enables running programs compiled for one architecture on another (e.g., running an ARM binary on an x86 machine). It is commonly used for cross-platform development, testing, and virtualization.

Much like QEMU, container2wasm provides CPU emulation, allowing Linux-based container workloads to be converted into Wasm binaries. This is particularly valuable because many Linux applications require substantial modifications—or even complete rewrites—to run as Wasm due to WASI's limited POSIX support.

Rather than requiring developers to manually port applications, container2wasm works by compiling CPU emulators—including QEMU itself—into Wasm. This enables existing Linux applications to be executed inside a Wasm runtime with minimal modifications. Figure 7.6 illustrates this process.

The higher degree of portability does come with a cost, though. In particular, you'll find that container2wasm applications, compared to their equivalent raw Wasm counterparts, have

- Lower performance due to the virtualization layer introduced by the CPU emulator.

- Larger binary sizes because of additional dependencies, such as the embedded CPU emulator and minimal Linux runtime.

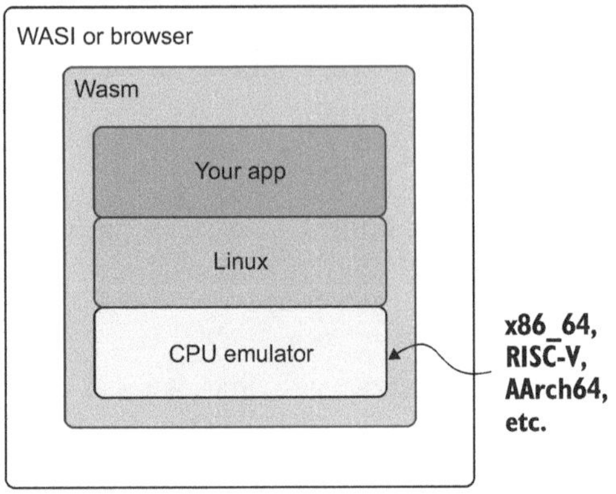

Figure 7.6 container2wasm encapsulates a CPU emulator to run Linux and Linux applications inside Wasm, enabling execution within either a WASI runtime or a browser environment.

Still, wasmifying a container allows you to use containers in ways that weren't previously possible. Beyond simply enhancing sandboxing and security, this approach opens up new possibilities. For example, you can now run an entire container inside the browser, creating in-browser development and testing environments where users can interact with a full Linux-based application without needing a local container runtime. It also makes offline-first computing much more practical. Applications that previously required a cloud backend—like collaborative document editors, CRM dashboards, or project management tools—can now run entirely in the browser and sync data back to the cloud when a connection is available.

Additionally, this technique enables secure, ephemeral execution environments. Think of things like running a confidential form-filling app, an online coding interview tool, or even short-lived data analysis tasks. These containers run in a fully isolated way, and once closed, they leave no trace on the user's device.

Now let's try wasmifying our first container!

7.6.2 Installing container2wasm

To start off, let's install container2wasm. At the time of writing, prebuilt releases are only available for Linux amd64 and arm64. If you're using Windows, you can run it through WSL. On macOS, since there's no native support, again, you'll likely need to provision a Linux environment to run it.

As of this writing, container2wasm's latest version is 0.8.3, so we'll be using that. Run the following command to begin the installation:

```
wget https://github.com/container2wasm/container2wasm/releases
➥ /download/v0.8.3/container2wasm-v0.8.3-linux-amd64.tar.gz
```

> **NOTE** If you're on an arm64 Linux machine instead of amd64, make sure to download the arm64 release by replacing amd64 in the link with arm64. You can find all available versions at https://mng.bz/gmWG.

After downloading the release, extract the archive with

```
tar -xvf container2wasm-v0.8.3-linux-amd64.tar.gz
```

Next, move the extracted binaries to a directory in your PATH so they can be used system wide:

```
sudo mv c2w c2w-net /usr/local/bin/
```

Ensure the binaries are executable by running

```
chmod +x /usr/local/bin/c2w /usr/local/bin/c2w-net
```

Now verify that the installation was successful by checking the version:

```
c2w --version
```

You should see output similar to

```
c2w version v0.8.3
```

Finally, clean up by removing the downloaded archive:

```
rm container2wasm-v0.8.3-linux-amd64.tar.gz
```

7.6.3 Using container2wasm

Now, we're all set up to start using container2wasm. In your chapter07/ directory, create a new folder for this project—let's call it hello-container2wasm/.

For this section, we'll set up a simple Python web server using Flask, a widely used web framework for building lightweight web applications and APIs.

Start by creating an app.py file inside the hello-container2wasm/ folder. Its contents should match the following listing.

Listing 7.6 app.py file for a simple Python web server

```
from flask import Flask

app = Flask(__name__)

@app.route('/')
def hello():
    return "hello from inside a container running on Wasm"

if __name__ == '__main__':
    app.run(host='0.0.0.0', port=8000)
```

In this file, we define a minimal Flask web server. The Flask object initializes the application, and we define a single route, /, which returns a simple text response when accessed. The final block ensures the server runs on all available network interfaces at port 8000, making it accessible from outside the container once deployed.

With this done, in the same folder, let's now create a `Dockerfile` to containerize our application. This file will define the environment and dependencies needed to run our Python web server inside a container. Your `Dockerfile` should look like the following listing.

Listing 7.7 Dockerfile for a simple Python web server

```
FROM python:3.9-slim

WORKDIR /app

RUN pip install flask

COPY app.py .

EXPOSE 8000

CMD ["python", "app.py"]
```

In this file, we define a lightweight containerized environment for our Flask application. We start from the `python:3.9-slim` base image, which provides a minimal Python runtime. We set the working directory to `/app`, install Flask using `pip`, and copy our `app.py` file into the container. The `EXPOSE 8000` instruction indicates that the application listens on port 8000, and the final `CMD` instruction runs the application when the container starts.

With the `Dockerfile` in place, you can now build your container image as you normally would by running

```
docker build -t python-wasm-webserver .
```

This will compile your image and store it locally. Next, we can use `container2wasm` to convert our newly built container image into a Wasm binary by running

```
c2w python-wasm-webserver python-wasm-webserver.wasm
```

NOTE This step can take a while.

Now that we have our Wasm binary, how do we run it? Theoretically, we could use Wasmtime directly, but there's a limitation: Wasmtime doesn't provide a built-in way to forward ports to the local host. This means that while we can execute the binary, we won't be able to interact with our web server.

Other runtimes, such as wazero (https://github.com/tetratelabs/wazero), offer this functionality out of the box. However, for convenience—since we already installed it—we'll use `c2w-net`. `c2w-net` is a wrapper around Wasmtime that enables networked applications to function properly by acting as a proxy.

Do this by running the following command:

```
c2w-net --invoke -p localhost:8000:8000 ./python-wasm-webserver.wasm --
➥net=socket
```

You might see some "failed" logs, but these can be ignored. After a short moment, you should see output similar to the following:

```
 * Serving Flask app 'app'
 * Debug mode: off
WARNING: This is a development server. Do not use it in a production
➥deployment. Use a production WSGI server instead.
 * Running on all addresses (0.0.0.0)
 * Running on http://127.0.0.1:8000
 * Running on http://192.168.127.3:8000
Press CTRL+C to quit
```

Now, in another terminal, run the following command:

```
curl http://127.0.0.1:8000/
```

This should return

```
hello from inside a container running on Wasm
```

And there it is! We just ran a Python Flask web server that was containerized and converted to Wasm, providing it with enhanced portability and security.

If you're interested in exploring more examples—especially its use in browsers—check out https://ktock.github.io/container2wasm-demo/. There you'll find demonstrations such as a full Debian image being wasmified and executed. Or, if you'd like to try it yourself, you can run

```
c2w ubuntu:22.04 ubuntu.wasm
```

Then, using Wasmtime, you can start a Wasm-encapsulated Ubuntu environment with

```
wasmtime ubuntu.wasm
```

This should give you a shell prompt, like

```
root@localhost:/#
```

With that, we've seen how container2wasm allows us to take existing Linux containers and convert them into Wasm binaries, making them more portable and secure. While this approach introduces some tradeoffs, such as increased binary size and performance overhead, it opens up new possibilities for running containerized workloads in constrained environments—including the browser.

Summary

- Containers and Wasm share similarities in providing portability and isolation, but Wasm eliminates the need for a guest OS, resulting in smaller binaries and faster startup times.
- Wasm containers use containerization principles to package and distribute Wasm binaries, integrating them into cloud-native ecosystems while maintaining Wasm's lightweight nature.
- The OCI now supports Wasm artifacts, enabling standardized distribution of Wasm components via OCI registries like GHCR.
- Unlike traditional container-based Wasm execution, wasmCloud packages an entire host environment inside a container, facilitating managed orchestration of Wasm components.
- container2wasm enables running Linux applications as Wasm binaries by encapsulating a CPU emulator, expanding Wasm's use cases to legacy applications and in-browser execution.

8 Scalability for Wasm with Kubernetes

This chapter covers

- Exploring the Custom Resource Definition and operator patterns in Kubernetes
- Extending Kubernetes to support Wasm workloads
- Using SpinKube to deploy Spin Wasm apps to Kubernetes
- Scaling Spin apps with Horizontal Pod Autoscalers
- Deploying wasmCloud applications to Kubernetes

Wasm has some clear advantages over containers. It's smaller, which makes it quicker to transfer over the network; it starts up faster; and it's built with a stronger security model. But despite all that, Wasm is still playing catch-up when it comes to the mature tooling and ecosystem that containers enjoy.

In the previous chapter, we looked at how to package Wasm applications as container images. Using the Open Container Initiative (OCI) image format, we tap into the rich tooling built for containers—most notably, Kubernetes.

Kubernetes is the standard way to manage containers in production. It takes care of scaling, load balancing, service discovery, and more. In this chapter, we'll look at how Wasm can plug into that same system and how we can take advantage of the Kubernetes feature set to run and manage Wasm workloads.

8.1 Kubernetes and Wasm

Imagine you're running an online game server that needs more instances during peak hours. You don't want to manually spin up new servers every evening and shut them down at night. Kubernetes can handle that for you. It watches how busy things are and scales up or down as needed. That's just one example of the kind of operational heavy lifting Kubernetes is built for.

If you've used Kubernetes before, you've probably used it to deploy containers—maybe a web app, an API, or even that same game server. That's what it's best known for. But Kubernetes isn't just a container orchestrator. At its core, it's an extensible API server that manages workloads through a well-defined architecture. As shown in figure 8.1, a Kubernetes cluster consists of two main parts: the control plane and the data

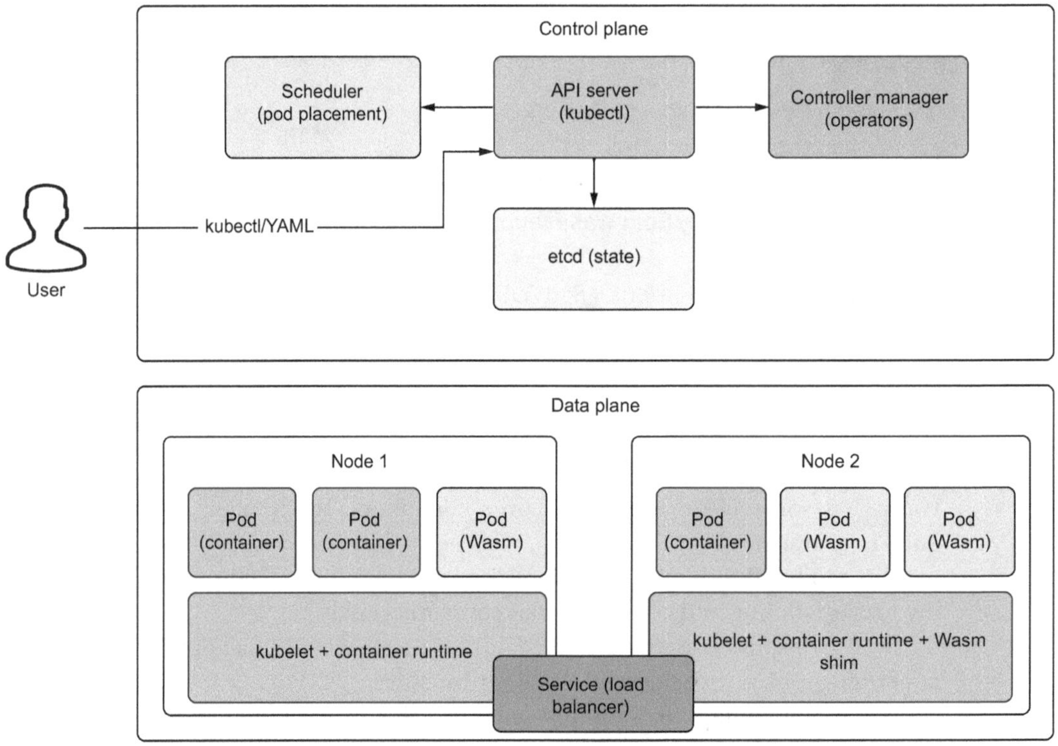

Figure 8.1 Kubernetes architecture showing the control plane (API server, scheduler, controller manager) and data plane (nodes with pods). The control plane manages cluster state and makes scheduling decisions, while the data plane runs the actual workloads. Users interact with the cluster through the API server, typically using `kubectl` commands or YAML manifests.

plane. The control plane makes all the decisions—where to place workloads, when to scale them, and how to respond to failures. The data plane is where your applications actually run, distributed across nodes that can host both traditional containers and, as we'll see, WebAssembly workloads.

Since version 1.7, when Custom Resource Definitions (CRDs) were introduced, Kubernetes has been capable of managing more than just containers—it can orchestrate pretty much anything. But there's no built-in concept of an "application" in Kubernetes. Instead, we compose apps from primitives like deployments, services, and config maps. CRDs let us extend that model by defining our own top-level resources—things that look and behave more like actual applications. We can then tweak their configuration the same way we would for native Kubernetes resources.

There are plenty of real-world examples of this pattern. Crossplane uses CRDs to model things like databases or storage buckets. KubeVirt does it for virtual machines. And we can do it for Wasm too.

Once a CRD is applied to our Kubernetes cluster, we can deploy our custom resources (CRs) just like we would any other Kubernetes object. But CRDs aren't the full story. Having a CRD and applying a CR is only useful if there's an operator—a controller running in the cluster that knows how to handle that CR. The operator interprets what the resource represents and acts accordingly. That might mean spinning up a deployment, wiring up networking, or handling day 2 concerns like updates and restarts.

As shown in figure 8.2, this is exactly how Wasm fits into Kubernetes today. Projects like Spin and wasmCloud have done the heavy lifting of defining CRDs and building operators, so we can simply apply them to our clusters and let Kubernetes take care of orchestrating our Wasm apps like any other workload.

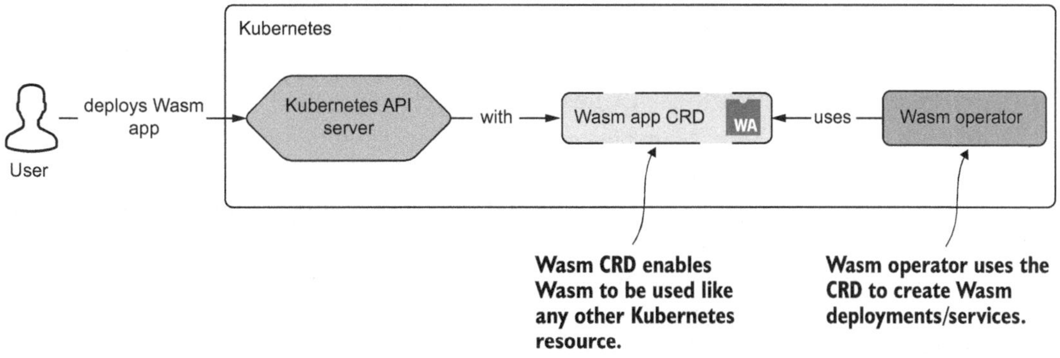

Figure 8.2 How a Wasm operator fits into Kubernetes: the user deploys a Wasm app by submitting a CR to the Kubernetes API server. This resource is defined by a Wasm-specific CRD, which is handled behind the scenes by a Wasm operator.

Kubernetes concepts for Wasm developers

While we'll introduce Kubernetes terms as they appear in context, a few concepts are worth understanding up front:

- *YAML manifests* are the format Kubernetes uses for its declarative configurations. You describe the desired state (e.g., "I want 3 replicas of my app running"), and Kubernetes figures out how to make it happen.
- *Deployments* are higher-level abstractions that manage groups of identical pods. Think of them as templates for your application instances that handle scaling, updates, and recovery automatically.
- *Services* provide stable networking for your pods. Since pods can come and go, services give them a consistent address and handle load balancing.
- *Namespaces* are logical partitions within a cluster. They're like folders in a filesystem—useful for organizing resources and keeping different projects or teams separated.

8.2 Running Wasm in Kubernetes with SpinKube

Now let's put what we've just learned into practice—starting with SpinKube. SpinKube is the Kubernetes integration for Spin, the Wasm framework we explored back in chapter 6. It brings Spin's developer-friendly tooling into the Kubernetes world using CRDs and operators under the hood.

Before we begin, it's worth noting that you'll need Spin installed on your system—we covered that in chapter 6. In this chapter, we'll extend Spin's capabilities by installing an official plugin called `kube`, which streamlines the process of deploying Spin applications to Kubernetes.

Other than that, to follow along with the rest of this chapter, you'll need a few more tools installed locally: `k3d` to spin up a local Kubernetes cluster, `kubectl` to interact with it, and *Helm* to simplify deploying resources to it. Once you've got those in place, we'll be ready to start working with SpinKube.

First, we'll install `k3d` to set up the Kubernetes cluster itself. `k3d` is a tool that makes it easy to run a local Kubernetes cluster by using Docker containers. It's fast, lightweight, and a great option for development and testing. At the time of writing, I've installed the latest available version: v5.8.3. You can find installation instructions here: https://k3d.io/v5.8.3/?h=installation#releases.

Next up is `kubectl`, the command-line tool used to interact with a Kubernetes cluster. You'll use it to apply configs, inspect resources, and run most Kubernetes-related commands throughout this chapter. Installation instructions are here: https://kubernetes.io/docs/tasks/tools/. Locally, I'm using

```
kubectl version --client
Client Version: v1.33.0
Kustomize Version: v5.6.0
```

Then, we'll need Helm. Helm is a templating tool that helps you generate the YAML needed to interact with the Kubernetes API. It's built for managing complex deployments without needing to handwrite pages of YAML. You can think of it as a way to bundle Kubernetes manifests together with configuration values, making deployment simpler and more repeatable.

> **NOTE** In some ways, Helm and CRDs solve similar problems—they both abstract complex Kubernetes deployments that would otherwise require writing large, complicated manifests. But while CRDs extend the Kubernetes API from the inside, Helm works on the client side. It prepares and sends the full set of objects—deployments, services, and so on—to the cluster in one go.

You can install Helm by following https://helm.sh/docs/intro/install/. I'm using the following version:

```
helm version
version.BuildInfo{Version:"v3.17.3",
➥GitCommit:"e4da49785aa6e6ee2b86efd5dd9e43400318262b",
➥GitTreeState:"clean", GoVersion:"go1.23.7"}
```

Finally, we'll install the Spin plugin that makes it easier to deploy Spin applications to Kubernetes. Assuming you already have Spin installed, run

```
spin plugins update
spin plugins install kube
spin plugins list --installed
```

You should see output similar to this (versions may vary):

```
cloud 0.11.0 [installed]
kube 0.4.0 [installed]
```

If you want to upgrade your plugin version to match this book, use the command `spin plugins upgrade` and choose the right version using their interactive picker. With that, we're ready to prepare our cluster for Wasm.

8.2.1 Preparing the cluster for SpinKube

A *cluster* in Kubernetes is the whole system: a control plane that manages the cluster state and a set of nodes that are running your workloads. When we say "deploy to Kubernetes," we mean deploying to a cluster. So, before we can deploy our Wasm application, we first need to set up a local Kubernetes cluster and prepare it with a few key components:

- Support tools like `cert-manager` to enable secure webhooks
- A `RuntimeClass` so Kubernetes knows how to launch Wasm workloads
- The CRDs and operator from SpinKube, which handle the actual orchestration

Let's go through those steps one by one.

CREATING THE CLUSTER

First, we'll create the Kubernetes cluster itself:

```
k3d cluster create wasm-cluster --image ghcr.io/spinframework/containerd-
➥shim-spin/k3d:v0.19.0 --port "8081:80@loadbalancer" --agents 2
```

This command creates a cluster named `wasm-cluster` using a custom `k3d` image that includes the `containerd-shim-spin` runtime we looked at in chapter 7. That's what lets Kubernetes run Spin-based Wasm workloads. It also exposes port 80 on the cluster's load balancer as port 8081 on your local machine and sets up two agent nodes—the physical or virtual machines where Kubernetes will actually run our workloads.

When we deploy our Wasm applications later, Kubernetes will package them into pods (the smallest deployable units in Kubernetes, each typically running a single container or Wasm module) and schedule these pods across our two nodes based on available resources.

INSTALLING SUPPORT TOOLS

Next, we need to install `cert-manager`—a Kubernetes add-on that automates the issuance and renewal of *TLS certificates*. SpinKube relies on it to secure its *admission webhooks*. These webhooks play a critical role: when you submit a CR like a Spin app, Kubernetes may call out to the operator's webhook to validate the configuration or apply defaults. That call must be made securely, and that's where TLS comes in.

You can install `cert-manager` with

```
kubectl apply -f https://github.com/cert-manager/cert-
➥manager/releases/download/v1.14.3/cert-manager.yaml
kubectl wait --for=condition=available --timeout=300s deployment/cert-
➥manager-webhook -n cert-manager
```

This sets up `cert-manager` and ensures its own webhook server is available. Later, the SpinKube operator will request a TLS certificate from `cert-manager` for its webhook service, so that the Kubernetes API server can communicate with it over HTTPS.

> **NOTE** TLS (Transport Layer Security) enables encrypted and authenticated communication between services—it's what puts the "S" in HTTPS. In Kubernetes, TLS is used not just for external traffic but also for securing internal components like webhooks.

DEFINING SPIN'S RUNTIME WITH RUNTIMECLASS

With that in place, the next piece we need is a `RuntimeClass`. Most of the time in Kubernetes, you don't need to think about container runtimes at all. When you deploy a pod, it just runs—usually using the default container runtime configured on the node, like containerd or CRI-O. But in our case, we're not running regular containers. We're deploying Wasm binaries, and those require adding a new, specialized runtime that knows how to execute them.

That's where `RuntimeClass` comes in. It's a standard Kubernetes resource that lets you explicitly tell Kubernetes which runtime to use for a particular workload. In our case, as shown in the following listing, we want to direct Kubernetes to use the `spin` runtime, which is provided by the containerd shim we set up earlier.

Listing 8.1 Spin `RuntimeClass`

```
apiVersion: node.k8s.io/v1
kind: RuntimeClass
metadata:
    name: wasmtime-spin-v2
handler: spin
```

This defines a new `RuntimeClass` called `wasmtime-spin-v2`. Any pod that specifies this `RuntimeClass` will be scheduled to use the `spin` handler, which runs Wasm binaries instead of standard containers.

You can install it with

```
kubectl apply -f https://github.com/spinframework/spin-
➥operator/releases/download/v0.5.0/spin-operator.runtime-class.yaml
```

That's all we need to get things working in our `k3d` setup. That's because, when we created the cluster, we used a custom image that includes the Spin-compatible containerd-shim on every node. With all nodes already equipped to run Wasm workloads, Kubernetes can freely schedule pods using the `wasmtime-spin-v2` `RuntimeClass` without any extra configuration.

In a production environment—where maybe not every node will have the Spin runtime installed—you'd likely want to be more selective. You'd typically label the compatible nodes and use a `nodeSelector` to ensure that only those nodes run Wasm workloads. That setup gives you tighter control over where these specialized workloads land, but for local development, we can keep things simple.

ADDING SPIN'S CRDS AND OPERATOR

Now that Kubernetes knows how to run Wasm workloads through our `RuntimeClass`, we need to introduce the resources that actually define what those workloads are. This is where SpinKube's CRDs come in.

Install them in your cluster with

```
kubectl apply -f https://github.com/spinframework/spin-
➥operator/releases/download/v0.5.0/spin-operator.crds.yaml
```

This manifest defines two key resource types that the operator will manage:

- `SpinAppExecutor` tells the Spin operator which executor to use when running a `SpinApp`. In practice, it links your workloads to the right runtime—in our case, the one specified by the `wasmtime-spin-v2` `RuntimeClass`. It also lets you control whether the operator should create a deployment, include default CA certificates, and so on.

- `SpinApp` is the main workload definition. It represents a Wasm application and exposes a set of options tailored to running it in Kubernetes. At the simplest level, you give it a container image, and the operator handles the deployment, pod, and service setup for you. But it also supports deeper runtime configuration, including
  - Image pull secrets for private registries
  - Liveness and readiness probes for health checking
  - Resource requests and limits
  - Spin variables for runtime configuration
  - Volume mounts to attach persistent storage
  - Autoscaling based on CPU or memory usage

Together, these CRDs give us the knobs and switches we need to configure and manage Wasm apps in a way that feels native to Kubernetes.

With our CRDs registered, we now need to bring in the component that will actually act on them. Remember, CRDs declare what you want in your cluster, but operators actually alter your cluster, adding or removing services so that the desired state in the CRD is reached. Defining a `SpinApp` or `SpinAppExecutor` doesn't do much on its own—the real logic lives inside the operator.

We'll install the Spin operator into the cluster using Helm:

```
helm install spin-operator --namespace spin-operator --create-namespace --
➥version 0.5.0 --wait oci://ghcr.io/spinframework/charts/spin-operator
```

This deploys the operator into its own namespace and wires it up to watch for `SpinApp` and `SpinAppExecutor` resources. From this point forward, whenever one of those resources is created or updated, the operator will respond accordingly—scheduling pods, provisioning services, and managing the lifecycle of our Wasm workloads.

To see what that looks like in practice, let's take a look at a `SpinAppExecutor` manifest.

Listing 8.2 `SpinAppExecutor` resource

```
apiVersion: core.spinkube.dev/v1alpha1
kind: SpinAppExecutor
metadata:
    name: containerd-shim-spin
spec:
    createDeployment: true
    deploymentConfig:
        runtimeClassName: wasmtime-spin-v2
        installDefaultCACerts: true
```

This resource tells the operator how Spin apps should be executed. In this case, we're asking it to use the `wasmtime-spin-v2` `RuntimeClass` we defined earlier, to automatically create a deployment, and to include a default set of CA certificates in the workload environment.

You can apply it with

```
kubectl apply -f https://github.com/spinframework/spin-
➥ operator/releases/download/v0.5.0/spin-operator.shim-executor.yaml
```

With this in place, the operator is fully equipped to handle incoming `SpinApp` resources—and to turn them into running Wasm applications inside our cluster.

8.2.2 Running a Wasm app in Kubernetes with SpinKube

With our cluster fully configured and the Spin operator ready to go, it's time to actually run a Spin application on Kubernetes.

To do that, we'll follow a simple pipeline:

1. Package our Spin app.
2. Push it to a container registry.
3. Scaffold the necessary Kubernetes resources using the Spin `kube` plugin.
4. Apply the generated manifest to our cluster.

If you followed along in chapter 6, you'll remember our `hello-world-spin` app—a minimal Spin application that responds to HTTP requests to any route with a plain-text message. We'll reuse that same app here to keep things simple.

With that, copy your `hello-world-spin/` directory into your `chapter08/` folder. Also, just to make things more obvious during testing, let's update the response message slightly.

Listing 8.3 `hello-world-spin/src/lib.rs`

```
use spin_sdk::http::{IntoResponse, Request, Response};
use spin_sdk::http_component;

#[http_component]
fn handle_hello_world_spin(req: Request) -> anyhow::Result<impl
➥ IntoResponse> {
println!("Handling request to {:?}", req.header("spin-full-url"));
Ok(Response::builder()
.status(200)
.header("content-type", "text/plain")
.body("Hello World from Spin in Kubernetes!")
.build())
}
```

We've updated the response body to indicate that the app is running inside Kubernetes.

Now, to apply our changes, from the root of the `chapter08/hello-world-spin/` folder, go ahead and rebuild the app:

```
spin build
```

> **IMPORTANT** Spin requires Rust 1.85.0 or later because some of its dependencies use Rust edition 2024. If you've been following along with Rust 1.84.0 (as recommended earlier in the book), you'll need to upgrade for this section. Install Rust 1.85.0 and its required components with `rustup install 1.85.0`, `rustup default 1.85.0`. You can verify the change with `rustc --version`.

With our app built, the next step is to publish it to a registry so that Kubernetes can pull and run it.

> **TIP** To push to a registry, you need to be authenticated. If you followed chapter 7, you should already be logged in to the GitHub Container Registry (GHCR).

Spin provides a simple command to push applications to a registry:

```
spin registry push ghcr.io/<your GH username>/serverside-wasm-book-
➥code/hello-world-spin:latest
```

This command uploads the app as an OCI image, similar to what we did with `wkg` before. Once the image is published, we're ready to generate the Kubernetes manifest for it.

> **IMPORTANT** Pushed packages are private by default. You'll need to change the package's visibility settings on GitHub to public for the following steps to work.

That's where the `kube` plugin comes in. We can use it to scaffold a `SpinApp` manifest that references the image we just pushed:

```
spin kube scaffold --from ghcr.io/<your GH username>/
➥serverside-wasm-book-code/hello-world-spin:latest
```

> **NOTE** If you'd rather skip building and pushing your own image, you can use mine instead: https://mng.bz/eB9q.

This generates a manifest like the one shown in the following listing, which defines a `SpinApp` resource pointing to the image we just pushed and tells the operator to use the `containerd-shim-spin` executor and run two replicas.

Listing 8.4 SpinApp manifest (scaffolded output)

```
apiVersion: core.spinkube.dev/v1alpha1
kind: SpinApp
metadata:
  name: hello-world-spin
spec:
  image: "ghcr.io/danbugs/serverside-wasm-book-code/hello-world-spin:latest"
  executor: containerd-shim-spin
  replicas: 2
```

Now that we have the manifest, we can deploy it to our cluster by piping the scaffolded output directly into `kubectl`:

```
spin kube scaffold --from ghcr.io/<your GH username>/
➥serverside-wasm-book-code/hello-world-spin:latest | kubectl create -f -
```

And that's it—you've just deployed your first Spin app to Kubernetes!

To check that it worked, run

```
kubectl get spinapps
```

You should see something like

```
NAME              READY DESIRED EXECUTOR
hello-world-spin 2      2       containerd-shim-spin
```

This output confirms that both requested replicas are up and running.

Now let's access the app. Since we didn't expose it through a load balancer or ingress controller, we'll use `kubectl port-forward` to connect locally:

```
kubectl port-forward svc/hello-world-spin 8083:80
```

Then, in another terminal, send a request to the app:

```
curl localhost:8083/
```

You should see

```
Hello World from Spin in Kubernetes!
```

That response confirms that our Spin app is up, running, and reachable from outside the cluster. We've gone from source code to live service, all through Kubernetes and Spin.

We're just getting started. Next, we'll take a closer look at how to scale these apps and explore some of the other runtime options SpinKube gives us.

8.2.3 Scaling Wasm in Kubernetes with SpinKube

So far, we've focused on getting a basic Spin application up and running in Kubernetes. But one of Kubernetes' core strengths is its ability to scale applications automatically based on demand—just like that game server we talked about at the start of the chapter. In this section, we'll see how to bring that same dynamic scaling to a Spin app.

Kubernetes supports a feature called the Horizontal Pod Autoscaler (HPA). The HPA watches metrics like CPU and memory usage and adjusts the number of replicas of your app to match the load. If your app is under pressure and needs more resources, it scales up. When things quiet down, it scales back down—saving resources and improving responsiveness.

To try this out, we'll build a new Spin app that can simulate load. That way, we can see the autoscaler in action.

CREATING A NEW APP

To get started, navigate to your `chapter08/` folder and create a new Spin app:

```
spin new
```

Select the `http-js` template for this demo—or use a different language if you'd like.

> **NOTE** If you need a refresher on creating new Spin applications, refer to section 6.5.1.

Name your app `scaling-spin`. If you chose the same template, your project folder should contain a file at `src/index.js` with the contents shown in the following listing.

Listing 8.5 src/index.js (`http-js` template)

```
import { AutoRouter } from 'itty-router';

let router = AutoRouter();

router
.get("/", () => new Response("hello universe"))
.get("/hello/:name", ({ name }) => `Hello, ${name}!`);

addEventListener("fetch", (event) => {
event.respondWith(router.fetch(event.request));
});
```

This app already has a couple of basic routes, but we'll add one more to simulate some CPU activity and trigger scaling behavior.

GENERATING LOAD WITH JAVASCRIPT

To generate CPU load, let's add a simple recursive Fibonacci calculator. It's intentionally inefficient—which is exactly what we want. Each request to this endpoint will put the CPU to work, creating the kind of sustained pressure that the autoscaler is designed to react to.

Add the following route after the `/hello/:name` handler:

```
.get("/load", () => {
  function fib(n) {
    if (n < 2) return n;
    return fib(n - 1) + fib(n - 2);
  }
  const result = fib(40); // Adjust this value to control CPU intensity
  return new Response(`fib(40) = ${result}`);
})
```

Every time we hit `/load`, this route burns a noticeable amount of CPU, which gives the autoscaler something to monitor and act on. Once you've added it, your full file should look like the following listing.

Listing 8.6 src/index.js (with load generator)

```
import { AutoRouter } from 'itty-router';

let router = AutoRouter();

router
    .get("/", () => new Response("hello universe"))
    .get('/hello/:name', ({ name }) => `Hello, ${name}!`)
    .get("/load", () => {
        function fib(n) {
            if (n < 2) return n;
            return fib(n - 1) + fib(n - 2);
        }
        const result = fib(40);
        return new Response(`fib(40) = ${result}`);
    })

addEventListener('fetch', (event) => {
    event.respondWith(router.fetch(event.request));
});
```

This route calculates the 40th Fibonacci number using a deliberately inefficient recursive algorithm.

PUBLISHING TO A REGISTRY

Once that's in place, in the `scaling-spin/` folder, build your app and push it to a container registry just like we did earlier:

```
spin build
spin registry push ghcr.io/<your GH username>/
➥ serverside-wasm-book-code/scaling-spin:latest
```

NOTE If you prefer, you can use my image for all the commands that follow: https://mng.bz/eB9q.

SETTING UP INGRESS

Before we scaffold the app, we need a way to send traffic into the cluster. Rather than using port forwarding like before, we'll set up an Ingress controller. This gives us a stable external endpoint to hit with requests.

Apply the provided Ingress configuration:

```
kubectl apply -f https://raw.githubusercontent.com/danbugs/
➥ serverside-wasm-book-code/refs/heads/main/chapter08/scaling-
➥ spin/ingress.yaml
```

NOTE An Ingress lets you route HTTP traffic to your services based on path or hostname. Unlike port forwarding, which is great for local development, Ingress is closer to how things would be set up in a real deployment.

The Ingress manifest we're applying is shown in the following listing.

Listing 8.7 Ingress resource

```
apiVersion: networking.k8s.io/v1
kind: Ingress
metadata:
  name: nginx
  annotations:
    ingress.kubernetes.io/ssl-redirect: "false"
spec:
  rules:
  - http:
      paths:
      - path: /
        pathType: Prefix
        backend:
          service:
            name: scaling-spin
            port:
              number: 80
```

This configuration tells Kubernetes to forward all HTTP traffic coming to / to the `scaling-spin` service on port 80. We're using a simple path prefix here, so any route—like `/load`—will be routed correctly.

SCAFFOLDING THE APP WITH AUTOSCALING

Now we're ready to scaffold our app using the `kube` plugin, just like before—but this time, we'll enable autoscaling with the `--autoscaler` flag and add resource constraints so the HPA has something to work with.

Here's the command we'll use:

```
spin kube scaffold
➥ --from ghcr.io/<your GH username>/serverside-wasm-book-code/scaling-
➥ spin:latest
➥ --autoscaler hpa
➥ --cpu-limit 100m
➥ --memory-limit 128Mi
➥ --cpu-request 50m
➥ --memory-request 64Mi
➥ --replicas 1
➥ --max-replicas 10
```

This tells SpinKube to

- Enable the HPA (`--autoscaler hpa`)
- Start with 1 replica, scaling up to 10 if needed

- Set CPU/memory requests and limits to give the scheduler and HPA room to make decisions

NOTE You can also use `--autoscaler keda` instead of HPA. KEDA is another autoscaling option that supports more event-driven triggers, like queue length or Kafka lag—not just CPU or memory usage. It's a good fit when your workloads respond to external systems or asynchronous traffic patterns.

This command will generate a manifest like the one shown in listing 8.8, which defines both a `SpinApp` and a `HorizontalPodAutoscaler` resource. The autoscaler watches CPU usage and scales the app between 1 and 10 replicas based on a target utilization threshold (defaulting to 60% unless otherwise specified).

Listing 8.8 `scaling-spin.yaml`

```
apiVersion: core.spinkube.dev/v1alpha1
kind: SpinApp
metadata:
  name: scaling-spin
spec:
  image: "ghcr.io/danbugs/serverside-wasm-book-code/scaling-spin:latest"
  executor: containerd-shim-spin
  enableAutoscaling: true
  resources:
    limits:
      cpu: 100m
      memory: 128Mi
    requests:
      cpu: 50m
      memory: 64Mi
---
apiVersion: autoscaling/v2
kind: HorizontalPodAutoscaler
metadata:
  name: scaling-spin-autoscaler
spec:
  scaleTargetRef:
    apiVersion: apps/v1
    kind: Deployment
    name: scaling-spin
  minReplicas: 1
  maxReplicas: 10
  metrics:
  - type: Resource
    resource:
      name: cpu
      target:
        type: Utilization
        averageUtilization: 60
  - type: Resource
    resource:
      name: memory
```

```
      target:
        type: Utilization
        averageUtilization: 60
```

Deploying the autoscaled app

Let's apply the manifest from listing 8.8 to the cluster:

```
spin kube scaffold --from ghcr.io/<your GH username>/serverside-wasm-book-
➥ code/scaling-spin:latest --autoscaler hpa --cpu-limit 100m --memory-
➥ limit 128Mi --cpu-request 50m --memory-request 64Mi --replicas 1 --max-
➥ replicas 10 | kubectl create -f -
```

Once the manifest is applied, we can confirm that the HPA was created and is tracking our deployment by running

```
kubectl get hpa
```

You should see something like this:

```
NAME            REFERENCE       TARGETS             MINPODS MAXPODS REPLICAS AGE
scaling-spin-   Deployment/     4%/60%, 33%/60%     1       10      1        114s
autoscaler      scaling-spin
```

This output shows that the autoscaler is watching the `scaling-spin` deployment. It's currently running 1 replica, but will scale up to 10 if CPU or memory usage crosses the configured thresholds.

Generating traffic

To test our scaling setup, we'll hit the `/load` route repeatedly to put pressure on the app. In chapter 6 (see section 6.3), we installed `oha`, a lightweight HTTP benchmarking tool. Let's use it here:

```
oha -c 40 -z 3m -t 5s http://localhost:8081/load
```

This command runs 40 concurrent connections for 3 minutes. Any individual request that takes longer than 5 seconds will time out. It's a good way to simulate sustained traffic and give the autoscaler something to respond to.

Verifying autoscaling behavior

After you've run `oha` and generated some load, Kubernetes should have responded by scaling up the deployment. To confirm that scaling took place, you can inspect the deployment history with

```
kubectl describe deploy scaling-spin
```

Even after the traffic stops, Kubernetes keeps a record of the scaling events. Here's an example of what that might look like:

```
  Type           Status  Reason
  ----           ------  ------
  Progressing    True    NewReplicaSetAvailable
  Available      True    MinimumReplicasAvailable
OldReplicaSets:  <none>
NewReplicaSet:   scaling-spin-797fbdb76 (10/10 replicas created)
Events:
  Type    Reason             Age   From          Message
  ----    ------             ----  ----          -------
  Normal  ScalingReplicaSet  27m   deployment    Scaled up replica set scaling
                                   -controller   ➥-spin-797fbdb76 to 1
  Normal  ScalingReplicaSet  18m   deployment    Scaled up replica set scaling
                                   -controller   ➥-spin-797fbdb76 to 2 from 1
  Normal  ScalingReplicaSet  17m   deployment    Scaled up replica set scaling
                                   -controller   ➥-spin-797fbdb76 to 4 from 2
  Normal  ScalingReplicaSet  17m   deployment    Scaled up replica set scaling
                                   -controller   ➥-spin-797fbdb76 to 8 from 4
  Normal  ScalingReplicaSet  17m   deployment    Scaled up replica set scaling
                                   -controller   ➥-spin-797fbdb76 to 10 from 8
```

This output confirms that HPA responded to the increased CPU load by scaling the number of replicas in stages—eventually reaching the maximum of 10.

And there we have it: a fully deployed, autoscaling Spin app on Kubernetes! We simulated traffic, watched the system respond, and saw the benefits of combining Wasm's efficiency with Kubernetes' operational tooling.

> **IMPORTANT** Now that you've completed the Spin example, you should revert to Rust 1.84.0 to maintain consistency with the rest of the book. Run `rustup default 1.84.0`. You can verify the change with `rustc --version`.

Next, we'll look at another approach to Wasm on Kubernetes with wasmCloud.

8.3 Running Wasm in Kubernetes with wasmCloud

Just like SpinKube, wasmCloud can run WebAssembly workloads in Kubernetes. And at first glance, the setup looks pretty familiar: install a few CRDs, apply some manifests, and let the operator manage your workloads. But under the hood, wasmCloud's model is a bit different.

The biggest difference, as we briefly saw in section 7.5, is that wasmCloud doesn't rely on a containerd-shim or, in this case, on a `RuntimeClass`. There's no equivalent to the containerd-shim-spin we used with Spin. Instead, wasmCloud deploys its full runtime environment inside the cluster. This includes the core wasmCloud host, a NATS message broker, and a component called `wadm` (i.e., wasmCloud application deployment manager).

Figure 8.3 illustrates this architectural difference. While SpinKube extends the container runtime layer to run Wasm directly in pods, wasmCloud takes a platform approach—deploying its complete application runtime as services within Kubernetes, then managing Wasm workloads through that platform layer.

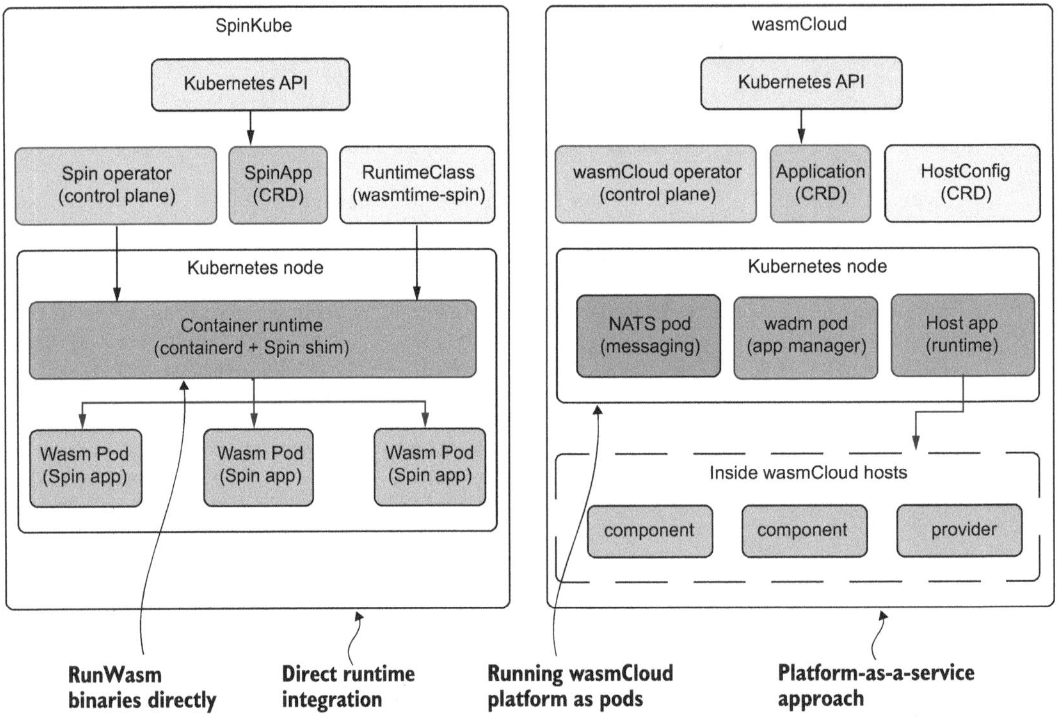

Figure 8.3 Architectural comparison of SpinKube and wasmCloud in Kubernetes. SpinKube (left) extends the container runtime with a Wasm shim to run Spin applications directly as pods. wasmCloud (right) deploys its platform components (NATS, `wadm`, and hosts) as regular Kubernetes pods, then orchestrates Wasm workloads within those hosts. Both approaches use CRDs and operators but integrate at different layers of the stack.

Let's see how that model plays out in practice.

8.3.1 Preparing the cluster for wasmCloud

To keep things simple, we'll reuse the same Kubernetes cluster we used earlier for Spin. There's no need to tear anything down—wasmCloud can be layered on top without conflict.

We'll install the wasmCloud platform using its official Helm chart, which includes all required services and configuration. It bundles together NATS, `wadm`, and the wasmCloud operator.

```
helm upgrade --install
➥wasmcloud-platform
➥--values https://raw.githubusercontent.com/wasmCloud
➥wasmcloud/main/charts/wasmcloud-platform/values.yaml
➥oci://ghcr.io/wasmcloud/charts/wasmcloud-platform:0.1.2
➥--dependency-update
```

To ensure everything's up and running before we continue, let's wait for the installed items to become available:

```
kubectl rollout status deploy,sts -l app.kubernetes.io/name=nats
kubectl wait --for=condition=available --timeout=600s deploy -l
➥ app.kubernetes.io/name=wadm
kubectl wait --for=condition=available --timeout=600s deploy -l
➥ app.kubernetes.io/name=wasmcloud-operator
```

Once ready, we can start using the wasmCloud operator to manage two key CRDs:

- `WasmCloudHostConfig` defines a host—a running instance of the wasmCloud runtime, just like the ones we'd create with `wash up`. Think of it like a replacement for Spin's `SpinAppExecutor`: it's what actually runs your app.
- `Application` represents a wasmCloud app. Remember those `wadm.yaml` files we've written in previous chapters? They are application CRs!

So, aside from creating hosts with `WasmCloudHostConfig`, deploying wasmCloud apps to Kubernetes is as simple as reusing the application specs we already built!

8.3.2 Running a Wasm app in Kubernetes with wasmCloud

Let's put it all together by deploying a simple wasmCloud app into our Kubernetes cluster.

Start by creating a new directory at `chapter08/hello-world-wasmcloud/`. Inside that folder, create a file named `wasmcloud-host.yaml` and add the contents from the following listing.

Listing 8.9 `WasmCloudHostConfig` CR

```
apiVersion: k8s.wasmcloud.dev/v1alpha1
kind: WasmCloudHostConfig
metadata:
  name: wasmcloud-host
spec:
  lattice: default
  version: "1.4.1"
```

This sets up a host named `wasmcloud-host`. This will be the actual process running your Wasm components—similar to how Spin's executor managed application pods.

Apply the host resource to your cluster from the `hello-world-wasmcloud/` folder:

```
kubectl apply -f wasmcloud-host.yaml
```

You can verify that it's active using

```
kubectl get wasmcloudhostconfig
```

You should see

```
NAME           APP COUNT
wasmcloud-host 0
```

At this point, your host is running, but it's not doing anything yet. To interact with it more directly, let's port forward the cluster's NATS port:

```
kubectl port-forward nats-0 4222
```

With that open, from another terminal, you can now use the full suite of `wash` commands—for example, with

```
wash get inventory
```

you'll get output listing the running host and its information:

```
Host ID              Friendly name
NBH2MFW...           cool-glade-4654

Host labels
hostcore.arch        x86_64
hostcore.os          linux
hostcore.osfamily    unix
kubernetes           true
...
```

NOTE For wash installation instructions, see chapter 6, section 6.1.

Now that we have our host ready, let's deploy the actual application.

We'll reuse the same app we created in chapter 6. From inside `chapter06/hello-world-wasmcloud`, assuming you've previously run `wash build` there, push your Wasm component to a registry:

```
wash push ghcr.io/<your GH username>/serverside-wasm-book-code/
➥hello-world-wasmcloud:v1 ./build/http_hello_world_s.wasm
```

This is similar to how we pushed Spin applications—just using the `wash` tool instead of `spin registry`.

NOTE Don't want to push your own image? Feel free to use mine: ghcr.io/danbugs/serverside-wasm-book-code/hello-world-wasmcloud:v1. If you decide to use your own registry, note that pushed packages are private by default. You'll need to change the package's visibility settings on GitHub to public for the following steps to work.

Next, copy the `wadm.yaml` file from your chapter 6 example into the `chapter08/hello-world-wasmcloud/` directory. There, we'll make a few changes:

1. Update the image path for the HTTP component to point to your registry.
2. Remove the custom `spreadscaler` setup. We originally used that to simulate multiple hosts for fault tolerance. Now that we have real Kubernetes replicas, we can rely on Kubernetes for scheduling and resiliency.
3. Change the HTTP server's address to `0.0.0.0:8080`. When running inside Kubernetes, using `127.0.0.1` can cause network errors because it won't bind to the container's external interface.

NOTE Want to see how Kubernetes handles fault tolerance? After deploying the app, run `wash get inventory`, then shut down one of the hosts with `wash down --host-id <id>`. You'll see all components migrate to the remaining host, with zero downtime—and Kubernetes will restart the failed pod automatically.

The final application file should look like the following listing.

Listing 8.10 wasmCloud application spec

```
apiVersion: core.oam.dev/v1beta1
kind: Application
metadata:
  name: rust-hello-world
  annotations:
    description: 'HTTP hello world demo in Rust, using the WebAssembly
    ➥Component Model and WebAssembly Interfaces Types (WIT)'
spec:
  components:
    - name: http-component
      type: component
      properties:
        image: ghcr.io/danbugs/serverside-wasm-book-code/
        ➥hello-world-wasmcloud:v1
      traits:
        - type: spreadscaler
          properties:
            instances: 10
        - type: link
          properties:
            namespace: wasi
            package: keyvalue
            interfaces: [store, atomics]
            target:
              name: kvnats
              config:
                - name: wasi-keyvalue-config
                  properties:
                    bucket: default
                    enable_bucket_auto_create: 'true'

    - name: httpserver
      type: capability
      properties:
```

Updates to use our image from the registry

Removes custom spreadscaler setup

```
        image: ghcr.io/wasmcloud/http-server:0.23.2
      traits:
        - type: link
          properties:
            target: http-component
            namespace: wasi
            package: http
            interfaces: [incoming-handler]
            source_config:
              - name: default-http
                properties:
                  address: 0.0.0.0:8080

    - name: kvnats
      type: capability
      properties:
        image: ghcr.io/wasmcloud/keyvalue-nats:0.3.1
```

Changes address as required for network access in Kubernetes

NOTE While editing the file, feel free to clean up unused annotations.

Back in the `chapter08/hello-world-wasmcloud/` folder, apply the app:

```
kubectl apply -f wadm.yaml
```

You can verify deployment with

```
kubectl get app
```

NOTE The `app` resource type isn't a built-in Kubernetes resource—it's specific to wasmCloud. We can use `kubectl get app` here because we applied wasmCloud's application CRD earlier. This CRD defines what a wasmCloud application looks like to Kubernetes, allowing us to manage Wasm applications using familiar `kubectl` commands.

This should return something like

```
APPLICATION        DEPLOYED VERSION      STATUS
rust-hello-world   01JVPDW…              Deployed
```

Or use `wash` for a more detailed view:

```
wash app status rust-hello-world
```

You should see output similar to the following:

```
rust-hello-world@ - Deployed
Name                                        Kind           Status
http_component                              SpreadScaler   Deployed
http_component -(wasi:keyvalue)-> kvnats    LinkScaler     Deployed
```

```
httpserver -(wasi:http)-> http_component    LinkScaler     Deployed
httpserver                                  SpreadScaler   Deployed
kvnats                                      SpreadScaler   Deployed
```

This breakdown shows which parts of the application were deployed, how they're connected, and whether everything came up successfully—great for debugging or just getting an overview. If something isn't working, try running `kubectl describe app rust-hello-world` to check its metadata and events.

Finally, to hit the app from outside the cluster, port forward the `wasmcloud-host` deployment:

```
kubectl port-forward deployment/wasmcloud-host 8080
```

Then, in another terminal window, try it out:

```
curl http://localhost:8080
```

And you should get

```
Hello! I was called 1 times
```

That's it—we've just run a full wasmCloud application in Kubernetes.

We reused the app from chapter 6, reused the deployment spec from earlier chapters, and deployed the wasmCloud host directly into our existing cluster. It's a different model than SpinKube, but it plays nicely with Kubernetes all the same—just from a slightly different angle.

The key difference comes down to architecture and tooling. SpinKube runs each Wasm binary in its own pod, treating Wasm workloads as first-class Kubernetes citizens. This means you can use `kubectl` for everything—from deployment to debugging to monitoring. wasmCloud takes a platform approach, where components run inside wasmCloud hosts, and you primarily interact through `wash` commands and `wadm` manifests.

This affects your operational workflow. With SpinKube, a failing Wasm workload looks like any other failing pod—you debug it with standard Kubernetes tools. With wasmCloud, you use commands like `wash app status` and work within the wasmCloud ecosystem to manage your applications.

Ultimately, the choice between SpinKube and wasmCloud on Kubernetes mirrors the decision we explored in chapter 6 (section 6.5.2). The tradeoffs between Spin's simplicity and wasmCloud's flexibility remain the same—Kubernetes just becomes another deployment target. If you chose Spin for its straightforward HTTP-focused approach, SpinKube extends that simplicity to Kubernetes. If you chose wasmCloud for its component model and provider ecosystem, those same benefits carry over when running on Kubernetes.

8.4 Running the SmartCMS example on Kubernetes

The time has come to take our SmartCMS application from earlier chapters and get it running on Kubernetes. The good news is we've already seen almost every piece we need. The process for deploying SmartCMS is very similar to what we did with the `hello-world-wasmcloud` app—just with a bit more wiring.

Here's the general plan:

1. Push the SmartCMS app to a registry so our cluster can pull it.
2. Modify the existing `wadm.yaml` to work with Kubernetes.
3. Deploy Ollama, the external large language model (LLM) backend we used in chapter 6.

Once that's in place, we'll fire it all up and run the app from a browser—just like we did before, but this time fully managed by Kubernetes.

8.4.1 Preparing the SmartCMS image and manifest

Start by pushing the SmartCMS component to a registry so that it can be accessed from within our cluster.

From inside the `chapter06/smart-cms/` folder, run

```
wash push ghcr.io/<your-GH-username>/serverside-wasm-book-code/
➥ smart-cms:v1 ./build/smart_cms_s.wasm
```

NOTE If you'd rather skip pushing your own image, you can use mine: https://mng.bz/Owqa.

Next, in your `chapter08/` directory, create a new folder called `smart-cms/`. Copy over the `index.html` and `wadm.yaml` files from `chapter06/smart-cms/` into this new directory.

Now we'll update the `wadm.yaml` manifest to reflect our Kubernetes setup. We need to make several key adjustments to adapt this app for Kubernetes:

- *Replace local references with registry images*—The local component reference needs to be replaced with the registry image we just pushed so Kubernetes can pull it at run time.
- *Remove local-only configurations*—The manual zone spread trait from our local setup is no longer needed; Kubernetes handles scheduling and fault tolerance for us.
- *Update networking for containers*—The HTTP server must bind to `0.0.0.0` instead of `127.0.0.1` to be accessible from outside the container.
- *Configure the Ollama provider*—Add a host field pointing to the Ollama Kubernetes service (not localhost, which would refer to the container itself).
- *Use prebuilt providers*—Replace the local Ollama provider build with a prebuilt version from a registry.

The following listing shows the updated manifest with these changes applied.

Listing 8.11 Updated SmartCMS application for Kubernetes

```
apiVersion: core.oam.dev/v1beta1
kind: Application
metadata:
  name: smart-cms
  annotations:
    description: "A smart CMS!"
spec:
  components:
    - name: http-component
      type: component
      properties:
        image: ghcr.io/danbugs/serverside-
➥ wasm-book-code/smart-cms:v1
      traits:
        - type: spreadscaler
          properties:
            instances: 100
        - type: link
          properties:
            namespace: wasi
            package: keyvalue
            interfaces: [store, atomics]
            target:
              name: kvnats
              config:
                - name: wasi-keyvalue-config
                  properties:
                    bucket: default
                    enable_bucket_auto_create: 'true'
        - type: link
          properties:
            target: ollama
            namespace: thomastaylor312
            package: ollama
            interfaces: [generate]
            target_config:
              - name: ollama-conf
                properties:
                  model_name: gurubot/tinystories-656k-q8
                  host: 'http://ollama:11434'
    - name: httpserver
      type: capability
      properties:
        image: ghcr.io/wasmcloud/http-server:0.23.2
      traits:
        - type: link
          properties:
            target: http-component
            namespace: wasi
            package: http
            interfaces: [incoming-handler]
```

Changes from local Wasm to registry image

Removes the local-only zone spread setup

Adds a host field for the Ollama provider

```
          source_config:
            - name: default-http
              properties:
                address: 0.0.0.0:8000          ← Changes 127.0.0.1 to 0.0.0.0 to
                                                  enable container networking
    - name: kvnats
      type: capability
      properties:
        image: ghcr.io/wasmcloud/keyvalue-nats:0.3.1

    - name: ollama
      type: capability
      properties:
        image: ghcr.io/danbugs/serverside-
          ➥ wasm-book-code/ollama-provider:v1      ← Updates provider to
                                                     use a public image
```

WARNING At the time of writing, the provider image used here only supports `x86_64-linux`. If you're running on a system with a different architecture—like an ARM-based Mac—this example likely won't work out of the box. You can check which architectures are currently supported by running `wash par inspect ghcr.io/danbugs/serverside-wasm-book-code/ollama-provider:v1`. If you're interested in compiling the provider yourself for a different architecture, you can see the changes I made to support Kubernetes (i.e., vendoring OpenSSL, compiling to a MUSL target) here: https://github.com/danbugs/ollama-provider/pull/1. Just like regular Wasm components, providers can be pushed to registries with `wash push`.

8.4.2 Preparing the Ollama dependency

To fulfill requests from the Ollama provider, we'll also need the Ollama service itself running in our cluster. Create a file named `ollama.yaml` in the same `chapter08/smart-cms/` folder, and populate it with the contents shown in the following listing.

Listing 8.12 Ollama deployment and service

```
apiVersion: apps/v1
kind: Deployment
metadata:
  name: ollama
  namespace: default
spec:
  replicas: 1
  selector:
    matchLabels:
      app: ollama
  template:
    metadata:
      labels:
        app: ollama
    spec:
```

```
      containers:
        - name: ollama
          image: ollama/ollama:latest
          ports:
            - containerPort: 11434
          env:
            - name: PRELOAD_MODELS
              value: "gurubot/tinystories-656k-q8"
            - name: OLLAMA_KEEP_ALIVE
              value: "12h"
          volumeMounts:
            - name: ollama-storage
              mountPath: /root/.ollama
          lifecycle:
            postStart:
              exec:
                command: ["/bin/sh", "-c", "for model in
                  $PRELOAD_MODELS; do ollama run $model \"\"; done"]
      volumes:
        - name: ollama-storage
          emptyDir: {}
---
apiVersion: v1
kind: Service
metadata:
  name: ollama
  namespace: default
spec:
  selector:
    app: ollama
  ports:
    - port: 11434
      targetPort: 11434
      protocol: TCP
```

Annotations: Preloads the TinyStories model (PRELOAD_MODELS); Service named "ollama" to match our app spec (name: ollama); Exposes port 11434 to match our app spec (targetPort: 11434).

This setup deploys a single Ollama container running the official image. It preloads the model we need, keeps it warm for reuse, and serves requests via HTTP. The service ensures it's accessible from other parts of our Kubernetes cluster—like the provider component from the SmartCMS app.

From inside the `chapter08/smart-cms/` folder, apply it to your cluster with

```
kubectl apply -f ollama.yaml
kubectl rollout status deployment/ollama --timeout=120s
```

8.4.3 Running the app

With everything in place, we're ready to deploy the SmartCMS app.

From inside the `chapter08/smart-cms/` folder, run

```
kubectl apply -f wadm.yaml
```

Then, in a separate terminal, if you haven't already, forward the NATS port:

```
kubectl port-forward nats-0 4222
```

This lets us use `wash` to inspect app status:

```
wash app status smart-cms
```

You should see all components listed with a status of "Deployed." If anything shows "Reconciling," give it a moment—things are still coming online:

```
smart-cms@ - Deployed

Name                               Kind            Status
http_component                     SpreadScaler    Deployed
http_component -(wasi:keyvalue)-> kvnats           LinkScaler      Deployed
http_component -(ollama)-> ollama                  LinkScaler      Deployed
httpserver -(wasi:http)-> http_component           LinkScaler      Deployed
httpserver                         SpreadScaler    Deployed
kvnats                             SpreadScaler    Deployed
ollama                             SpreadScaler    Deployed
```

Once everything looks good, `port-forward` the app so you can use it locally:

```
kubectl port-forward deployment/wasmcloud-host 8000
```

Now just open the `index.html` file in your browser. You should be able to create stories, retrieve them, and even generate new ones using the LLM backend—just like you did in chapter 6.

> **NOTE** If something goes wrong, your first stop should be the logs: `kubectl logs -l app.kubernetes.io/instance=wasmcloud-host -c wasmcloud-host`.

That's it—you just deployed your SmartCMS app, complete with LLM inference, onto a Kubernetes cluster using wasmCloud.

Take a moment to reflect on how far we've come. Back in chapter 2, we were manually working with Wasm memory just to use a string. In chapter 3, we had to handcraft hosts to even run a Wasm component. Now we're orchestrating an entire multiservice Wasm application—complete with autoscaling, component linking, and model-backed generation—on a distributed system!

Summary

- Wasm can reuse mature, battle-tested components of the container ecosystem, like Kubernetes. This helps solve problems where there's no good Wasm-native solution yet.
- CRDs and operators enable Kubernetes to manage noncontainer workloads, including Wasm apps, using native patterns for orchestration and scaling.

- SpinKube integrates Spin with Kubernetes, providing CRDs and an operator that understands how to deploy, scale, and manage Spin applications using Kubernetes-native primitives.
- The Spin `kube` plugin streamlines deployment by scaffolding Kubernetes manifests for Spin applications, making it easy to move from local dev to production.
- Kubernetes' HPA can be integrated with Spin apps, allowing replicas to scale dynamically based on CPU and memory load.
- Unlike SpinKube, wasmCloud does not rely on a specialized container runtime; instead, it deploys its full host environment inside the cluster and manages apps through NATS and `wadm`.

9 The future of Wasm

This chapter covers

- Applying Wasm to confidential computing scenarios
- Securing Model Context Protocol AI agents with Wasm
- Running Wasm at the edge for low-latency compute
- WASI 0.3 async updates on the path to WASI 1.0

In the previous chapter, we walked through getting our Wasm applications running inside a Kubernetes cluster. Pair that lesson with everything else you've learned—starting from simple Wasm modules and custom hosts and stretching to Wasm components and generic hosts like wasmCloud—and you now have all the pieces you need to put a Wasm app into production while talking to the services already living in your cluster and the wider Kubernetes ecosystem.

This chapter wraps up our journey with SmartCMS and pulls back the curtain on new frontiers: confidential computing, AI/machine learning (ML), and edge compute. We'll also take a look at the upcoming WASI 0.3 release and how it lays the groundwork for a stable, long-term WASI 1.0.

9.1 SmartCMS closing remarks

From a sketch on paper to a production-ready service, SmartCMS grew chapter by chapter. We began in chapter 2 by drafting a minimal WebAssembly Interface Types (WIT) contract that defined our core content API. Chapter 3 turned that contract into code with a JS guest served by a custom Rust host. Chapter 4 added intelligence with an ML guest that, through composition, ran alongside the original component. Chapter 5 swapped our bespoke ML interface for the `wasi:nn` spec, giving the model a portable runtime. Chapter 6 handed the application to wasmCloud for more generic development—no custom hosts required—and chapter 8 wrapped up the journey by containerizing the service and launching it inside Kubernetes. The result is the architecture shown in figure 9.1.

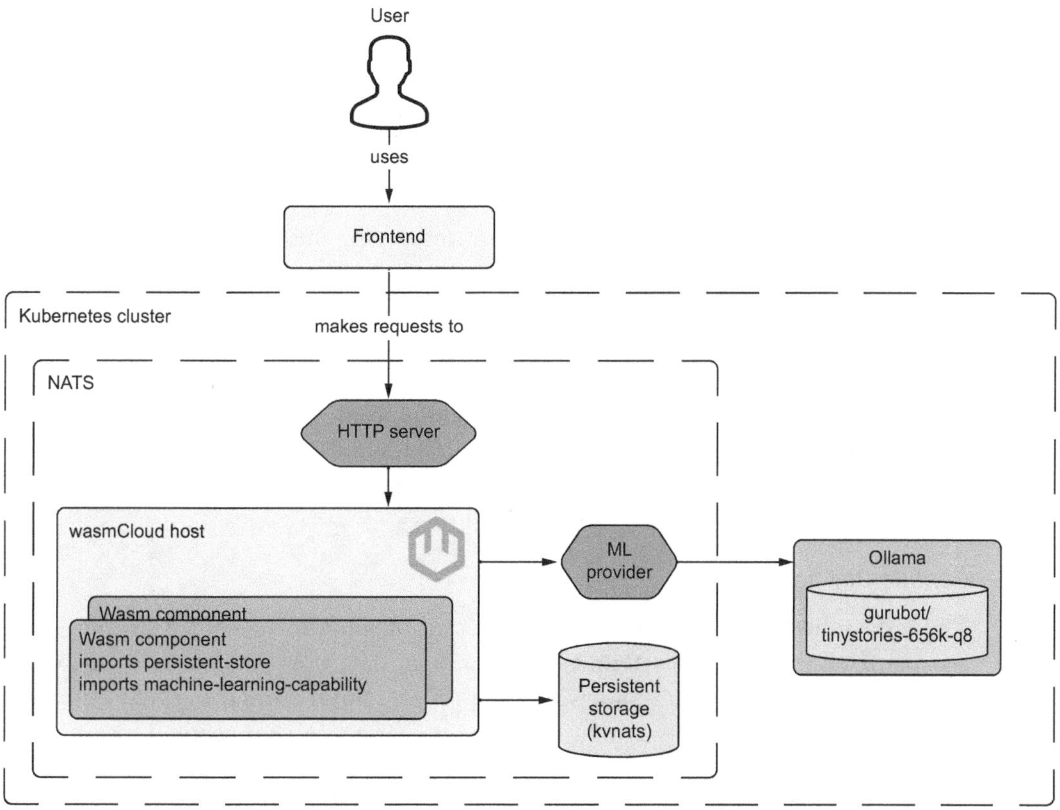

Figure 9.1 Final architecture of SmartCMS deployed in Kubernetes. The frontend interacts with a wasmCloud host via an HTTP server. Inside the host, Wasm components use capability providers for storage and ML. The ML provider delegates inference to Ollama, while persistent storage is handled by `kvnats`.

If you'd like to take SmartCMS a step further, you've got a few options. One path is adding new features by building your own provider or tapping into the many premade ones listed here: https://mng.bz/YZya. For example, you could experiment with the built-in logging provider or try swapping out the key-value store—maybe use Redis instead of NATS!

> **TIP** To get started building your own provider, run `wash new provider <provider-name>`. You can also scaffold a provider from a specific template using something like `wash new provider my-provider --template-name custom-template-go`. Check out other available template names here: https://mng.bz/GwqJ.

Another way to level up SmartCMS is by integrating it more deeply with the broader Kubernetes ecosystem. For example, you could add observability using tools like Prometheus for metrics, Grafana for dashboards, or Jaeger for distributed tracing. You might also bring in Argo CD to manage deployments through GitOps workflows or use Gatekeeper to enforce cluster policies. These additions can help bring SmartCMS closer to a production-grade deployment, giving you greater visibility, control, and automation.

Speaking of production—if you're ready to get your SmartCMS into other people's hands, head over to appendix B. There we'll walk through deploying SmartCMS to the Azure Kubernetes Service. Or, if you just want to see it in action, check out my own deployment at https://sswasm.com!

With that, thanks for joining the ride in developing and deploying SmartCMS. I hope it gave you a practical, real-life lens on each chapter's topics. Next up, let's look at some future areas where I see Wasm having an effect.

9.2 What's next for Wasm?

There are plenty of areas that stand to benefit from Wasm's growth beyond the browser—whether it's for its language agnosticism, sandboxed execution, or portability. In this section, we'll highlight a few of these spaces that either didn't come up earlier in the book or deserve a bit more spotlight.

9.2.1 Confidential computing

These days, just about everyone uses the cloud in some form—and with that shift, a massive amount of personal and organizational data now lives on someone else's infrastructure. But it wasn't always that way. When cloud computing first emerged, the idea of storing sensitive data on someone else's servers seemed risky—even unacceptable.

Now that cloud adoption is nearly universal, securing that data—whether it's code or content—is more critical than ever. Figure 9.2 introduces the data security triad, which highlights the three key states where data is vulnerable to compromise: at rest, in transit, and in use.

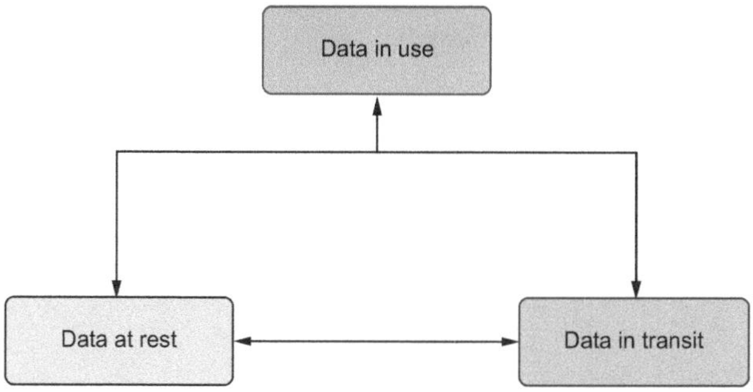

Figure 9.2 The three states of data: at rest, in transit, and in use. Each state represents a potential point of vulnerability where data can be exposed or compromised if not properly protected.

Some parts of the triad are fairly well understood and protected today. *Data in transit*—like information moving between your browser and a server—can be encrypted using protocols like TLS, keeping it safe from prying eyes during transmission. *Data at rest*—stored on disk or in the cloud—can be secured using encrypted filesystems or managed key storage systems offered by most cloud providers.

But *data in use* is a tougher nut to crack. This is data that's actively being processed in memory—when encryption can't protect it and traditional defenses fall short. That's where *confidential computing* comes in: it's a growing area focused on keeping data secure even while it's being used.

Think about it this way: right now, when a computer processes data, it typically pulls it into memory (RAM) in clear text. At that point, the data could be read or copied by anyone who can access and inspect RAM directly—like a malicious actor or even the cloud provider itself.

Confidential computing tackles this problem through something called a *trusted execution environment* (TEE), or *enclave*. These enclaves use special CPU extensions to encrypt memory access on the fly, so even while the data is in use, it's still protected from threats outside the enclave.

> **NOTE** These CPU extensions for confidential computing are already supported by most major processor vendors. For example, Intel supports this through SGX (Software Guard Extensions), AMD through SEV (Secure Encrypted Virtualization), ARM provides TrustZone and the newer Confidential Compute Architecture (CCA), and RISC-V has support via Keystone. These features are increasingly common in modern cloud environments.

One powerful use case for confidential computing is *secure multiparty collaboration*. Imagine you work at an institution developing an AI model and you want to train it on sensitive hospital patient data. Your model is proprietary, so handing it over to the hospital isn't an option. On the flip side, the hospital can't share its patient records with you due to strict confidentiality regulations.

This is where a TEE can help. By running the model and the data together inside a secure enclave, neither party has to expose their sensitive assets. Figure 9.3 illustrates how this setup works.

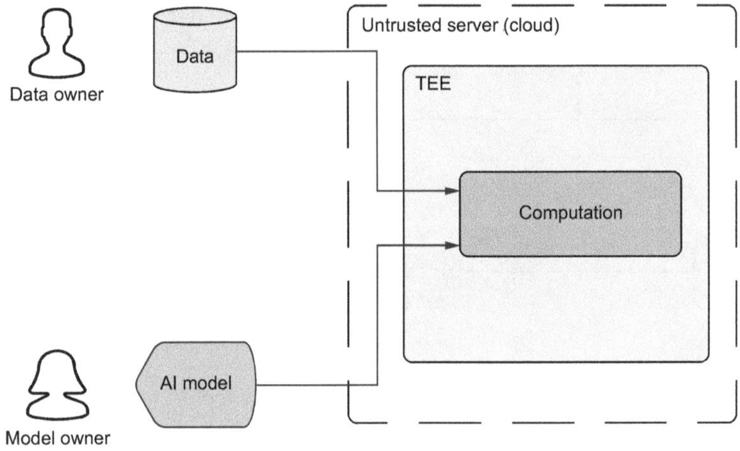

Figure 9.3 Secure multiparty computation using a TEE. Sensitive data and proprietary models are loaded into an enclave within an untrusted server. The computation runs securely inside the TEE, keeping both inputs confidential from the hosting environment.

An example of a system that enables this kind of secure enclave interaction is CoCoS.ai (https://cocos.ai/), an open source platform developed with partial support from the ELASTIC project—funded by the European Union's Horizon Europe Research and Innovation Program—and presented at WasmCon 2024.

With CoCoS.ai, collaborators define who the data providers and result consumers are up front. Then, approved data providers upload their data to the enclave, where computation—possibly supplied by a separate third party—is carried out securely. Once the task completes, only the authorized result consumers can access the output, closing the loop on a secure multiparty compute cycle.

So where does Wasm fit into all this? A good way to think about a TEE is like a stripped-down, bare-metal machine. By default, it has no built-in tooling or environment—just a minimal, secure shell. To run computations, we need to load everything ourselves.

We could drop in a full Linux kernel and userspace, but that introduces a lot of complexity and potential vulnerabilities. In security terms, this expands the *trusted computing base (TCB)*—the entirety of the code and systems that need to be trusted to keep data safe inside the enclave.

Wasm is a great fit here because it can run in small, purpose-built runtimes with far fewer moving parts. Instead of booting an OS, we can just drop in a Wasm module/component and a minimal runtime. This keeps the TCB tight and focused, which is exactly what we want in confidential computing scenarios.

But that's not all. The CPU extensions that power these enclaves—like Intel SGX and AMD SEV—are typically exposed through low-level C or C++ APIs, since they're designed to interact closely with hardware. That means if you're not working in those languages, you're pretty much out of luck when it comes to using those features directly.

This is another place where Wasm shines. Because it's language agnostic, you can write your application logic in a language you're comfortable with—Rust, Go, you name it—and compile it to Wasm. That Wasm binary can then run inside the enclave via a compatible runtime, letting you interact with confidential computing features without writing C code or dealing with the system-level APIs.

Finally, one more benefit Wasm brings to TEEs is multitenancy. Because Wasm runs in a sandboxed environment, it's possible to execute multiple tenants' code safely within the same enclave. This opens the door to shared, confidential compute environments where different parties can run their logic side by side—without risking data leakage or interference.

Overall, confidential computing is still an emerging field, but it's already showing real promise—especially when paired with technologies like Wasm. By combining hardware-enforced isolation with Wasm's lightweight, portable, and language-agnostic execution model, we get a practical foundation for building secure, privacy-respecting applications in sensitive environments. Whether it's collaborative AI, secure data processing, or sandboxed services in the cloud, this space is ripe for innovation—and Wasm is well positioned to play a central role.

9.2.2 AI and machine learning

Earlier in the book, we used `wasi:nn` to connect a Wasm component to an ML backend. But with AI moving as fast as it is, there's a lot more ground to cover. In this section, we'll take a closer look at two efforts that are shaping how AI and Wasm interact: `wasi-gfx` and the Model Context Protocol (MCP).

WASI-GFX

`wasi-gfx` is a WASI proposal that bundles several packages—`wasi:webgpu`, `wasi:frame-buffer`, `wasi:surface`, and `wasi:graphics-context`—into a unified graphics and compute interface. Its aim is to bring the same security and portability benefits of Wasm from the CPU world to the GPU.

The proposal targets several key goals: secure GPU compute, Wasm-based UI rendering, graphics in GPU-less environments, and AI use cases not covered by `wasi:nn`. Its sweet spot is in scenarios where you need low-level GPU access, want to work with unsupported `wasi:nn` backends, or are doing things like training and fine-tuning models directly.

To see it in action, check out the browser playground with example workloads here: https://wasi-gfx.github.io/playground/.

Model Context Protocol

One fast-growing area in AI is the rise of AI agents—autonomous or semiautonomous models that can plan, reason, and act to achieve specific goals. These agents aren't just enhanced chatbots; they're designed to interact with tools, access files, call APIs, and sometimes even perform actions on the host machine.

In November 2024, Anthropic introduced the MCP, a proposal aimed at standardizing how agents interface with their environments. Think of MCP as doing for agents what

REST did for web services: it defines a consistent model for accessing resources, tools, and data. In MCP, a server exposes a set of resources and tools, and an agent (the client) interacts with them according to a clear, structured context. This setup ensures that an agent knows exactly what it can access and how it should interact with its environment.

But as with any powerful abstraction, there's risk. If you give an agent access to a system without guardrails, things can go sideways—fast. A common example is *prompt injection*, where a malicious file or input manipulates the agent into performing actions it shouldn't, like deleting data or exfiltrating secrets.

Now imagine implementing the MCP server with Wasm. Because this server is responsible for exposing tools and resources to the agent, we can define those capabilities precisely using WIT. This lines up perfectly with the only-what-you-need security model from chapter 3—where each Wasm component is given access only to the specific interfaces it requires. On top of that, Wasm's sandboxed execution ensures that even if the agent misbehaves or is compromised, its interactions are limited to the tightly scoped capabilities exposed by the server. It's a strong foundation for building secure, predictable environments for intelligent agents—and one that's well worth keeping an eye on.

NOTE For an example of building MCP servers with Wasm components and WIT-defined capabilities, check out wassette: https://github.com/microsoft/wassette.

9.2.3 Compute at the edge

The *edge* is a layer of infrastructure that sits between end users and centralized cloud servers. It's made up of data centers distributed across many locations—often run by Content Delivery Networks (CDNs) like Fastly, Cloudflare, or Akamai—and it exists to reduce latency by bringing computation physically closer to users. In the context of web applications, these edge nodes are the "in-between" spots, usually positioned within or near ISPs.

To make this concrete, imagine you're running a blog. If it's a static site with just HTML files, serving it from the edge is straightforward—the CDN caches your files at hundreds of locations worldwide, so readers in Tokyo get your content from a nearby Tokyo server instead of your origin server in Virginia.

Traditionally, CDNs used this edge layer only to cache and serve static content like images, scripts, and HTML. But modern web experiences demand more than static files. People expect real-time updates, dynamic personalization, and interactive features that respond instantly. Consider adding a comment system to that blog: comments need to be fetched from a database, chronologically ordered, nested for replies, and filtered for spam. In the traditional model, every comment request would travel back to your centralized database, adding latency that slows down page loads.

This is where compute at the edge comes in—running actual application logic at these distributed CDN locations. Instead of just serving cached files, edge computing platforms now let you execute code right where the request arrives. For our blog example, you could run your entire comment system at the edge, processing and serving comments from the same location that delivers your blog posts. Your readers get both static and dynamic content from the nearest edge location, making the entire experience feel instantaneous.

While edge computing has many incarnations—from autonomous vehicles making split-second decisions locally to IoT sensors processing data before sending it upstream—web applications focus on a specific pattern. Traditional web applications receive requests at a CDN, do some lightweight processing (like blocking bots or malicious traffic), and then forward the request to a centralized server for the heavy lifting. But with edge compute, you can handle more of that logic directly at the CDN location, eliminating the roundtrip to your backend servers. This saves those precious milliseconds that make the difference between a sluggish and a snappy user experience.

But edge computing isn't a full replacement for your backend. Edge environments often have limits: no full database access, smaller memory footprints, and stricter execution times. So, you typically use them for specific slices of logic—not your whole app. You can see how this interaction plays out in figure 9.4.

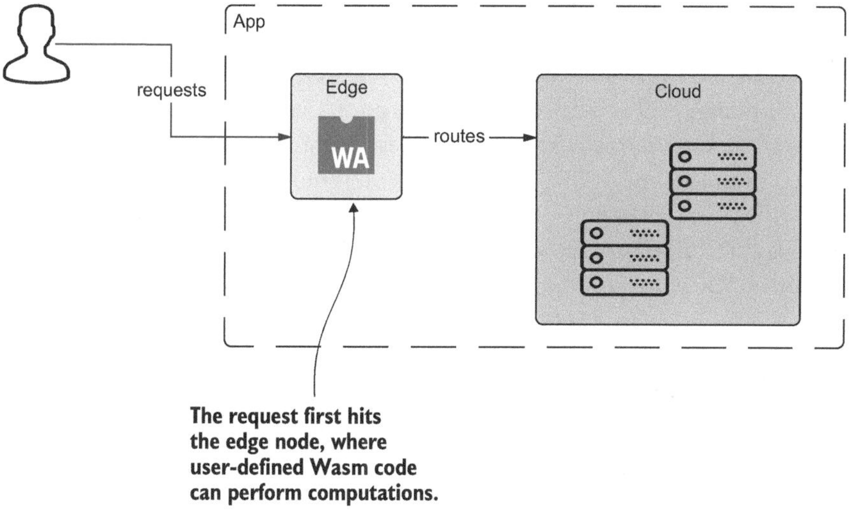

Figure 9.4 Request flow with edge compute. Incoming requests first hit the edge node, where user-defined Wasm code can perform logic before routing to the centralized cloud backend.

Wasm is a great fit for these environments. It offers a compact, secure way to ship multi-language workloads to constrained environments like edge nodes. Platforms like Fastly Compute compile your code to Wasm and then run it on edge nodes using runtimes like Wasmtime.

To understand the scale and purpose, consider a global e-commerce platform like an online retailer serving millions of customers across continents. Major CDN providers typically operate 100 to 300 edge locations worldwide—Cloudflare has about 330 cities, Fastly has about 430 strategic locations, and Akamai boasts over 4,000 locations. For our e-commerce platform, this means their code runs in all these places simultaneously.

Here's how edge computing helps their operations:

- *A/B testing*—When launching a new checkout flow, they can instantly route 10% of, say, Japanese users to the experimental version while keeping everyone else on the current flow.
- *Rate limiting*—During flash sales, malicious actors might try to buy up inventory with bots. Edge nodes can identify and block these patterns instantly, protecting inventory for real customers without overwhelming the central order processing system.
- *Geo personalization*—European visitors see prices in euros with VAT included, while US visitors see dollars with sales tax calculated by state—all computed at the edge based on the user's location.
- *Auth filtering*—Premium members get priority access during high-traffic events. The edge validates their membership tokens and routes them to dedicated back-end resources, while nonmembers might see a "please wait" queue.

The power isn't just in any individual feature—it's in how they compose. That same e-commerce platform can combine these capabilities: validate membership, apply regional pricing, enforce rate limits, and run experiments, all in milliseconds at the edge location nearest to each customer. This creates a responsive, personalized experience that would be impossible if every decision required a roundtrip to a central server.

In short, Wasm gives you a secure and portable way to run this custom logic across hundreds of locations worldwide—without needing to manage full servers at each point of presence. You write your logic once, then compile it to Wasm, and it runs identically whether it's serving customers in São Paulo, Stockholm, or Singapore.

9.3 What's next for WASI?

So far in the book, we've worked with WASI 0.1 and 0.2. These early versions helped define how components can interact with system-like interfaces in a structured, portable way. WASI 0.2, in particular, was the first version to adopt the component model, which we've leaned on throughout the SmartCMS example.

The next major step is WASI 0.3, which is currently in development and may land in late 2025. Its biggest contribution is native support for asynchronous operations. Unlike earlier versions that relied on manually modeling async behavior using state machines or resource juggling, WASI 0.3 brings asynchrony directly into the type system with built-in `future<T>` and `stream<T>` primitives. These types can appear in component function signatures, allowing async behavior to be expressed directly and naturally across languages.

The goal is to make asynchronous components interoperable across toolchains without needing glue code. A Rust component using `async/await` could be used from Python or C#, and the host runtime handles the async machinery behind the scenes. WASI's host supplies the runtime, while the guest interacts with it through a standard ABI. Under the hood, this is managed using *waitables*—handles that represent in-progress operations. A guest can block on a waitable or return a special code to tell the host to pause its task and resume it later, freeing up the host to run other work in the meantime.

This approach simplifies interface definitions. For example, the `wasi:http` interface in 0.2 needed over a dozen resource types to manually model async behavior. With native `future` and `stream` support, that interface can be redefined with just a few types and a single handler.

WASI 0.3 won't be a one-off release. The plan is to periodically release backward-compatible updates (0.3.1, 0.3.2, etc.) as new features are added. These updates are expected to include

- *Cancellation*—Support for canceling ongoing operations, integrated with language-native patterns like C#'s `CancellationToken` or JavaScript's `AbortSignal`.
- *Stream optimizations*—Adding support for common stream patterns like splicing, skipping, and caller-provided buffers to improve performance and reduce memory copies.
- *Threads*—First cooperative (nonpreemptive) threads to allow concurrency within a single OS thread—important for getting toolchains like `wasi-libc` working safely. Later, preemptive threading will be added via the *shared-everything-threads* proposal (https://mng.bz/z2pA) to enable parallelism across CPU cores.

These changes set the stage for WASI 1.0, which could arrive as early as 2026. That release would mark the start of long-term stability guarantees, but it's not just about maturity—it's about solidifying the foundations for building modern, high-performance, server-side Wasm applications.

9.4 Staying in the loop

Wasm is moving fast, and it can be tricky to keep up with all the progress—especially around the component model and WASI. If you want to follow the latest developments, the best place to start is the Bytecode Alliance blog: https://bytecodealliance.org/articles/. It covers major updates, proposals, and announcements from the team shaping much of the Wasm standards work.

For deeper technical discussions or proposal feedback, you can follow relevant GitHub topics in the Bytecode Alliance org (https://github.com/bytecodealliance) or even join in directly on the Bytecode Alliance's Zulip chat: https://bytecodealliance.zulipchat.com/. It's open to the public and a good space for asking questions or following active design threads.

If you're more into hands-on examples or walkthroughs, I occasionally post tutorials and updates on my YouTube channel (http://youtube.com/c/danlogs), where I focus on topics like Rust and Wasm in practice.

It's also worth keeping an eye on community conferences like WasmCon (https://events.linuxfoundation.org/wasmcon/) and Wasm I/O (https://wasm.io/). These events often feature demos of bleeding-edge tools, talks from folks building the standards, and real-world case studies that can help you stay grounded in how all this tech is being used.

Finally, thanks for coming with me on this journey. Whether you followed along chapter by chapter or dropped in to skim a few sections, I hope this book helped you understand what server-side Wasm is capable of—and maybe even inspired a few ideas of your own. There's a lot of exciting work ahead, and the ecosystem could use more folks building, experimenting, and asking good questions.

If you've got feedback on the book—typos, ideas, questions, or suggestions—you can drop a note in the book's live forum (https://livebook.manning.com/forum?product=chiarlone) or open an issue in the book's GitHub repository (https://github.com/danbugs/serverside-wasm-book-code). I'd love to hear what you think.

Summary

- Wasm in confidential computing enables secure, multiparty execution using TEEs—hardware-enforced secure enclaves that protect data even while it's being processed. Wasm's minimal runtime and language-agnostic nature make it ideal for these constrained environments, keeping the TCB small while enabling multiple tenants to run securely side by side.
- AI/ML use cases for Wasm are expanding beyond `wasi:nn`. The wasi-gfx proposal brings GPU compute capabilities for training and fine-tuning models, while the MCP—a standard for how AI agents interact with tools and resources—pairs naturally with Wasm's sandboxed execution to create secure environments for autonomous agents.
- Wasm fits naturally into edge compute environments, where its compact size and sandboxed security match the constraints of CDN-distributed execution across hundreds of global locations. Edge platforms like Fastly Compute compile your code to Wasm for use cases, including A/B testing, rate limiting, geo-personalization, and auth filtering—all running milliseconds away from users without managing full servers at each location.
- WASI 0.3 introduces native async support via built-in future<T> and stream<T> types, eliminating the need for complex state machines and resource juggling. This simplifies interface design, enables cross-language async interoperability, and sets the foundation for WASI 1.0's stability guarantees expected around 2026.

appendix A Required tools

You can use this appendix as a quick reference for installing all the tools used throughout the book.

A.1 Rust

To install Rust, see https://www.rust-lang.org/learn/get-started.

NOTE We use `rustc 1.84.0 (9fc6b4312 2025-01-07)`. If you already have Rust installed, you can install this specific version with `rustup install 1.84.0` and then set it as default with `rustup default 1.84.0`. For some Spin sections, we use Rust version 1.85.0. You can follow the same steps to install it and swap between different Rust versions as needed.

A.1.1 Target installation

Here are the Rust targets used in this book and how to install them:

- `wasm32-unknown-unknown`—`rustup target add wasm32-unknown-unknown`
- `wasm32-wasip1`—`rustup target add wasm32-wasip1`
- `wasm32-wasip2`—`rustup target add wasm32-wasip2`

A.1.2 Cargo installs

These are the Cargo-based tools we'll install as needed:

- *Cargo component*—`cargo install cargo-component@0.20.0 --locked`

- *Wasm tools*—`cargo install wasm-tools@1.227.1 --locked`
- *Wasmtime*—`cargo install wasmtime-cli@30.0.0 --locked`
- *WASI-Virt*—`cargo install wasi-virt --git https://github.com/bytecodealliance/WASI-Virt --rev b662e419 --locked`
- *WAC*—`cargo install --locked wac-cli@0.6.1`
- *Wasm Hex Dump*—`cargo install wasm_hex_dump@0.1.0 --locked`
- *Wash*—`cargo install --locked wash-cli` (installs the latest version)
- *Oha*—`cargo install oha@1.4.7 --locked`
- *Wkg*—`cargo install wkg@0.10.0 --locked`

A.2 Git LFS

To install Git LFS, see https://git-lfs.com/.

A.3 Docker

There are two ways you can install Docker:

- *Docker Engine*—Lightweight, CLI-focused: https://docs.docker.com/engine/install/
- *Docker Desktop*—Includes Docker Engine with a GUI: https://docs.docker.com/desktop/

NOTE The recommended version is Docker 28.0.0, build f9ced58. You can verify your version with `docker --version`.

A.4 JS toolchain

If you're on Linux, macOS, or Windows Subsystem for Linux, install nvm with

```
curl -o- https://raw.githubusercontent.com/nvm-sh/nvm/v0.40.2/install.sh | bash
```

Restart your terminal; then install Node version 22 (along with npm) by running

```
nvm install 22
```

If you're on Windows, download the installer from https://github.com/coreybutler/nvm-windows, and follow the same steps.

After setting up Node and npm, install JavaScript's Wasm toolchain with

- `jco`—`npm install -g @bytecodealliance/jco@1.10.2`
- `componentize-js`—`npm install -g @bytecodealliance/componentize-js@0.17.0`

A.5 Python toolchain

To install Python, check out https://mng.bz/KwqO. At the time of writing, the book uses Python version 3.12.3.

A.6 Spin

Install Spin from https://developer.fermyon.com/spin/v3/install.

NOTE We use `spin 3.2.0 (c9be6d8 2025-03-24)`. To stay consistent, use this version while following along.

To prepare for Kubernetes deployment, install the Spin plugin:

```
spin plugins update
spin plugins install kube
spin plugins list --installed
```

You should see output similar to this (versions may vary):

```
cloud 0.11.0 [installed]
kube 0.4.0 [installed]
```

A.7 Ollama setup

Install instructions are at https://ollama.com/.

Then pull the model used in the book with

```
ollama pull gurubot/tinystories-656k-q8
```

A.8 regctl

To install on Ubuntu using Snap, run

```
sudo snap install regclient
```

At the time of writing, this installs regctl version 0.8.0. For other operating systems, follow https://regclient.org/install.

A.9 container2wasm

Install with

```
wget https://github.com/container2wasm/container2wasm/releases/download/
v0.8.3/container2wasm-v0.8.3-linux-amd64.tar.gz
```

NOTE If you're on an arm64 Linux machine instead of amd64, make sure to download the arm64 release by replacing amd64 in the link with arm64. You can find all available versions at https://mng.bz/9yqr.

After downloading the release, extract the archive with

```
tar -xvf container2wasm-v0.8.3-linux-amd64.tar.gz
```

Next, move the extracted binaries to a directory in your PATH so they can be used system-wide:

```
sudo mv c2w c2w-net /usr/local/bin/
```

Ensure the binaries are executable by running

```
chmod +x /usr/local/bin/c2w /usr/local/bin/c2w-net
```

Now verify that the installation was successful by checking the version:

```
c2w --version
```

You should see output similar to the following:

```
c2w version v0.8.3
```

Finally, clean up by removing the downloaded archive:

```
rm container2wasm-v0.8.3-linux-amd64.tar.gz
```

A.10 Kubernetes setup

Start by installing `k3d`, a Docker-based local Kubernetes cluster tool. It's fast, lightweight, and great for development/testing.

We use version v5.8.3: https://k3d.io/v5.8.3/?h=installation#releases.

Next, install `kubectl` to interact with your cluster: https://kubernetes.io/docs/tasks/tools/.

We use

```
kubectl version --client
Client Version: v1.33.0
Kustomize Version: v5.6.0
```

Then install Helm by following https://helm.sh/docs/intro/install/.

We use

```
helm version
version.BuildInfo{Version:"v3.17.3",
GitCommit:"e4da49785aa6e6ee2b86efd5dd9e43400318262b",
GitTreeState:"clean", GoVersion:"go1.23.7"}
```

appendix B Deploying the SmartCMS to Azure Kubernetes Service

In this appendix, we'll walk through how to deploy the SmartCMS app to Azure Kubernetes Service (AKS).

B.1 Prerequisites

For this section, you'll need a few tools installed. Most are covered in appendix A. The only new one is the Azure CLI, which you can install by following the steps here: https://mng.bz/jZNe.

You'll also need an Azure account and an active subscription. If you don't already have one, you can create both by following this guide: https://mng.bz/WwQW.

Next, you'll need a Kubernetes cluster on Azure. To set it up, follow the instructions at https://mng.bz/8XqD. Follow the guide up to, but not including, the Deploy the Application step.

Once your cluster is up and running, grab the public IP assigned to it with

```
az network public-ip list --query "[?starts_with(resourceGroup, 'MC_') &&
➥ ipAddress!=null].{Name:name, ResourceGroup:resourceGroup, IP:ipAddress}"
➥ -o table
```

You'll get output that looks like

```
Name          ResourceGroup             IP
------------  ------------------------  -----------
715a31e6-...  MC_sswasm_sswasm_westus2  4.155.90.17
```

Next, assign a DNS name to your cluster's public IP:

```
az network public-ip update
➥--resource-group <YOUR PUBLIC IP'S RG>
➥--name <YOUR PUBLIC IP'S NAME>
➥--dns-name <YOUR DESIRED PUBLIC IP'S DNS NAME>
➥--query "dnsSettings.fqdn"
```

Replace <YOUR DESIRED PUBLIC IP'S RG> with the resource group name, <YOUR PUBLIC IP'S NAME> with the public IP's name from the previous command (i.e., the value in the leftmost column), and <YOUR PUBLIC IP'S DNS NAME> with a DNS name of your choice (e.g., danbugssmartcms).

Make sure to save the FQDN output from this command (e.g., danbugssmartcms.westus2.cloudapp.azure.com)—you'll need it for the Ingress configuration later.

> **NOTE** Aside from setting up the cluster, I've already built a Docker image for the frontend and pushed it to GitHub's Container Registry (GHCR). You can find it here: ghcr.io/danbugs/smartcms-frontend:v1. The source code is available at https://mng.bz/EwYR.

B.2 Preparing the cluster

Now that your Kubernetes cluster is up and running, it's time to set it up for SmartCMS. We'll install some tools, configure networking, and get things ready to run our app. Make sure you're logged into GHCR, following https://mng.bz/NwEd if necessary.

First, install the wasmcloud-platform Helm chart:

```
helm upgrade --install wasmcloud-platform
➥--values https://raw.githubusercontent.com/wasmCloud/wasmcloud/main/
➥charts/wasmcloud-platform/values.yaml
➥oci://ghcr.io/wasmcloud/charts/wasmcloud-platform:0.1.2
➥--dependency-update
```

Next, set up the Ingress controller. This will allow HTTP traffic to flow into the cluster. Replace <YOUR PUBLIC IP HERE> with the IP address you obtained in the previous section:

```
helm upgrade --install ingress-nginx ingress-nginx/ingress-nginx
➥--namespace ingress-nginx --create-namespace
➥--set controller.replicaCount=2
➥--set controller.nodeSelector."kubernetes.io/os"=linux
➥--set defaultBackend.nodeSelector."kubernetes.io/os"=linux
➥--set controller.service.externalTrafficPolicy=Local
➥--set controller.service.loadBalancerIP="<YOUR PUBLIC IP HERE>"
```

After deploying, it may take a few minutes for the Ingress controller's external IP to show up. You can check its status with

```
kubectl get svc -n ingress-nginx
```

To enable HTTPS, install `cert-manager`:

```
kubectl apply
➥-f https://github.com/cert-manager/cert-manager/releases/latest/
➥download/cert-manager.yaml
kubectl wait --namespace cert-manager
➥--for=condition=Available deployment/cert-manager --timeout=120s
```

Once `cert-manager` is available, you'll need a `ClusterIssuer` so it can request TLS certificates from Let's Encrypt.

> **NOTE** Let's Encrypt is a free certificate authority that issues trusted SSL/TLS certificates. It uses the ACME protocol to prove that you control the domain.

Replace `<YOUR EMAIL HERE>` with your email address to receive expiration warnings.

Listing B.1 Let's Encrypt `ClusterIssuer` for TLS

```
apiVersion: cert-manager.io/v1
kind: ClusterIssuer
metadata:
  name: letsencrypt-prod
spec:
  acme:
    email: <YOUR EMAIL HERE>
    server: https://acme-v02.api.letsencrypt.org/directory
    privateKeySecretRef:
      name: letsencrypt-prod
    solvers:
      - http01:
          ingress:
            class: nginx
```

Save this to a file called `cluster-issuer.yaml`, then apply it with

```
kubectl apply -f cluster-issuer.yaml
```

Finally, deploy the wasmCloud host configuration. This gets your backend runtime set up and ready:

```
kubectl apply -f https://raw.githubusercontent.com/danbugs/serverside-wasm-
book-code/refs/heads/main/app_c/setup/wasmcloud-host.yaml
```

B.3 Deploying the SmartCMS

Now that the cluster and Ingress are ready, it's time to deploy the SmartCMS system. It consists of a few backend services, a frontend, and an Ingress that ties it all together.

B.3.1 Deploying the backend components

Apply each of the backend YAML files:

```
kubectl apply
-f https://raw.githubusercontent.com/danbugs/
➥serverside-wasm-book-code/refs/heads/main/app_c/backend/ollama.yaml
kubectl rollout status deployment/ollama --timeout=120s

kubectl apply
➥-f https://raw.githubusercontent.com/danbugs/
➥serverside-wasm-book-code/refs/heads/main/app_c/backend/wadm.yaml
kubectl apply
➥-f https://raw.githubusercontent.com/danbugs/
➥serverside-wasm-book-code/refs/heads/main/app_c/backend/wasmcloud-api.yaml
```

NOTE Most of this is the same as chapter 8; one difference is that we now expose the `wasmcloud-api` service through an Ingress route instead of using `kubectl port-forward`. This is a more production-friendly approach and integrates with TLS.

B.3.2 Deploying the frontend

Apply the frontend YAML file:

```
kubectl apply
➥-f https://raw.githubusercontent.com/danbugs/
➥serverside-wasm-book-code/refs/heads/main/app_c/frontend/frontend.yaml
```

This deploys the static frontend, which will serve the UI for the SmartCMS.

B.3.3 Configuring Ingress

To route external traffic to your services, create an Ingress configuration. Save the following listing as `ingress.yaml`, replacing `<YOUR PUBLIC IP'S FQDN>` with the FQDN we obtained in the prerequisites section.

Listing B.2 An example Ingress resource for SmartCMS

```
apiVersion: networking.k8s.io/v1
kind: Ingress
metadata:
  name: nginx
  annotations:
    cert-manager.io/cluster-issuer: letsencrypt-prod
spec:
  ingressClassName: nginx
  tls:
    - hosts:
        - <YOUR PUBLIC IP'S FQDN>
      secretName: sswasm-tls
  rules:
    - host: <YOUR PUBLIC IP'S FQDN>
      http:
        paths:
          - path: /api
```

```
            pathType: Prefix
            backend:
              service:
                name: wasmcloud-api
                port:
                  number: 8000
          - path: /
            pathType: Prefix
            backend:
              service:
                name: smartcms-frontend
                port:
                  number: 80
```

Apply it with

```
kubectl apply -f ingress.yaml
```

Once everything is set up, you'll be able to access the SmartCMS frontend at `https://<YOUR PUBLIC IP'S FQDN>`. To see my own deployment, visit: https://sswasm.com/. For an overview of the deployed Smart CMS system, see figure B.1.

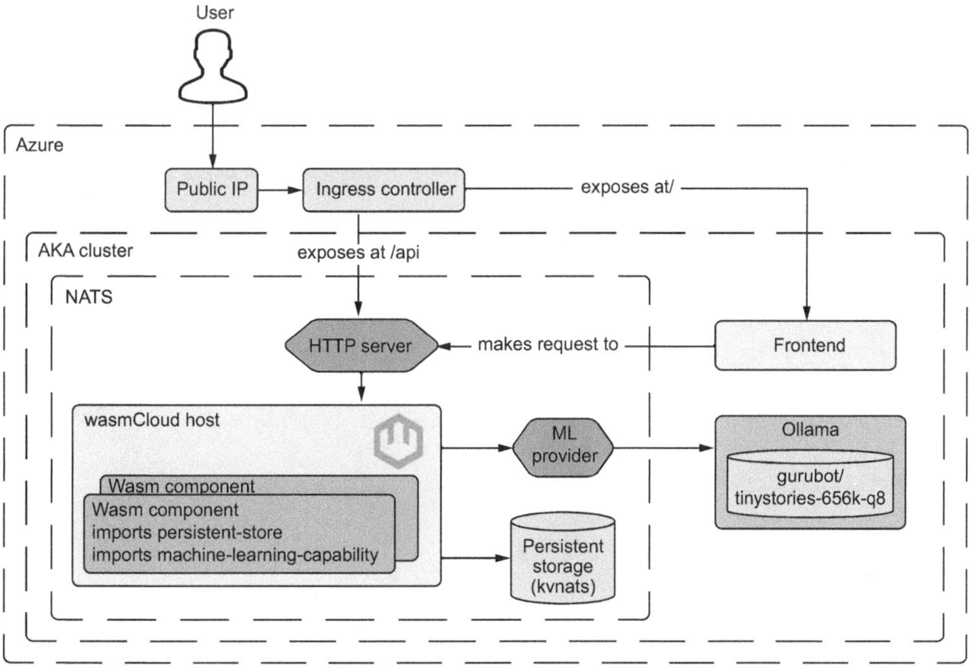

Figure B.1 The full SmartCMS deployment architecture on Azure. The Wasm component runs inside a wasmCloud host within an AKS cluster, communicating with persistent storage and a machine learning provider. Traffic enters through an Ingress controller mapped to a public IP, routing API requests to an HTTP server and frontend assets to the web UI. Inference is powered by an Ollama-hosted model.

And that's it! You've deployed a Wasm backend service to a Kubernetes cluster running on a public cloud—and made it accessible to the world. You configured networking, installed essential tooling like wasmCloud and `cert-manager`, and even set up HTTPS using trusted TLS certificates.

afterword

When we first started working on WebAssembly in Firefox, along with our colleagues in Chrome, Safari, and Edge, we were, as Dan mentioned at the beginning of this book, primarily interested in providing a safe, portable, standards-based alternative to native browser NPAPI, ActiveX, and PPAPI plugins. Already this was a challenging goal for both technical and browser-political reasons—several attempts in this direction had already been made, and all had failed to achieve cross-browser adoption. Fortunately, with Emscripten and asm.js already being used in production, we had a nice, focused goal for our initial release: provide something functionally equivalent but more efficient and less weird than asm.js that existing Emscripten users could target by simply flipping a flag.

At the same time, given the explosive growth of JavaScript *outside* the browser, driven by the adoption of Node.js, we thought that maybe, just *maybe*, WebAssembly might also be useful outside the browser as well. For what? We weren't sure; after all, outside the browser there is no prohibition on running native code or the ever-present need for sandboxing of malicious code, which had been the prime motivators for WebAssembly inside the browser. But just in case, the WebAssembly standards group included "non-web embedding" use cases in its initial goals and design documents. What this mostly boiled down to was not baking in any hard dependencies on JavaScript or Web APIs into core WebAssembly. Instead, all interactions between WebAssembly and the rest of the browsers were carefully factored out into separate, optional, layered specifications that nonbrowser embeddings were free to ignore. This layering discipline also helped us to keep the core WebAssembly specification relatively small and self-contained, which in turn has encouraged formalization, proofs of soundness, mechanized reasoning, and a growing body of academic study and research.

What has been pleasantly surprising since the release of WebAssembly in browsers is that this initial suspicion—that WebAssembly could provide unique value even outside the browser—has turned out to be true. As Dan explains in the preceding pages, compared to popular mainstream alternatives like containers, WebAssembly offers a smaller size, lower cold start times, better portability, and simpler sandboxing, all of which can lead to cost savings, which has become increasingly important in recent years. We've seen these benefits play out in a number of other software domains, which Dan has helpfully given us a tour of throughout this book.

As exciting as it is to see WebAssembly spreading outside the browser, it has also created the clear and present need to beef up the foundational standards to fill in the gaps left by the absence of JavaScript and web APIs. This is the role of the Component Model and WASI standards proposals that Dan has thoroughly introduced throughout the book. It is my belief that as we progress from the release of 0.3, which Dan describes in the final chapter, to the subsequent stable 1.0 release, we'll see self-reinforcing, exponential growth as each popular language, framework, package, and platform provides upstream, out-of-the-box support for WebAssembly as another instruction set and operating system—a special one based on vendor-neutral open standards, rigorous formal foundations, capability-based security, and extreme portability. By explaining the concepts, big ideas, and nuts and bolts of WebAssembly, WASI, and the WebAssembly Component Model with approachable language and examples, this book is an invaluable tool for kicking off this exponential growth.

—LUKE WAGNER

COCREATOR OF WEBASSEMBLY AND DISTINGUISHED ENGINEER AT FASTLY

index

A

B

C

X

Y

RELATED MANNING TITLES

WebAssembly in Action
by Gerard Gallant

ISBN 9781617295744
448 pages, $49.99
November 2019

Rust Servers, Services, and Apps
by Prabhu Eshwarla

ISBN 9781617298608
328 pages, $59.99
July 2023

Rust Web Development
by Bastian Gruber

ISBN 9781617299001
400 pages, $49.99
December 2022

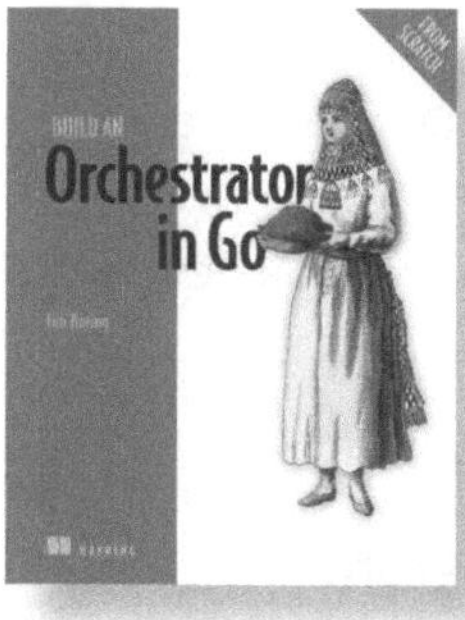

Build an Orchestrator in Go (From Scratch)
by Tim Boring

ISBN 9781617299759
288 pages, $59.99
March 2024

For ordering information, go to www.manning.com